Text and Context

Acta Universitatis Stockholmiensis

Stockholm Studies in Russian Literature

23

TEXT AND CONTEXT

ESSAYS TO HONOR

NILS ÅKE NILSSON

Edited by

Peter Alberg Jensen
Barbara Lonnqvist
Fiona Björling
Lars Kleberg
Anders Sjöberg

Almqvist & Wiksell International 1987
Stockholm – Sweden

© Stockholm Studies in Russian Literature 1987

ISBN 91-22-00879-9

Almqvist & Wiksell International

Printed with the aid of a grant from Längmanska kulturfonden

Printed in Sweden by

gotab   Stockholm 1987

TABULA GRATULATORIA

Nils Åke Nilsson's friends and colleagues wish to congratulate him on the occasion of his seventieth birthday, September 1st, 1987.

Erik Adrian
Zsuzsanna Bjørn Andersen

Henryk Baran
Gösta Berg
Märta Bergstrand
Henrik Birnbaum
Nils Bjervig
Fiona Björling
Per-Arne Bodin
Liisa Byckling
Jostein Børtnes

Sten Carlsson
Roland Castenberg
J Douglas Clayton

Staffan Dahl
L'ubomír Ďurovič

Thomas Eekman
Erik Egeberg
Aleksandra Eiche
Jan van der Eng
Kjell Espmark

Henrik Panum Falkentorp
Jerzy Faryno
Aleksandar Flaker
Zbigniew Folejewski

Arne Gallis
Boris Gasparov

Sven R Gustavsson
Roger Gyllin

Aage A Hansen-Löve
Hans Hertz

Kazimiera Ingdahl

Robert Louis Jackson
Hillevi och Gunnar Jacobsson
Bengt Jangfeldt
Gunnar Jarring
Halina Jelinska
Ole Husted Jensen
Peter Alberg Jensen
Kurt Johansson
Inge Jonsson
Knud Jordal
Harry Järv

Urpu-Liisa Karahka
Lennart Kjellberg
Geir Kjetsaa
Lars Kleberg
Gustav Korlén

Marja Leinonen
Anna och Henryk Lenczyc
Anja och Hans Lidberg
Siegfried Lienhard
Elsa och Örjan Lindberger
Sven Linnér
Anna Ljunggren

3

Magnus Ljunggren
Jørgen Lund
Bengt A Lundberg
Siri Sverdrup Lunden
Zhanna Lundman
Elisabeth Löfstrand
Barbara Lönnqvist
Erik Lönnroth
Håkan Lövgren

Vladimir Markov
Elsa Melin
Israel Mittelman
Bertil Molde
Peter Ulf Møller

Barbro Nilsson
Eja Nilsson

Olof Paulsson
Jaroslav Pavlík
Thomas Petersen
Thore Pettersson
Erkki Peuranen
Karin Pontoppidan-Sjövall

Helge Rinholm
Cecilia Rohnström

Charles Rougle
Velta Rūķe-Draviņa
Åke Runnquist
Carl Hugo Ryrberg

Anders Sjöberg
Miloslava Slavickova
Eigil Steffensen
Thure Stenström
Carl Stief
Stig Strömholm
Hagar Sundberg

Kiril Taranovsky
Victor Terras
William Mills Todd III

Andrzej Nils Uggla

René Wellek
Siw Wesslén
Thomas G Winner
Dean S Worth

Bodo Zelinsky

Margareta och Stig Åkerberg

4

Table of Contents

J. Douglas Clayton

'Tis folly to be wise: The Semantics of *um-* in Griboedov's *Gore ot uma*

One of the striking aspects of *Gore ot uma* by A. S. Griboedov is its title, which seems to sum up in its pithiness the main problem of the play, as well as exemplifying that aphoristic quality that commentators have seen as a principal feature of the text.[1] This is not to say, however, that the interpretation of the title is clear-cut, for while the semantics of *gore* ('woe') are simple and can be seen to have their fulfilment in the discomfiture of Čackij, those of *um* are not, and their analysis reveals the complexity of the predicament in which the hero finds himself.

The following study is intended to throw some light on the semantics of *um* and its derivatives as they are used in the play.[2] These derivatives are (in descending order of frequency):

um: 42 instances; distribution of forms: *uma* – 20 (63, 69, 78, 116, 117, 119, 119, 138, 138, 139, 139, 140, 141, 143, 144, 144, 145, 158, 163, 172); *um* – 9 (76, 79, 84, 88, 102, 115, 117, 119, 162); *ume* – 5 (68, 137, 146, 158, 160); *umy* – 2 (83, 149); *umu* – 2 (99, 125); *umom* – 2 (101, 102); *umov* – 1 (115); *umiškom* – 1 (157).

umnyj: 14 instances (including one verbal and one substantival derivative); distribution of forms: *umen* – 3 (74, 78, 116); *umnyj* – 2 (149, 157); *umnee* – 2 (116, 161); *umnejšimi* – 1 (154); *umnoj* – 1 (155); *umny* – 1 (115); *poumnel* – 1 (113); *umnogo* – 1 (77); *umna* – 1 (73); *umnikov* – 1 (172).

umet': 9 instances; distribution of forms: *umel* – 4 (72, 88, 119, 150); *umeet* – 1 (77); *sumela* – 1 (79); *umejut* – 1 (100); *sumeju* – 1 (110); *umet'* – 1 (116).

bezumnyj: 8 instances; distribution of forms: *byzumnyj* – 3 (144, 160, 172); *bezumnych* – 2 (145, 147); *bezumnym* – 2 (169, 172); *bezumnye* – 1 (139).

poloumnyj: 1 instance (136).

Apart from these words, the following are etymologically related to *um-:* *razumnik* (99), *sumasšedšij* (140), *sumasšestvija* (116), *vrazumiš'* (142), *obrazumljus'* (170). Including these there is a total of 79 instances of the *um-* root in the play. Words that are semantically close, but not etymologically related include *umudrilis'* (73), *mudreno* (83), *premudrogo* (149), *rassudok* (108), and the negative *glupogo* (77), *glupee* (84), and *glupet'* (91). The word *sumatocha* (74) is not etymologically related to *um-*, but its similarity to such words as *sumasšestvie* suggests that we should consider it in this context (as an example of 'folk etymology' on Griboedov's part).

The very frequency and variety of the forms suggests one assumption from the outset – that the text is motivated at least in part by a long conceit or pun on the meaning of the word *um*. The fact that different characters participate in this suggests that there is a textual unity in the play that transcends any particularities of speech.[3] Additional, more precise questions need to be posed, however, namely – what exact shades of meanings are given to the word in the play; to whom are the qualities of *um* (in its various meanings) attributed, and to what effect; where is this notion of *um* derived; and how is this use of the word reflected, if at all, in the work of other Russian writers.

'Mind, intellect, wits' are English equivalents of *um* listed in *The Oxford Russian-English Dictionary*. It is the term 'wit' that translators have generally preferred in translating the title into English. In Griboedov's text, the ambiguous semantics of the word are exploited to the full. There are three basic semantic fields that can be distinguished in the play. The first of these is also the most straightforward, namely the meaning of *um* as 'mind', as in the numerous uses of the expression *sojti s uma* – 'to go out of one's mind' (and its derivative, the substantive *sumasšestvie*). Other related uses are the idiomatic phrase: 'na um teper' prišla' – 'she came to mind' (79); and: 'naši robkie . . . umy' – 'our timid minds' (83). This meaning is only tangentially related to the two following ones, but the coincident use of the term *um* adds to the complexity and the density of the conceits in the text. We will refer to this meaning as um^1.[4]

The second and third meanings bring us to the centre of the ideological conflict that underlies the text. Essentially, both of these refer to the *contents* of the mind. Thus, um^2 refers to the commonsensical, traditional notions of old Moscow, as expounded by Famusov in his speech in II.5:

A naši staricki?? – Kak ich voz'met zador,
Zasudjat ob delach, čto slovo – prigovor.

––––––––––

Prjamye kanclery v otstavke – po umu! (99).

This no-nonsense conception of *um*, of which Famusov himself is the salient example in the play, along with his sister-in-law Chlestova and his prospective son-in-law Skalozub, grows out of um^1 – if you are in your *um*, then you will share this common wisdom. It favours wealthy suitors, nepotism, corruption, foreign fashions, and comfortable self-satisfied opinions.

um^3 is that insight into the nature of prejudice and justice that marks Čackij and singles him out from the Moscow environment. His reaction to the speech of Famusov defines his position: 'Doma novy, no predrassudki stary' (100). It is strongly associated with education and enlightenment, as we see in Famusov's and Chlestova's complaints about the various pedagogical establishments that have sprung up in Moscow (145). As Bilinkis re-

8

marks, 'Čackij's speech and that of Famusov belong emphatically to different linguistic spheres and can in no way be mixed up'.[5] Čackij's um^3 can almost be compared to Hamlet's conscience, and leads him to see through and criticise the hypocrisy of Famusov's um^2. Essentially, Čackij is a representative of decembrist thinking, a movement that was in many ways an application of the eighteenth-century enlightenment in the sphere of social justice, and advocated the *rational* organisation of society. That is to say, Čackij's um^3 is a critique of um^2 based on reason. It is *not* an irrational, *bezumnyj* Romantic revolt against authority. A parallel can be found in the paradoxical relationship between the older (Shishkovite and politically reactionary) and the younger (decembrist) archaists. Both groups advocated eighteenth-century classical forms in literature, and both represented mutually hostile continuations of the (by now conservative) ideology of the enlightenment.[6] This is why, at certain points, Čackij's views sound startlingly similar to those espoused by his ostensible opponent, Famusov, e.g.in his speech on foreign influences at the end of Act III:

> Puskaj menja of"javjat staroverom,
> No chuže dlja menja naš sever vo sto krat
> S tech por, kak otdal vsë v obmen na novyj lad:
> I nravy, i jazyk, i starinu svjatuju,
> I veličavuju odeždu na druguju –
> Po šutovskomu obrazcu ... (148)

One of the most complex uses of the word *um* is in the title of the play. We could assume that um^3 is shared by the author too, since the title is the only fragment of the authorial voice that is included in the dramatic text. That is to say, the author expresses as it were his rueful solidarity with Čackij. From this point of view, the change of title from the threatening *Gore umu* to *Gore ot uma* reflects a subtle shift in the notion of *um* – from a pernicious tendency that must be eradicated (foreshadowing, perhaps, the execution and exiling of the decembrist leaders), to a characteristic given by fate, the consequences of which must be endured. The title is potentially ambiguous, however – perhaps it could mean um^2. That is to say, we may understand it to suggest that the woes of society come from Famusov's old-fashioned common-sensical *um*. The ambiguity is important, since the desirability of the one or the other depends on one's point of view. The change in title, it should be noted parenthetically, eliminated, by the insertion of the preposition, any tendency to link *gore* and um^3 (or um^2 – again, depending on one's perspective) into *gore-um*, although, tantalizingly, the two words dance around each other, e.g., in Sofija's speech:

Kogda ž pečal'noe ničto na um nejdet,
Zabylis' muzykoj, i vremja šlo tak plavno;
  Sud'ba nas budto beregla;
  Ni bespokojstvo, ni somnen'ja . . .
  A gore ždet iz-za ugla (77).

The noun *um* has an opposite – *sumasšestvie* – only in the meaning *um*[1]. It is significant that the Romantic terms *bezumstvo*, *bezumie*, and *bezumec*, which play such a key role in the poetic semantics of Puškin and Lermontov are not attested in the play. These form the Russian equivalent of the French *folie* and, more important still, the German *Wahn[sinn]* (the adjective *bezumnyj* assuming for these writers the meaning of the German *dämonisch*). The Russian expressions are more evocative than their German and French equivalents in that they contain, in their formation, the *um-/bezum-* opposition. The use of cognates in the Russian also ensures a certain tidiness and, at the same time, a resonance that is a motive force in the word-play of Griboedov's text (and that later writers exploit to such advantage).

The absence of Romantic connotations and terms places Griboedov firmly in the neo-classical context, in which the healthful notion of reason, rather than the creative idea of the demonic, possessed genius, was paramount. Čackij is driven, not by a noble folly, but by a higher definition of reason. In this he is totally unlike Puškin's heroes such as Evgenij (in *Mednyj vsadnik*) or Germann in *Pikovaja dama*, or Lermontov's lyrical hero in the poem 'Beleet parus.' True, his notion of reason seems to others like madness (*sumasšestvie*), yet the differences are crucial. Thus, in the ball sequence (137-43), the rumour spreads that Čackij has gone mad ('S uma sošel'); this is a perversion of Sofija's original remark 'On ne v svoem ume' (literally, 'he is not in his mind'). It is Zagoreckij who introduces the term *bezumnyj* (139): 'Ego v bezumnye uprjatal djadja-plut' (139), but here the word is a synonym of *sumasšedšij*, and the connotation is still 'clinical', not the Romantic idea of the possession of the individual by some divine folly.

Derived from the root *um-* is the adjective *umnyj* and its various subforms. The adjective is important because it offers the possibility of an evaluative sequence: *umnyj* – *poloumnyj* – *bezumnyj*. The basic meaning of *umnyj* is 'smart, intelligent'. As such Famusov uses it to describe Madame Rosier (73); Sofija denies the quality in Skaluzub (77) but finds it in Čackij (78). When Čackij wonders whether Molčalin can have acquired it (113 & 116) it becomes clear that there is a *double entendre* at work. To become *umnyj* is a code-word in Čackij's vocabulary for becoming disaffected – a decembrist. Apparently Čackij thinks Molčalin may have become one during the former's absence. He muses on the 'transformations' that he has witnessed:

Est' na zemle takie prevraščen'ja
Pravlenij, klimatov, i nravov, i umov,
Est' ljudi važnye, slyli za durakov:
Inyj po armii, inyj plochim poėtom,
Inyj ... Bojus' skazat', no priznany vsem svetom,
   Osobenno v poslednie goda,
      Čto stali umny chot' kuda (115).

In this meaning *umnyj* becomes identified with a version of um^3, and um^3 is in turn made more specific by Čackij's subsequent reference to 'umnyj narod' in his attack on foreign fashions (149). It is important to note, however, that this use has a nuance, for example in Repetilov's description of his new acquaintances:

Pozdrav' menja, teper' s ljud'mi ja znajus'
S umnejšimi!! ...
U nas est' obščestvo, i tajnye sobran'ja
   Po četvergam. Sekretnejšij sojuz ... (154–155);

and in his comment:

Da umnyj čelovek ne možet byt' ne plutom (157).

We have to do here with a perversion or vulgarization of the notion of critical reason for which Čackij stands. He is as repelled by these fashionable adherents of club decembrism – represented by the buffoon Repetilov or (God forbid) Molčalin – as he is by the Famusov circle, the representatives of um^2. This gives a special meaning to the descriptions of Čackij as *bezumnyj* (e.g., 160, 172), for we now perceive him as equally alienated from the traditional and the debased-decembrist forms of *um*; and to Famusov's complaint:

   nynče, pušče, čem kogda,
Bezumnych razvelos' ljudej, i del, i mnenij (145)

– one person's *bezumnyj* is another's *umnyj*. Poor Čackij is *bezumnyj* both to Famusov and to the Repetilov decembrists, the *umnejšie*.

A secondary question concerns the use of the verb *umnet'*. It connotes social skill, *savoir faire*, or even cunning, as in the following remarks by Sofija about Čackij:

On slavno
Peresmejat' umeet vsech;
Boltaet, šutit, mne zabavno (77):

and Čackij's comment about Molčalin:

Kakoju vorožboj umel k nej v serdce lezt' (119);

or it can mean the individual's ability to exert self-control and manipulate his/her own emotions, e.g. Liza's remark about how Sofija's aunt went grey when she was abandoned by her Frenchman:

chotela schoronit'
Svoju dosadu, ne sumela (79).

In this meaning it is used not only by Liza, but by Čackij about himself:

Ot sumasšestvija mogu ja osterečʼsja;
Puščusʼ podalee prostytʼ, ocholodetʼ,
Ne dumatʼ o ljubvi, no budu ja umetʼ
Terjatʼsja po svetu, zabytʼsja i razvlečʼsja (116).

Clearly, this ability is part of *um*[1]; it suggests the intelligence that some of us have that enables us to 'live by our wits' in the world, and the primacy of intelligence over the emotions (for good – to overcome the devastations of unrequited love – or evil – to seduce in cold blood the object of one's machinations).

The use of *umet'* here reinforces the *um* conceit in the play, and adds to the function of the play as a discourse on reason. Čackij shows the noble use to which reason can be put – the suppression of passion, and the cultivation of that 'Roman' virtue that Lotman singles out as a feature of the decembrist ethos.[7] Contrasted with this is the self-serving hypocrisy of Molčalin – who uses his reason for selfish purposes.

The last aspect of the use of the *um-* root that I would like to examine is who uses the root most frequently, and about whom. The following list treats all the word-forms together and omits the other roots listed above. In some cases the object of the remark is guessed at. The speaker is indicated in italics and the object of the comment in roman.

Author
Čackij: 63
Famusov
Liza: 68, 69
Famusov: 72
Mme Rosier: 72
indeterminate: 73, 88, 99, 145
Kuzʼma Petrovič: 89
Moscow girls: 100

12

Čackij: 101, 169, 172, 172
Anna Alekseevna (Čackij's mother): 144
Sofija
Molčalin: 74, 117
Sofija: 76, 110
Skalozub: 77
Čackij: 77, 78, 116, 117, 137
Liza
Liza: 79
Chlestova: 79
Čackij
Čackij: 84, 102, 116, 116, 163, 172
Čackij & Sofija: 83
indeterminate: 102, 115, 115, 119, 149, 172
Molčalin: 113, 115, 116, 116, 119, 119, 119
Russians: 149
Natal'ja Dmitrievna Gorič
Platon Michailovič Gorič: 125
Chlestova
Famusov: 136
Čackij: 143, 144, 147
indeterminate: 145, 146
*G. N.**
Čackij: 138, 138, 139
*G. D.**
Čackij: 139
Zagoreckij
indeterminate: 139
Čackij: 140, 140, 141, 144, 160, 160
Grafinja vnučka Chrjumina
Famusov: 150
Repetilov
club decembrists: 154, 155, 158
indeterminate: 157, 162
Repetilov: 157
Knjaginja Tugouchovskaja
Čackij: 161

From this (admittedly imperfect survey) several points stand out. First, the large number of uses by different characters about other characters suggests that *um* is considered a principal trait in the definition of character in general. A typical example of this is Sofija's remark about Skalozub: 'On slova umnogo ne vygovoril srodu' – to which Liza offers her own nuance: 'Da-s, tak skazat' rečist, a bol'no ne chiter'' (77). Second, there is a large number of instances (fifteen in all) where the object is indeterminate. These include both turns of speech, proverbs, and, more significantly, generalisations about the spreading of *um* or its absence among the population (e.g., Famusov: 'nynče, pušče, čem kogda, bezumnych razvelos' ljudej, i del, i mnenij' [145]). Third, it is not surprising that the character about whom there are the most conjectures concerning his *um*, both by others and by himself, is Čackij (31 instances, including one in which he includes Sofija). The only other character with a significant concentration is Molčalin, Čackij's rival and the character who is contrasted with Čackij in the play (9 instances).

Concerning the frequency with which different characters use the root, it is again not surprising that Čackij heads the list (21 instances), given his preoccupation with reason (both his own and that of others, especially Molčalin). It is more interesting that Famusov is second (15 instances). This seems to confirm my view of Famusov and Čackij as the definers of the two different kinds of *um* – um^2 and um^3 respectively. It is significant that Famusov's remarks are not particularly concerned with Čackij (only 4 instances – two of them on the last page). Rather, Famusov serves as the general definer of old-fashioned common sense in his remarks on the behaviour of different individuals. It is not Famusov but Zagoreckij who spreads the news of Čackij's madness, as we can see from the concentration of six references to him. Famusov's concurrence with this judgment is reserved until the last speech of the play.

It is by no means an easy matter to resurrect the literary semantics of a play written under complex circumstances a century and a half ago. Nevertheless, I believe it is safe to conclude that the problem of the definition of *um* is the central one in the play. The subtleties and nuances that the root acquires in the usage of different characters are by no means exhaustively served by the above analysis, which is meant to illustrate the fact that the language of the play, although differentiated in the mouths of the different characters (as numerous 'realist' critics have pointed out), is nevertheless manipulated with considerable artifice to focus on the central ideological problem.

NOTES

1. First and most notably Puškin, who in 1825 remarked of the verses: 'half of them are destined to become proverbs' (quoted in V. Filippov, 'Jazyk dejstvujuščich lic "Gorja ot uma",' in A. S. Griboedov, *Gore ot uma: P'esa, stat'i, kommentarii,* edited by N. Piksanov and V. Filippov [Moskva: 'Iskusstvo,' 1946], 136). Puškin's opinion is echoed by, for example, S. M. Petrov (*Gore ot uma: Komedija A. S. Griboedova* [Moskva: 'Prosveščenie', 1981], 70).
2. For this analysis I have used the text of the play in A. S. Griboedov, *Sočinenija v stichach* (Leningrad: Sovetskij pisatel', 1967), 63–172, to which all subsequent page numbers in parentheses refer.

3. In this respect my argument differs from those of Jean Bonamour, who stresses the individualization of the language in the play (*A. S. Griboedov et la vie littéraire de son temps* [Paris: Presses Universitaires de France, 1965], 350), and P. Šabliovskij, who examines the use of language to produce character-traits ('Jazyk dejstvujuščich lic komedii "Gore ot uma",' *Russkij jazyk v sovetskoj škole*, No. 4, 1929, 64–78).

4. This is the equivalent to meaning 1 –'myslitel'naja sposobnost' čeloveka' – in the *Slovar' jazyka Puškina*, IV (Moskva: Gosudarstvennoe izdatel'stvo inostrannych i nactional'nych slovarej, 1961), 691.

5. Ja.S. Bilinkis, 'K voprosu o chudožestvennom novatorstve A. S. Griboedova v "Gore ot uma". (Problema "charakterov" i "obstojatel'stv")' *Učenye zapiski Tartuskogo universiteta*, 78 (1959), 105.

6. For more on this, see Ju. N. Tynjanov, 'Archaisty i Puškin,' in *Archaisty i novatory* (Leningrad, 1929; reprint: München: Wilhelm Fink Verlag, 1967), 87–227.

7. See Jurij M. Lotman, 'Theater and Theatricality in the Order of Early Nineteenth-Century Culture,' in Henryk Baran, ed., *Semiotics and Structuralism: Readings from the Soviet Union* (White Plains, N. J.: International Arts and Sciences Press, 1976), 33–63.

Boris Gasparov

The Apocalyptic Theme in Puškin's "Count Nulin"

"Count Nulin" is one of the most mysterious of Puškin's works, even given the complexity and semantic polyvalency typical for all of his oeuvre. On the surface, the poem seems to reflect quite obviously (even too obviously) the poet's turn to the "realistic" style. This aspect of the poem was emphasized by Belinskij, who praised it highly as a direct predecessor of the "natural school", and whose interpretation has been followed in numerous monographs on Puškin ever since. Nevertheless, a set of scenes in the "Flemish" style is hardly what one would expect of a Puškinian *poéma* written in the same year as "Boris Godunov" and the fourth and fifth Chapter of "Eugene Onegin". This discrepancy looks even more striking if we consider the particular circumstances in which the poem was written – with remarkable rapidity – during the day and night of December 13–14, 1825.

At the beginning of December Puškin learned about the death of Aleksander I. His letters of December 4–6 (to P. Katenin and P. Pletnev) reflect the poet's excitement and anticipation of radical changes both in the political situation and in his own life. Puškin's agitation grew even stronger upon receiving a letter from I. Puščin who called him to St.-Petersburg "for a rendez-vous"[1] (such an invitation being charged with clear implications, since Puškin was forbidden to leave Michajlovskoe). After receiving the letter, Puškin decided to go to Petersburg incognito; he probably would have arrived there on the night of December 13, just on the eve of the Decembrist uprising. However, he encountered many omens which eventually made him give up the whole affair: he met a priest, a hare crossed his path, etc.[2] (we should especially keep this hare in mind for the purpose of further analysis). In this state of anxiety, frustration and premonitions about upcoming events Puškin wrote, on the very day he would have arrived in Petersburg (the day whose date was probably perceived by him as one of the bad omens), his comic poem whose "Flemish" façade, as well as the parodic imitation of Shakespeare's "Rape of Lucrece", seem to be most inappropriate to the circumstances.

To make the confusion even worse, Puškin later (probably in 1830) sketched a commentary to his poem ("A Note on 'Count Nulin' "), in which it was pointedly indicated that a connection between this literary joke and the events in the wake and in expectation of which it had been written, did exist:

16

At the end of 1825 I was in the country. While reading "Lucrece", a rather weak poem by Shakespeare, I reflected: what if it had occurred to Lucretia to give Tarquinius a slap? Perhaps it would have had the effect of cooling off his resolution, and he would have been forced to retire shamefully from the field? Lucretia would then not have stabbed herself, Publicola would not have become enraged, Brutus would not have driven out the kings, and the world and its history would have been different. And so we owe the republic, the consuls, the dictators, the Catos, and Caesar to a titillating incident, not unlike one that recently took place in the vicinity here, in Novorževskij District. The idea of parodying history and Shakespeare occurred to me; I could not resist the double temptation and in two days finished this tale.[3]

I have the habit of recording the year and day on my papers. "Count Nulin" was written on December 13 and 14. Sometimes there are strange coincidences in this world. (*Byvajut strannye sbližen'ja.*) /XI, 188/[4]

It is also worth mentioning that Puškin's poetic epistle to Puščin in Siberia, written a year later, was dated by the author December 13, 1826,[5] which was the anniversary – not of the uprising itself, but of the meeting of the two friends which would have occurred had Puškin come to Petersburg, and of the creation of "Count Nulin" (whose manuscript actually bore the same date: December 13, 1825).

M. O. Geršenzon and B. M. Ėjchenbaum, who were the first to direct attention to the hidden serious meaning of the comic poem intimated in the author's commentary, both came to the conclusion that "Count Nulin" somehow reflects Puškin's meditations on the laws and paradoxes of history.[6] Later, Ju. M. Lotman specified the subtextual meaning of the "Note" implied by the literary source of its last phrase (a letter by Laurence Sterne): ". . . on the night of December 14, 1825 he pondered on history's laws and on the possibility for a chain of trifle accidents to jeopardize a great event."[7] However, these commentaries explain the meaning of the "Note" rather than the poem itself; it still remains unclear, in which particular way the poem's earthy characters and "Flemish" scenery represent expectations of a great historical event and its probably negative outcome with which Puškin was apparently preoccupied while creating "Count Nulin". To answer this question, we must take into account the broader context in which this poetic message was produced.

First of all, "the idea of parodying Shakespeare" relates "Count Nulin", in a paradoxical way, to "Boris Godunov" (finished a few months earlier), since the "Shakespearean" character of this historical drama was emphasized by the author more than once.[8] "Boris Godunov" was dedicated to events whose imprint on Russian cultural memory bore clear Apocalyptic overtones. Besides providing many clues for the Apocalyptic background of

17

the plot and main characters in the drama itself, Puškin directly indicated this association in his letter to P. Vjazemskij dated July 13, 1825 (NB the date):

> My tragedy is before me. I cannot restrain myself from copying out the title: "A Comedy About the Real Misfortune to the Moscow State, About the Tsar Boris, and About Grishka Otrepiev, Written by God's Servant Alexander the Son of Sergej Pushkin in the Year 7333, on the Site of the Ancient Fort of Voronich." What do you think of it?[9] /XIII, 128/

The date 7333 (which truly corresponds to 1825, according to the Old Russian chronological system) is charged with allusions to Apocalyptic prophecies: it is one third of the eighth (presumably the last) millennium which has passed, and it amounts exactly to a half of "the number of the Beast". (In the past, the year 1492 – i.e., 7000 – had been determined as the date of the Antichrist's coming and the end of the world; after it had passed, further calculations, aimed at predicting the ultimate date within the eighth millennium, usually employed the number 666 and its derivatives.) This background to Puškin's tragedy also provides some clues to the meaning of his comic poem.

The name of the poem's heroine is introduced in an ostensibly casual way which in fact focuses the reader's attention on it:

> К несчастью, героиня наша . . .
> (Ах! я забыл ей имя дать.
> Муж просто звал ее Наташа,
> Но мы – мы будем называть
> Наталья Павловна) . . .   /V, 4/

/Unfortunately, our heroine . . . Ach, I've forgotten to give her a name. Her husband used to call her Natasha, informally, but we – we shall call her Natalja Pavlovna/.

This name has a double connotation in Puškin's oeuvre. During the first decade of his work, it was invariably associated with a genuinely Russian and folkloric (or low-class) female character: from the poem "To Natal'ja" (1813) dedicated to a serf actress, to the ballad "The Bridegroom" (1825), whose heroine is "Nataša, a merchant's daughter".[10] On first glance, Natal'ja Pavlovna does not correspond to this *emploi:* she is discussed as being negligent of "ancestral customs" *(otečeskij zakon)*, having been brought up by "an emigrée Falbala". The name Falbala, however, literally means 'fringe, ornamentation'; it suggests the true character of the heroine's europeanism. Even the count's praise of her fashionable garment points out its ornamental components:

18

Позвольте видеть ваш убор;
Так... рюши, банты, здесь узор;
Все это к моде очень близко.   /V, 7/

/let me see your attire. Well, the ruches, the bows, and the adornment over here – all of this is very close to the latest fashions/.

Nataša's healthy rustic nature shows itself through the veneer of "fashionable" european ornamentation, just as her ruddy complexion cannot help being seen through her make-up: *"Lica rumjanec derevenskij–zdorov'e kraše vsech rumjan."* (Her rustic rosy cheeks, a picture of health which is more pretty than any make-up) /V, 9/.

Another meaning of the name Natal'ja, which was indicated explicitly in Puškin's later works, is associated with the image of the Madonna; cf. the poem "Madonna" (1830) addressed to the poet's bride Natal'ja Nikolaevna Gončarova, and also the fact that Puškin had initially chosen the name Natal'ja for the heroine of his poem "Poltava" (1828), then changed it to *Maria*. Apparently, "Count Nulin" was the first of Puškin's works in which this new meaning of the name (which was probably due to its association with French *natal*) emerged. The double connotation of the name of the poem's heroine is suggested by the fact that she is actually given the *two names*, Nataša and Natal'ja Pavlovna, corresponding to the two alternative meanings.

Thus, the heroine of the poem represents (in the most ironic way) the syncretic image of "Russia" and "Madonna" (*Bogorodica*) – a synthesis typical for the Russian cultural tradition. She is an impersonation, however ludicrous, of the "sacred Rus' " whom count Nulin curses in his speeches (*"Svjatuju Rus' branit"*) and on whom he later launches his unsuccessful attack.

Nataša's husband is not given a name. However, his colorful portrait is presented in the poem's introductory passage which depicts the preparations for the hunt:

Выходит барин на крыльцо,
Все, подбочась, обозревает;
Его довольное лицо. ...
Приятной важностью сияет. ...
Вот мужу подвели коня.   /V, 3/

/The master comes out at the porch; his hands akimbo, he surveys the whole scene. His contented mien is radiant with pleasant solemnity ... Now, his steed is brought to him/.

Three years later, Puškin used, with remarkable consistency (though with a totally different connotation), the same details for the portrait of Peter the Great in the midst of the battle of Poltava ("Poltava", Chant III):

Выходит Петр. Его глаза
Сияют. Лик его ужасен.
Движенья быстры. Он прекрасен,
Он весь, как Божия гроза.
Идет. Ему коня подводят.   /V, 56/

/Peter comes out, his eyes radiant, his step agile. He is sublime; his whole being is like God's storm. His steed is brought to him/.

Both portraits of a horseman with a radiant face are reminiscent of the image of the Horseman in the ultimate battle in the Apocalypse:

> And I saw heaven opened, and behold a white horse; and he that sat upon him was called Faithful and True ... His eyes were as a flame of fire, and on his head were many crowns; and he had a name written that no man knew but he himself.   /Rev. 19:11–12/

Similar traits of the image of the Apocalyptic Horseman were also present in Puškin's poetic portrait of Napoléon – "the bellicose horseman (*vsadnik brannyj*)" and "the man of destiny (*muž sudeb*)" – given in two poems of 1824 on the subject and in the draft of the tenth Chapter of "Eugene Onegin" (1830).

These associations cast an odd light on the whole introductory scene of "Count Nulin". Its first phrase, apparently announcing the beginning of the hunt ("It's time, it's time! the horns are blowing" – *Pora, pora! roga trubjat*), suggests an association with the Apocalyptic catastrophe whose advent is announced by the trumpets. The whole scene – people and beasts (horses, dogs) gathered before the porch, on which the master stands with his "radiant" and "solemn" face – is reminiscent of the description of the heavenly throne in the Revelation. The very fact of the husband's nameless-ness corresponds to the image of the Horseman whose name "no man knew but he himself". (Napoléon also remains nameless in all the Puškin poems mentioned above, as do Tat'jana's and Donna Anna's husbands in the two other works whose plot exhibits certain parallels with the "Count Nulin" triangle: the eighth Chapter of "Eugene Onegin"[11] and "The Stone Guest", both written in 1830.)

The design of the introductory episode is reproduced in another scene of the poem which is usually considered the most striking example of Puškin's newly-achieved "realism": the portrait of Natal'ja Pavlovna sitting in front of the window and surveying the scene below (in the yard), in which people and different kinds of beasts (meticulously described) are involved. Even the book which Natal'ja Pavlovna holds opened – the fourth volume of an "ancient" and "long, long, long" story – can be interpreted as an ironic allusion to the Book of Destiny whose reading is apportioned by the sequence of the seven seals. The scene is interrupted by a "sudden" sound of the bell (a correlate of the horns having blown at the beginning of the poem) which announces the appearance of count Nulin.

Such are the circumstances under which the main protagonist enters the scene. His name apparently refers to his outright insignificance; but at the same time, it connects the "new Tarquinius" with his prototype – *Sextus* Tarquinius, since they both possess names derived from Latin numerals. The "new Tarquinius' " advent occurs under the zero-name which disguises his original name.

On his first appearance, the count hobbles (because of an accident with his carriage). There is a long list of articles he brought with him from Paris. Among them is "the horrible book by Guizot" (*s užasnoj knižkoju Gizota*), which is probably one of the French historian's treatises arguing that the fall of monarchy as a form of government is imminent; the ironical epithet used by Puškin not only refers to the book's political notoriety in the context of Russian life, but also adds an "infernal" connotation.

Another of the count's attributes is "the latest song by Béranger". Only a few months before, in July 1825, Puškin had proposed in a letter to Vjazemskij a practical joke aimed at scaring his uncle, in which Béranger's blasphemous song would have been involved:

What song from Béranger did Uncle Vasily Lvovich translate?
It wasn't *Le Bon Dieu,* was it? Declare to him as a secret that in Petersburg he is being suspected of it, and that an investigative commission is already being prepared ...[12]   /XIII, 185/

It is quite probable that the same song is meant in the poem.

The traditional Russian Apocalyptic pattern (which had been formulated at least since the XVI century) suggested that the Antichrist would come from the West. At the beginning of Napoléon's campaign in 1812, Satan's itinerary had been described in numerous poetic and publicistic works with even higher precision: the Antichrist would come (actually did come, in the image of Napoléon) from Paris – the "new Babylon". This mythological pattern remained overpowering among Russian writers (including young Puškin) during the first years after Russia's victory. Within this pattern, the French revolution was also incorporated into the Apocalyptic succession of events, since it was Napoléon's dramatic transformation from a symbol of liberty to a tyrant whose "villainous mantel" (*zlodejskaja porfira)* imposed a cruel yoke on all peoples that confirmed the Apocalyptic essence of the whole epopee. Puškin did not abandon this pattern in his "libertarian" poetry of 1818–1824, even though his sympathy had shifted to the defeated and banished "Satanic figure" from the "sacred forces" which had caused its downfall. This background is relevant for understanding the symbolism of count Nulin's itinerary and adventure.

Thus, count Nulin has come from Paris; his destination is ironically called by archaic and solemn names: he is going to "Petropol' ", and scornfully calls his native land "*svjataja Rus*'" to which he addresses his "curse". The apparent purpose of his trip, as decribed in the poem, is to show himself as a "prodigious beast".

> Себя казать, как *чудный зверь*,
> В Петрополь едет он теперь.   /V, 6/

/Now he is going to Petropolis to show himself like an exotic (literally *prodigious*) beast./

The motif of the "beast" persistently, though inconspicuously, accompanies count Nulin throughout the whole poem. Thus, at the end of the poem, the returning husband announces that he set dogs on the hare; later, in anger, he promises to set dogs on the adventurous count as well. The parallelism between the two episodes implies the comparison of the count to a hare. Such is one of his incarnations as a "beast" (remember the hare which emerged as a bad omen on the day prior to writing the poem).[13] The even more mocking scene of "setting dogs" on the count occurs in Natal'ja Pavlovna's bedroom, when her spitz's barking causes Nulin to flee and abandon the whole affair. In this confrontation with the dog, he represents another beastly incarnation – a cat, to which he is compared when approaching the bedroom (the comparison itself being a parodic periphrasis of the comparison of Tarquinius with a lion in Shakespeare's poem[14]).

To sum up, count Nulin arrives (preceded by the horns' blowing and the bell's ring) in his Western costume (which makes him look like an exotic, or prodigious, beast), equipped with infernal attributes, such as "the horrible book" and a blasphemous song which proclaim the end of monarchy and of God's realm. He utters curses against "sacred Rus' " and prepares to appear in its capital called by its ancient Greek name. On his way, he attempts to make a conquest of the heroine who is temporarily abandoned by her husband (the features of the latter revealing a comic representation of the image of the Russian emperor and Apocalyptic "man of destiny"). Nulin is nothing less than a new incarnation of Sextus Tarquinius, and therefore the outcome of his undertaking seems to be prearranged: it has already been written in the book (Shakespeare's "rather weak poem"). But at a crucial point, the heroine who at first glance appeared quite prepared to follow the rules of the "titillating" plot, suddenly makes a move which is quite in accordance with the core of her rustic nature but which is totally unexpected,

22

considering the veneer of her appearance and behaviour. This climactic event – the slap in the count's face – has broken the development of the prototypical plot; and thereafter, nothing has happened: no "republic, consuls, dictators, Catos, and Caesar" are to come into existence. The heroine remains in possession of her imperious and nameless husband. As the last lines of the poem suggest, their marriage is far from being an ideal one, but still, for one reason or another, its harmony is not to be broken by a chain of events similar to those which caused the fall of the Roman Empire.

During the first year of his life in Michajlovskoe (the fall of 1824 – fall of 1825), Puškin often portrayed himself as a "prophet" whose vision embraces the hidden meaning and future outcome of current events. Of course, most of Puškin's remarks on this topic were made in the form of jokes; however, sometimes the meaning of those jokes corresponded to the meaning of his most serious and solemn poetic works of that period. For instance, Puškin ironically compared his precipitous transfer from Odessa to Michajlovskoe with Mahomet's "flight from Mekka to Medina"; consequently, a manuscript he had lost in a card game in Odessa and was unable to recover because of his sudden departure, was called his "Koran" (letter to Vjazemskij of November 29, 1824). But at the same time Puškin wrote his solemn "Imitations of the Koran" charged with transparent allusions to his own destiny and mission.[15] Likewise, Puškin was only half-joking when he wrote to Žukovskij explaining his refusal to undergo an operation: "I shall not die; that is impossible; God wouldn't want *Godunov* to be destroyed with me." (Letter of October 6, 1825) /XIII, 236/.[16] This prophetic mood was reinforced by the message about Aleksander's death. In the excited letter to Pletnev (4–6 December, 1825) Puškin referred to this event as proof of his prophetic gift; by this he meant his poem "Andrej Šen'e", written in the summer of 1825, in which the persecuted poet was depicted as making a prophetic statement about the coming end of the "tyrant", his tormentor:

Dear fellow! I am a prophet, by golly a prophet! I shall order my *André Chénier* published in Church Slavonic letters in the name of the Father and the Son, etc. [17] /XIII, 248/

The "Apocalyptic prophecy" of "Count Nulin", fulfilled in the most dramatic way, could not have been presented in any other form but as a parody whose protagonists appeared most ludicrously unfit for their roles in the battle between the heavenly and infernal forces. It was quite typical for Puškin to make his most important and revealing statements in a cryptic form, often in the disguise of a joke, obscenity, blasphemy, etc. Nevertheless, the statement had been made, and its imprint can be felt on many of Puškin's important later works, such as "Poltava", the last chapter of

"Eugene Onegin", the two poems written on the events of the Polish uprising and surrender of Warsaw, and "The Bronze Horseman".

NOTES

1. See the story of this letter in: *Zapiski dekabrista N. I. Lorera*, ed. by M. N. Pokrovskij, Moscow, 1931, p. 189. M. A. Cjavlovskij (*Letopis' žizni i tvorčestva Puškina*, v. 1, Moscow, 1951, p. 655) suggests the possible date of Puškin's receiving the letter: between December 5 and 13.
2. An account of this event was given by M. P. Pogodin (*Prostaja reč' o mudrenych veščach*, 3rd ed., Moscow, 1875, sect. II, p. 24). Pogodin's story was confirmed by P. A. Vjazemskij in a letter to Ja. K. Grot; see: *Puškinskij licej (1811-1817). Bumagi I-go kursa, sobrannye J. K. Grotom*, St. Petersburg, 1911, p. 107.
3. Up to this point the English text is quoted from: William Harkins, ed. & transl., *Three Comic Poems by Alexander Pushkin*, Ann Arbor, 1977, p. 47. In the translation of the last sentence, a phrase from L. Sterne, quoted by Puškin, was used (Laurence Sterne, The letter to Ignatius Sancho of July 27, 1766; see also note 7).
4. The numbers in straight brackets indicate volume and page in: A. S. Puškin, *Polnoe sobranie sočinenij*, v. I-XVII, AN SSSR, 1937–1959. The italics in all examples are mine.
5. /III, 1133/. See also: I. I. Puščin, *Zapiski o Puškine. Pis'ma*, Moscow, 1956, p. 85.
6. M. O. Geršenzon, Graf Nulin, 2nd ed. in: M. O. Geršenzon, *Stat'i o Puškine*, Moscow, 1926, pp. 42–49; B. M. Èjchenbaum, O zamysle "Grafa Nulina", *Vremennik Puškinskoj komissii*, v. 3, Moscow-Leningrad, 1937, pp. 349–357.
7. Ju. M. Lotman, Tri zametki k puškinskim tekstam, *Vremennik Puškinskoj komissii 1974*, Leningrad, 1977, p. 90.
8. M. P. Alekseev, Shakespeare und Puschkin, *Shakespeare-Jahrbuch*, Weimar, Bd. 104 (1968), pp. 141–174; Gerhard Dudek, Die Bedeutung von Puschkins Shakespeare-Rezeption für die Entwicklung der russischen Nationalliteratur, i b i d., Bd. 116 (1980), pp. 26–35.
9. English translation is taken from: *The Letters of Alexander Pushkin*, Translated by Thomas Shaw, The University of Wisconsin Press, 1967, p. 230.
10. Cf. the analysis of this meaning of the name Nataša in: V. F. Chodasevič, *Poètičeskoe chozjajstvo Puškina*, v. 1, Leningrad, 1924, pp. 75–76.
11. A parallelism between the finales of "Count Nulin" and "Eugene Onegin" is noted by D. D. Blagoj (*Duša v zavetnoj lire. Očerki žizni i tvorčestva Puškina*, Moscow, 1977, p. 219).
12. Th. Shaw, o p. c i t., p. 227.
13. The same bad omens (a hare which he wished to be hunted down and a priest) confronted Puškin once more eight years later during his trip to the Uralian provinces where he was collecting materials for the "History of Pugačev". Puškin wrote about these incidents to his wife (letters of September 14 and October 2, 1833):

    I'm in Simbirsk again. Night before last I left, setting out for Orenburg. I had barely gotten out onto the highway when a hare ran across in front of me. . . . I would give a great deal to be a borzoi; I certainly would have hunted down that hare. /XV, 80/

    As I was approaching Boldino, I had the gloomiest premonitions. . . . After entering the boundaries of Boldino, I met some priests, and I became as irritated with them as at the Simbirsk hare. /XV, 83/

    (Th. Shaw, o p. c i t., pp. 610 & 612).
    During this October in Boldino, Puškin wrote "The Bronze Horseman".
14. W. Harkins, o p. c i t., p. 41.

15. Personal allusions in "Imitations of the Koran" have been thoroughly studied in the following works: N. V. Fridman, Obraz poėta-proroka v lirike Puškina, *Učenye zapiski MGU*, v. 118, book 2, Moscow, 1947, pp. 88–98; B. V. Tomaševskij, *Puškin. Materialy k monografii. Kn. 2 (1825–1836)*, Moscow-Leningrad, 1961, pp. 42–45; Walter N. Vickery, Toward an Interpretation of Pushkin's "Podrazhanija Koranu", *Canadian-American Slavic Studies*, v. XI (1977), pp. 61–74.
16. Th. Shaw, o p. c i t., p. 259.
17. Th. Shaw, o p. c i t., p. 267.

Jostein Børtnes

On Puškin's Response to Liturgical Poetry: "Otcy pustynniki i ženy neporočny" and Saint Ephraim the Syrian's Penitent Prayer

It was in the summer of 1836, while staying at a villa on Kamennyj Ostrov, the fashionable holiday resort of St.-Petersburg high society, that Puškin wrote his paraphrase of Saint Ephraim the Syrian's Penitent Prayer, only half a year before his death on 29 January 1837. The poem, "Otcy pustynniki i ženy neporočny" belongs to a small group of short, meditative lyrics that were all completed here within the short span of a few weeks, from the beginning of June to the end of July. The other poems are "Kak s dreva sorvalsja predatel' učenik" ("Podražanie italijanskomy") – a variation of the *topos* "what happened to Judas in Hell" – "Kogda velikoe sveršalos' toržestvo" ("Mirskaja vlast' ") – in which the *topos* "if Christ came back now" is combined with the *stabat-mater* motif – and the anarchistic "Nedorogo cenju ja gromkie prava" ("Iz Pindemonti"). None of these poems was published by the poet himself, but posthumously, "Otcy pustynniki" under the title "Molitva" by Žukovskij in 1837, in Puškin's owe journal, the *Sovremennik* (V:319).

Until recently, the poems have always been treated separately, but it now looks as if they were meant to form a cycle. In the autographs, some of them carry Roman numerals, and N. V. Izmajlov, to whom we owe a special study of the manuscripts, has identified the poems in the following order: II "The Prayer", III "Imitated from the Italian", IV "The power of this world", and VI "From Pindemonte". I and V have not been identified.[1]

In spite of the similarities between the four poems, it is difficult to see what should have constituted their cyclic unity. They are all written in Alexandrine couplets, but so are many other of Puškin's poems from this period, this being his favourite metre for meditative verse during the last years of his life. Thematically, the first three of the poems are closely connected. They are all variations of motifs from the liturgy, and in their original context, the three liturgical motifs virtually form a sequence: Saint Ephraim's Prayer, repeated several times in all the services of the Great Lent, is read for the last time on Easter Wednesday, when the Judas motif makes its first appearance in the liturgy. Judas' betrayal is the central motif of the Maundy-Thursday service, whereas the *stabat-mater* motif has its place in the Good-Friday liturgy, the re-enactment of Christ's confrontation with the powers of this world and His Crucifixion. In the context of the liturgy there is thus an inner progression from one motif to the next which must be felt by all Orthodox readers of Puškin's poems.[2]

But this liturgical contiguity of the motifs makes it all the more difficult to see how the sixth poem, "From Pindemonte", could fit into the cycle. After all, this vehement attack on all forms of secular government, with its final paean to individual freedom, to the beauty of nature and of art, has no parallel in the liturgy. Moreover, the sequential coherence of the first three poems, so self-evident from a liturgical viewpoint, is not equally obvious when seen in the context of Puškin's verse. His adaptation of the old Church Slavonic prayer in the first poem is very different, both in tone and in thematic development, from the burlesque treatment of the Judas theme in the second, and from the scourging irony of the juxtaposition of the Crucified Christ with soldiers from the imperial guard in the third. The common liturgical background of the poems serves rather to underline their poetic dissimilarity.[3] In view of this, we shall not try to pursue the question of their cyclic character any further at this point, but focus instead on the interpretation of the "Prayer", Puškin's paraphrase of Saint Ephraim's prayer in Church Slavonic translation known by heart by Orthodox Russians today as in the days of the poet:

Гꙋ́и и влⷣко живота моегѡ, дꙋхъ празаности, оунꙑ́нїа, любоначалїа, и празанословїа не даждь ми.

Дꙋ́хъ же цѣломꙋдрїа, смиреномꙋдрїа, терпѣнїа, и любве, даруи ми рабꙋ твоемꙋ́.

еи гꙋ́и црⷭю, даруи ми зрѣти моа прегрѣшенїа, и не осуждати брата моегѡ, ꙗко благословенъ еси во вѣки вѣкѡвъ, аминъ.

Like its Greek exemplar, the Church Slavonic translation has lost the syllabism of Ephraim's Syrian text. The Church Slavonic version copies the rhythmic prose of its Greek prototype.[4]

That Puškin's adaptation is very close to the Church Slavonic exemplar, strikes us as soon as we read the poem, here reproduced from the Academy edition of Puškin's Collected Works (III:1, 421):

1 Отцы пустынники и жены непорочны,
2 Чтоб сердцем возлетать во области заочны,
3 Чтоб укреплять его средь дольных бурь и битв,
4 Сложили множество божественных молитв;

5 Но ни одна из них меня не умиляет,
6 Как та, которую священник повторяет
7 Во дни печальные Великого поста;
8 Всех чаще мне она приходит на уста
9 И падшего крепит неведомою силой:
10 Владыко дней моих! дух праздности унылой,
11 Любоначалия, змеи сокрытой сей,
12·И празднословия не дай душе моей.
13 Но дай мне зреть мои, о Боже, прегрешенья,
14 Да брат мой от меня не примет осужденья,
15 И дух смирения, терпения, любви
16 И целомудрия мне в сердце оживи.

Like so much of Puškin's mature poetry, with the exception of *The Bronze Horseman* and the "Exegi monumentum", the "Prayer" has never been popular with critics. It is usually passed over in silence, and when it is mentioned, it is mostly for negative reasons. It has become an "accepted truth" that Puškin's rendering of Saint Ephraim's prayer is a failure. In the two books on Puškin that have come out in English in the last two decades, Magarshack's from 1967, and Bayley's from 1971, the latter claimed to be the first critical assessment in English of the whole range of Puškin's writings, there is not a single reference to the poem. The reason for this neglect may be the cavalier rejection of the "Prayer" in Mirsky's brilliant Puškin monograph from 1926. To this provocative scholar, who maintained that in spite of his longings for a Christian inner life, Puškin's nature "remained pagan", the poem could only be an embarrassment and he needed all his rhetorical prowess in order to reduce both its artistic and its biographical significance:

> That Christian emotions were in substance alien to him may perhaps be best illustrated by his very well-known paraphrase of one of the most beautiful and profound of the prayers of the Eastern Church – the Penitent Prayer of St. Ephraim of Syria. It is certainly one of the very few of Pushkin's adaptations which is distinctly inferior to its original.[5]

One of the few Western scholars who has challenged this negative assessment of Puškin's "Prayer", is Stender-Petersen, himself a great connoisseur both of Russian and of Church Slavonic poetry. He regarded this poem as one of the finest examples of Puškin's mature verse, praising in particular its subtle balance of modern and archaic elements, "executed with a wonderful sureness of touch".[6]

It is this combination of liturgical rhetoric with Puškin's own religious symbolism that determines the structure of the "Prayer". In their intersection lies the key to its poetic significance.

The network of elements selected from the two sources has to be seen against the background of pervasive features common to the poem as a whole. The most salient of these is the transposition of the solemn prose of the liturgical prayer into a regular continuum of eight Alexandrine couplets with alternating feminine and masculine rhymes, and with the obligatory caesura, or intonational break, after the third foot.

With the exception of two couplets (lines 9–10 and 15–16), all the end rhymes of the poem are grammatical, bringing together words from the same parts of speech, words with identical endings, or endings similar in sound and with different but contiguous grammatical functions (e.g. $_5$'umil*jaet*' $_6$'povtor*jaet*', with correspondence both in sound and meaning, but $_{13}$'pregre-*šen'ja*' $_{14}$'osužden'ja', where likeness of sound conceals a functional difference between the nominative plural and the genitive singular). This pattern is broken only at two crucial points in the poem, $_9$'*siloj*' $_{10}$'*unyloj*', and $_{15}$'*ljubvi*' $_{16}$'*oživi*'. In both pairs the rhyme is antigrammatical, juxtaposing in the first case a feminine noun in the instrumental singular with the genitive feminine singular of an adjective, in the second the genitive singular of the feminine noun "*ljubov'* " and the imperative second person singular of the perfective verb "*ožit'* ". The first of these deviations marks the boundary between the poet's *prothesis* and the *paraphrase* proper, the second marks the end of the whole poem by rhyming a noun quoted in the liturgical text ($_{15}$ '*ljubvi*') with a word not found in the Church Slavonic original but central to Puškin's own religious vocabulary ($_{16}$'*oživi*').

In his handling of the compulsory caesura, Puškin introduces an alternation between masculine and dactylic breaks, a device granted by the conventions of the six-footed Russian iamb and exploited by Puškin with great subtlety.[7] A masculine caesura means that the last downbeat of the first hemistich falls on the last syllable before the pause, whereas a dactylic caesura has the last downbeat on the proparoxytonic syllable of the first hemistich. Between these two alternatives (feminine caesura is impossible in Russian prosody) there is a rhythmical difference, masculine caesurae often being combined with a rhythmical pattern of four main downbeats and an intonational pause after the break, giving it a "heavy" character, in contrast to the dactylic variant, usually combined with three main downbeats and no pause, giving it a "lighter" quality.[8]

In the "Prayer" the alternation between these rhythmical impulses creates a pattern that does not coincide, but interacts with the regular succession of feminine and masculine end rhymes in a complex structure that also involves the syntactic units of the text, defined by the "strong" punctuation marks employed in the poem: the colon in the middle, marking the borderline between prothesis and paraphrase, the two semicolons in the former, and the two full stops in the latter:

29

End rhymes
and punctuation: $_1$A,$_2$A,$_3$b,$_4$b;$_5$C,$_6$C,$_7$d;$_8$d$_9$E:$_{10}$E,$_{11}$f,$_{12}$f.$_{13}$G,$_{14}$G,$_{15}$h$_{16}$h.
Caesurae: D m m D m D D m m m D D m m D D

The scheme shows a correlation between masculine end rhymes, dactylic caesurae, and "strong" punctuation in a system interrupted only in the middle of the poem, on either side of the colon, where masculine caesurae are followed by feminine endings in the second distichs. This deviation, emphasizing the transition from prothesis to paraphrase, coincides with a pattern of sound repetition between the last stressed syllables of the hemistichs not found elsewhere in the poem: $_8$'onA' $_8$'ustA', $_9$'krepIt' $_9$'sIloj', $_{10}$'moIch' $_{10}$'unYloj'.

The correspondence between rhythmical phrasing and syntactic segmentation reflected in our scheme, implies that the regular continuum of Alexandrine couplets may be divided into sections of varying length comparable to the division of a poem into stanzas. The primary division of the "Prayer" is given by the dichotomy of prothesis and paraphrase. These units are in their turn subdivided into smaller segments, three in the first and two in the second half of the poem, yielding the following pattern:

I(1-4);II(5-7);III(8-9):V(10-12).V(13-16).

Our next task will be to see whether this pattern, delineated by the rhymes, caesurae, and punctuation of the poem, may be found also in the distribution of sound patterns and verbal categories. In doing this, we shall try to apply Roman Jakobson's analytical method, as summarised by Paul Kiparsky:

> Jakobson views a poem as having a kind of constituent structure, characterized relationally in terms of succession (aa bb), alternation (ab ab) and enclosure (abba). It is possible that the right way to visualize these structures is in terms of binary branching of hierarchical tree representations. He states the distribution of linguistic elements over those relational structures by quantifying expressions that include *all Xs, no Xs, the only X*. This then means that it is a relevant structural fact about the poem that, say, all finite verbs occur in the second half, or that it contains no animate nouns.[9]

In the "Prayer", sound figures play a prominent part in the segmentation of the text. The accumulation of composite nouns with similar desinences in the paraphrase, and the absence of such nominal compounds in the prothesis, create a clear-cut, morphonological contrast between these two main parts: $_{11}$'Ljubonačalija' $_{12}$'prazdnoslovija' $_{13}$'pregrešen'ja' $_{14}$'osužden'ja' $_{15}$'smirenija' $_{15}$'terpenija' $_{16}$'celomudrija'. With the exception of "osužden'ja", all these *homoioteleuta* are quoted from the liturgy. The *homoioteleuton*, a major device both in Byzantine and Slavonic rhetoric, is closely related to the grammatical end rhymes that Puškin has chosen for his poem. How closely, may be seen from lines 13–14, where two *homoioteleuta, "pregrešen'ja"*, taken over from the original, and *"osužden'ja"*, supplied by the poet in replacement of the Church Slavonic infinitive, have been integrated into the system of end rhymes, so that the rhetorical and the poetic uses of *homoioteleuta* are no longer distinguishable.

Alliteration – the repetition of the same sound or syllable in two or more words of a line or a group of lines – is another sound figure favoured by Puškin. The recurrence of the four sonorants *m, n, r, l,* and the *d*-alliterations that permeate the whole poem, form a background against which less frequent sound sequences become all the more effective.

Syllables containing the sounds '*ž*' and '*c*' occur only in I and V, defining these segments as the *outer*, in contrast to the *inner* parts of the poem, the segments II, III, and IV: I $_1$'*(O)tCY*' $_2$'*serdCEm*', V $_{16}$'*CElomudrija*' $_{16}$'*serdCE*'; I $_1$'*I'ŽEny*' $_4$'*(S)lOŽIli*' $_4$'*mnOŽEstvo*' $_4$'*bOŽEstvennych*', V $_{13}$'*(B)OŽE*' $_{14}$'*OsUŽDEn'ja*' $_{16}$'*OŽIvi*'. (In this connection it is worth noting that the version of the "Prayer" published by Zhukovsky in the *Sovremennik,* has $_9$'*svežit*' instead of $_9$'*krepit*', with the *ž*-alliterations including the central, third segment as well, combining I, III, and V as the *odd* segments against the *even* ones, II and IV, leaving it to the '*c*'-repetitions to mark the opposition between inner and outer).

In our version of the poem, the distinction between *odd* and *even* segments is signalled on the sound level by the occurrence in the even segments II and IV of reiterative sound sequences containing the combination – '*dn*' – and '*čal*' –, absent from the three odd segments: II $_5$'*ODNA*', $_7$'*(V)O DNI*', IV $_{10}$'*(V)ladyko DNEJ*' $_{10}$'*prAZDNOsti*' $_{12}$'*prAZDNOslovija*'; II $_7$'*pE-ČAL'nye*' $_{11}$'*(L)juboNAČALIja*'.

II and III are bound together by the repetition of '*šč*' – II $_6$'*SVJAŠČEnnik*' III $_8$'*VSECH ČAŠČE*', whereas its hard equivalent '*š*', occurring in III, V, and IV, affirms the borderline status of the central segment: $_9$'*padŠEgo*' $_{12}$'*duŠE*' $_{13}$'*pregreŠEn'ja*'.

A special correspondence in the sound make-up of the poem is formed between the three odd segments by the reiteration of two roots found in I, one in III, the other in V: I $_2$'*SERDCEm*' and $_3$'*uKREPljat*', the first root reappearing in III $_9$'*KREPit*', the second in V $_{16}$'*SERDCE*'. These correspondences point to a thematic propinquity of the odd as opposed to the even segments.

Puškin's late meditative poetry is characterised by a distinct predominance of grammatical devices at the cost of metaphoric imagery of the kind usually associated with poetic language.[10]

The "Prayer" is no exception in this respect. The only metaphoric, "lexical trope" in the whole poem is the allegorical image of the serpent, well-known both from traditional Christian symbolism and from Puškin's own religious idiom. Inserted into the liturgical text as a definition of the concept of *philarchia*, ₁₁*'Ljubonačalija, zmei sokrytoj sej'*, it brings this particular sin into the sphere of the poet's own religious thought.

Moving on to the syntactic structuration of the poem, we see that the initial segment occupies a special place. Its main clause has been divided into two parts, the subject being contained in I₁, the predicate in I₄, thus embracing the two infinitive clauses of purpose occupying I₂ and I₃, together forming a syntactic parallelism introduced by the anaphoric *"Čtob"*. Both infinitives are imperfective, the first intransitive, the second transitive, the first, ₂*'vozletat''*, a verb of motion denoting an upward surge into invisible regions reached by the heart only, the second focusing the attention on the heart as the object towards which the action is directed.

At its first mentioning, ₂*'serdcem'*, the heart is a mere vehicle, its *peripheral status* being expressed by the instrumental.[11] The central theme in this part of the first segment is expressed in the verb – *"vozletat' "* – the upward movement away from this world. In the next line, however, the focus of vision has been shifted from the vertical movement upwards to the accusative object ₃*'ego'*, referring to the "heart" in its lowly terrestrial sphere, ₃*'sred' dol'nych bur' i bitv'*.

The closed structure of the first quatrain is underlined by the finite verb, ₄*'Složili'*, its perfective preterit showing that there is no direct contact between the event described by it and the *here* and *now* of the lyrical "I" of the poem. This contact is only established with the introduction of the present tense in II and III: ₅*'umiljaet'* ₆*'povtorjaet'* ₈*'prichodit'* ₉*'krepit'*. With the exception of ₆*'povtorjaet'*, related to the subject of the relative clause, ₆*'svjaščennik'*, these finites are all governed by pronominal subjects referring to the one particular prayer that has been singled out from the others referred to in I, and defined in II: ₆*'ta'*, ₈*'ona'*, the object being the lyrical "I", first directly, ₅*'menja'*, then indirectly, ₈*'mne'*, and finally represented by the metonymic ₉*'padšego'*, describing the lyrical "I" in his role as the penitent sinner.

In the tense correlation between the present and the preterit, it is the latter that is the *marked* term, the present tense being in itself indefinite in regard to time.[12] In contradistinction to the finite preterit of the first segment, the present finites in II and III do not define events or actions from the point of view of time, but in their spatial relationship to the lyrical "I". In II this relationship is external – the lyrical "I" being affected by the prayer read by the priest during Lent. In III the relationship has been internalised, and the prayer comes back to the lyrical hero in his own memory. Segments II and III are contiguous stages in the act of penitence.

The relationship between these two stages is expressed by the religious meaning of the verbs ₅*'umiljaet'* and ₉*'krepit'*, as well as by the substantival participle ₉*'padšego'*, the only participle in the poem, used, as we have already seen, metonymically about the lyrical hero as the "fallen man" in the Christian sense of the word. In modern Russian, the verb *"umiljat' "* means "move emotionally". Its Church Slavonic equivalent *"oumiliti"*, however, translates the Greek *"katanussō"*, *"to stab"*, used metaphorically of the feeling of pain connected with anxiety or remorse, *"be deeply moved"* in this religious sense, and, more explicitly, *"move to repentance"*. In the religious context of the "Prayer", ₅*'umiljaet'*, a *hapax legomenon* in Puškin, has to be understood in its religious significance, expressing the pangs of contrition with which repentance begins. In contrast, ₉*'krepit'* in its Church Slavonic context means *"strengthen"* in the sense of *"comfort'*, thus denoting the power of prayer to bring about a spiritual renewal in the "fallen man". The movement inwards from the liturgical environment of II towards the "inner man" of the lyrical "I" in III, implies a relationship of similarity and contrast between the two stages, in addition to their spatial contiguity.

Opposed to the finites of the prothesis, which are all in the indicative, the first part of the paraphrase has not a single indicative, and its only verb form is the negative imperative ₁₂*'Ne daj'*. When used in its conative function, as an appeal, the imperative corresponds to the vocative, in Puškin's poem to the invocation of God the ₁₀*'Vladyko dnej moich'* in the first line of the paraphrase, and to the direct appeal ₁₃*'o Bože'* in the second part, where the imperative is repeated in its positive form, ₁₃*'daj'*. The master-slave relationship between God and his servant in Saint Ephraim's original, has significantly been left out and replaced by another relationship, more congenial to the poet's religious outlook, that between the masculine 'duch', the divine spirit coming from the life-giving *Vladyko dnej moich* and the feminine *'duše moej'*, synecdochically replacing the "mi" of the original.

The only finite non-imperative of the paraphrase, ₁₄*'primet'*, is perfective like the only finite in the initial segment, ₄*'Složili'*, but unlike this, it is singular and non-preterit, its perfective present denoting a future possibility dependent on the fulfilment of the wish expressed in the imperative clause. Introduced by the archaic conjunction ₁₄*'Da'* in its Church Slavonic meaning of "in order to", this subordinate clause varies the motif of purpose found in the two *"Čtob"*-clauses in I, and it is significant that Puškin removed the paratactic infinitive of the liturgy – *"i ne osuždati brata moego"* – into the centre of his paraphrase, simultaneously changing it into a subordinate clause with *"brat moj"* as the subject, *"ot menja"* emphasizing the involvement of the lyrical "I" much more forcefully than in the original, making the clause of purpose dependent on the contrition of the lyrical hero, and not, as in the Church's prayer, on God's will only. No less significant is Puškin's transformation of the Christian relationship to one's *"brat"*, or neighbour, into a precondition for the final appeal for new life, the imperative ₁₆*'oživi'* rhyming with ₁₅*'ljubvi'* and functionally corresponding to the two invocations of God, one in the beginning and one in the middle of the supplication.

The perfective past of the initial segment, complete and separated from the *here* and *now* of the lyrical "I", is thus counterbalanced in the final segment by verbal forms expressing a timeless relationship between God and man, and a potential change in the situation of the penitent hero. But in the central segment this change has already taken place, brought about by the *"nevedomoju siloj"* of the words of the prayer. There is thus a parallel between the present indicative of III and the potential modality of V, just as there is a parallel between II and IV: The detestation of past sins implicit in II$_5$'*umiljaet*', is equivalent to the deprecative imperative IV$_{12}$'*Ne daj*', the supplication of deliverance from evil, whereas the confirmative III$_9$'*I padšego krepit*' finds its counterpart in the positive V$_{13}$'*No daj*', followed by the prayer for the resurrection of Christian virtues in the heart of the penitent, where the heart, once a vehicle and a direct object, has become the goal of the divine movement: $_{16}$'*v serdce oživi*'.

It is a characteristic feature of Puškin's prothesis that the lyrical "I" is never referred to in the nominative. The subject of the lyrical utterance never appears as the grammatical subject in the poem, only in the oblique cases.

The lyrical hero of the "Prayer" is not a "doer", but an "undergoer", the agent being the feminine and inanimate prayer, represented by the pronouns $_6$'*ta, kotoruju*' and $_8$'*ona*'. This switching of roles – we would expect the active subject of transitive verbs like *"umiljaet"* and *"krepit"*, as well as a verb of motion like *"prichodit"* to be an animate being – "suggests an element of personification".[13] The prayer, once composed by one of the desert fathers in the striving of his heart towards a higher reality beyond the world of the senses, comes back to the poet invested with a divine power, *"nevedomoju siloj"*, the epithet being a Church Slavonic equivalent of the Greek *"adēlos"* ("unknown" in the sense of "invisible", "not seen"), and thus corresponding to the *"zaočny"* in the initial couplet. These two epithets, both signifying a divine presence, have a demonic, negative antonym in *"sokrytoj"* in $_{11}$'*Ljubonačalija, zmei sokrytoj sej*" characterising the serpent of *philarchia*.

Puškin's version of Saint Ephraim's prayer differs from the original not only in the arrangement of minor details, but in its basic pattern, which in Puškin is determined by the soul-spirit motif and by the motif of spiritual death and regeneration. With the help of these motifs, Puškin has transformed the text of the liturgy in the context of his own religious experience, projecting onto the old Penitent Prayer his own vision of penitence and spiritual resurrection.

This is not the place for a detailed discussion of this pattern and its role in Puškin's *oeuvre*. Let me confine myself to mentioning two of his poems about spiritual death and regeneration – the stanzas addressed to A. B.

Kern, "Ja pomnju čudnoe mgnovenie", and the "Prorok". The latter poem is particularly interesting in connection with the paraphrase of Saint Ephraim's prayer, since it too is a paraphrase of a liturgical text, the vision in the Prophet Isaiah of the seraphim flying down and touching the prophet's mouth with burning coal:

> I kosnulsja ust moich, i skazal: vot, ėto kosnulos' ust tvoich, i bezzakonie tvoe udaleno ot tebja, i grech tvoj očiščen (Is. 6:7, according to the modern Russian translation).

This verse, quoted from the end of the passage paraphrased in "The Prophet", is cchocd in lines eight and nine of the "Prayer":

8 Vsech čašče mne ona prichodit na usta
9 I padšego krepit nevedomoju siloj:

In view of this correspondence, the occurrence in the passage in Isaiah of the verb *"umilichsja"* in the meaning of *"katanenugmai"*, or, in the modern Russian Bible, *"pogib ja"*, and the reference to the prophet's *"nečisti ustně"*, help us to illuminate Puškin's paraphrase:

> I skazal ja: gore mne! pogib ja! ibo ja čelovek s nečistymi ustami, i živu sredi naroda takže s nečistymi ustami, – i glaza moi videli Carja, Gospoda Savaofa (Is. 6:5).

Clearly, Puškin has sought, and found a meaning in the prayer he knew so well from the liturgy, by juxtaposing it with the passage from the Prophet Isaiah that ten years earlier had made such an impact on him that he paraphrased it into "The Prophet", one of his greatest poems, composed according to the same pattern as the one underlying "Otcy pustynniki i ženy neporočny". Furthermore, both poems reflect a common tendency in the lyric poems of his mature period, when the lyrical hero loses his central position, at the same time as the poet seeks to conceal his role as author by presenting his own works as imitations or paraphrases. The poetry written in these years is not lyric in the sense of expressing the feelings and emotions of the lyrical "I", but poetry about feelings and emotions. By the same token, Puškin's "Prayer" is not a direct expression of the author's remorse and repentance, but a poem about the religious significance of contrition and prayer.

However, like "The Prophet", Puškin's "Prayer" is also a poem about the poet's role in society. The sudden transition in the last lines of the prothesis from the peripheral first person $_8$'Vsech čašče mne ona prichodit na usta', to the third person object ₉'I padšego krepit', is highly ambiguous. The "fallen man" here undoubtedly refers to the lyrical "I" as "the other" in relation to the voice speaking through his lips. But the inspired poet also addresses his message to "the other" in a more general sense: the fallen man who hears the prayer spoken by his lips is strengthened by its divine power. Again, the passage from Isaiah and Puškin's paraphrase of it comes to mind:

"Vosstan', prorok, i vižd', i vnemli,
Ispolnis' voleju moej,
I, obchodja morja i zemli,
Glagolom žgi serdca ljudej".

In a discussion of Puškin's response to the liturgical poetry of the Orthodox Church, it is worth noting that the passage that inspired Puškin's "Prophet" and helped him to find a deeper meaning in the Penitent Prayer he so often had heard repeated during Lent, also inspired one of the earliest and finest examples of Church Slavonic poetry, Saint Constantine-Cyril's Encomium to Saint Gregory the Theologian, reconstructed by N. S. Trubetzkoy[14] and analysed by Roman Jakobson:

Ѿ григоре, тѣломь | чловѣче, а дѹшеѭ | анѣеле! |||
тъı бо, тѣломь | чловѣкъ съıи, | анѣелъ ѣви сѧ, ||
ѹста бо твоѣ, | ѣко единъ | отъ серафимъ, ||
бога прославѣѭтъ | и вьсь миръ | просвѣщаѭтъ ||
правъıѧ вѣръı | казаниемь, | тѣмь же и мене, ||
припадаѭщь | къ тебѣ лѭбъвиѭ | и вѣроѭ, ||
приими и бѫди ми | просвѣтитель | и ѹчитель! || 15

The last two lines of the poem are, according to Jakobson, directly connected with Isaiah's vision in 6:3 and 6:5–8, i. e. the passage paraphrased by Puškin. In Constantine's Encomium, the lips, 'usta' are a synthesis of body and soul, and their juxtaposition with the heavenly seraphim is a juxtaposition found in Isaiah's vision and in Puškin as well. In the Eulogy, as in Puškin, man's communion with the heavenly powers acquires the meaning of "a purification bestowed from on high on the lips called to praise God and bring the prophetic message to the people".[16]

Puškin's response to the poetry of the Orthodox Church was thus a response that carried over into nineteenth-century Russian literature not only the central message of the Christian faith, the message of man's spiritual rebirth, but also its poetic means of expression.

NOTES

1. See N. V. Izmajlov, "Liričeskie cikly Puškina konca 20–30-ch godov", *Očerki tvorčestva Puškina,* Leningrad: Nauka, 1975, pp. 213–269. In the ongoing discussion, S. A. Fomičev has recently argued in favour of putting the poem "From Pindemonte" in the first place, a solution he first put forward in 1974, maintaining that the number IV is a misreading of No 1 in the autograph. S. A. Fomičev, *Poėzija Puškina: tvorčeskaja ėvoljucija,* Leningrad: Nauka, 1986, pp. 266–282.
2. This liturgical coherence is emphasised by V. P. Stark, "Stichotvorenie 'Otcy Pustynniki i ženy neporočny . . .' i cikl Puškina 1836 g.", *Puškin: issledovanija i materialy,* t. X, Leningrad: Nauka, 1982, 193–203.
3. A different view is taken both by Fomičev and Stark, interpreting the cycle in close connection with Puškin's own biography and with the fate of his Decembrist friends. Particularly interesting on the cycle as a poetic representation of the fate of the exiled Decembrists and their wives is Fomičev's discussion, op. cit., pp. 273ff. A recent non-biographical interpretation of the cycle is E. A. Toddes, "K voprosu o kamennoostrovskom cikle", *Problemy puškinovedenija,* Riga: LGU, 1983, 26–44.
4. See S. S. Averincev, "U istokov poėtičeskoj obraznosti vizantijskogo iskusstva", *Drevnerusskoe iskusstvo: problemy i atribucii,* Moscow: Nauka, 1977, pp. 421–454.
5. D. S. Mirsky, *Pushkin,* London: Routledge, 1926, p. 213.
6. Ad. Stender-Petersen, *Den russiske litteraturs historie,* II, Copenhagen: Gyldendalske, 1952, p. 174.
7. A. Kvjatkovskij, *Poėtičeskij slovar',* Moscow: Sov.Ėnc., 1966, p. 331.
8. See S. M. Bondi, "Šestistopnyj jamb Puškina", *Puškin: issledovanija i materialy,* t. XII, Leningrad: Nauka, 1986, pp. 5–27.
9. Paul Kiparsky, "Roman Jakobson and the Grammar of Poetry", *A Tribute to Roman Jakobson 1896–1982,* Berlin: Mouton/de Gruyter, 1983, pp. 27–38.
10. See Roman Jakobson, *Selected Writings,* III, The Hague: Mouton, 1981, in particular "Poėzija grammatiki i grammatika poėzii", pp. 63–86, and "O 'Stichach, sočinennych noč'ju vo vremja bessonnicy", pp. 378–387.
11. For the general meaning of the Russian cases, see Roman Jakobson, "Beitrag zur allgemeinen Kasuslehre: Gesamtbedeutungen der russischen Kasus", *Selected Writings,* II, The Hague: Mouton, 1971, pp. 23–71.
12. Roman Jakobson, "Zur Struktur des russischen Verbums", *Selected Writings,* II, The Hague: Mouton, 1971, pp. 3–15.
13. "einen gewissen Beigeschmack der Personifizierung", Roman Jakobson, op. cit., p. 36.
14. N. S. Trubetzkoy, "Ein altkirchenslavisches Gedicht", ZfSLPh, 11 (1934), pp. 52–54.
15. Roman Jakobson, "Pochvala Konstantina Grigoriju Bogoslovu", *Selected Writings,* VI, 1, Berlin: Mouton, 1985, pp. 207–239.
16. ibid. , p. 227.

Robert L. Jackson

Tjutčev's "V razluke est' vysokoe značen'e ...":
The Timeless Dream and the Timebound Moment

> We are such stuff as dreams are made on,
> and our little life is rounded with a sleep.
>
> Shakespeare, *The Tempest,* IV. 1

В разлуке есть высокое значенье –
Как ни люби, хоть день один, хоть век,
Любовь есть сон, а сон – одно мгновенье,
И рано ль, поздно ль будет пробужденье,
А должен наконец проснуться человек,

"Here are some bad verses expressing something even worse", Tjutčev wrote to his wife with reference to his poem of August 6, 1851.[1] The poem is in no sense a bad one; on the contrary, it is a masterpiece in miniature. Whether it expresses something on the somber or pessimistic side is another question. In any case, Tjutčev's subjective reaction to his poem does not alter its rich poetic and philosophical texture.

"V razluke est' vysokoe značen'e" is a philosophical poem about the pathos of parting and time. The poet perceives the parting of lovers as a prefiguration of man's ultimate parting from life. The dream of love stands for the dream of life. Life, like love, is a dream from which there is an inevitable awakening. The awakening is to time and mortality. Yet the awakening also carries intimations of immortality. The poem, however, seems finally to suggest that immortality lies in the dream of love and life, that is, in the timeless realm of poetry, all that man must return to eternity. What is certain is that the act of parting is laden with "lofty meaning" (vysokoe značen'e).

The poem consists of five lines and thirty two words. Six words are used twice, thus reducing the poem's working vocabulary to twenty six words. The poem is marked by an extraordinary compression and interaction of parts. It is a micro-universe and, as a poem, as a marvel of compression, illustrates the paradox of the timeless dream embedded in the timebound "moment".

The core of the poem – lines 2, 3 and 4 – asserts that love is a dream from which there is an inevitable awakening. The two framing lines of the poem – lines 1 and 5 – stand in direct relationship to one another. The opening line speaks of the "lofty meaning" (vysokoe značen'e) of parting – an allusion to death and resurrection – while the final line discloses that meaning in the veiled metaphor of "waking up" (prosnut'sja). The dash (–) at the end of the opening line establishes the line's privileged status as signaler of the poem's – and man's – solemn concern.

Lines 2 and 4 use groups of words that stand in direct relation to one another and give expression to the notion of noumenal time: "chot' den' odin, chot' vek/I rano l', pozdno l' ". Line 3 – the middle of the poem – speaks of the paradox of the timeless dream (son), that is, of phenomenal time, and has as its center of gravity the dream or sleep (son/a son).

Lines 2, 3 and 4 break down into two syntactical-semantic units separated by a caesura in the third line of the poem: "Kak ni ljubi, chot' den' odin, chot' vek,/Ljubov' est' son /caesura/, a son – odno mgnoven'e,/ I rano l', pozdno l' budet probužden'e". "However /long/ one loves, be it for a single day or for a lifetime,/ Love is a dream"; that is , in loving, or in love, one is plunged into a dream world that is timeless. "But the dream is a moment,/ And sooner or later there will be an awakening"; that is, the dream of love is actually but an instant, a single moment in man's temporal existence; on awakening one is returned to noumenal time. The abstract noun, "probuž-den'c", means "awakening" in the literal sense, but it carries the figurative meaning of "coming to one's senses", waking up to the reality or hard truth.

"A dolžen nakonec prosnut'sja čelovek". In the final line of the poem, the poet speaks unambiguously of man's "waking up": the verb "prosnut'sja", with its root "son", means exactly to wake up from a dream or sleep. Though seemingly a mere reiteration of the thought contained in line 4, the closing line establishes its own independent semantic field. The poet's thought on the dream-like character of love has led him into an even more profound meditation on the inevitable ending of the dream of life. Thus the poem comes full circle back to the first line that alludes to the "lofty meaning" of parting.

The notion of "parting" (razluka – with its root in "lučit' – to splinter) in the poem is both structural and thematic. The caesura in line 3, falling between "son" and "a son", evenly divides the poem into two groups of sixteen words each. But the matter goes beyond the poet's obvious delight in formal symmetries; the poet has invested this pivotal caesura, this non-verbal "space", with metaphysical meaning, indeed, with the poem's most significant statement: falling between two "sleeps" (son//a son) this caesura constitutes a ghostly Pascalian embodiment of the transience of human life. Man's existence is but a "moment" between two sleeps of eternity. Thus the poet has converted poetic "space" into time.

One of the most brilliant accomplishments of the poet is the manner in which he puts to use the word "son" with its alternate though closely related meanings of "sleep" and "dream". "Son" is certainly intended to be understood as "dream" in the syntactic – semantic context of line 3. But "son" as "sleep", as a metaphor for death, is very active in the poem's subtext. The use of the words "probužden'e", and, in particular, "prosnut'sja", serve to bring out the meaning of "sleep" in "son". But the poet has laid the groundwork for this association in the opening line of his poem where he poses in the reader's mind the question of the "vysokoe značen'e" of parting. By line 3 the answer – "son" – is advanced phonologically: the stressed vowel -o- and the syllable -so- in "vysokoe" (certainly the most portentous word in the line) recurs significantly in "son/a son" – the two sleeps between which man lives out his lifetime. The "vysokoe značen'e" of parting is solemn and sonorous "son" (sleep) – a fact made explicit only in the poem's final line. The dominant sense of "son" in line 3, however, is that of "dream". Man's awakening from his dream of love (ljubov' est' son), that is, his consciousness of his dream as "one moment", is signalled phonologically by the unpleasant cluster of consonants "mgn" in the word "mgnoven'e"; after the sonorous "son/a son" this is indeed an unpleasant "awakening" (probužden'e). Thus by line 3 the poet has prepared the way phonologically for the harsh message of lines 4 and 5.

The ultimate fact in man's existence is his mortality. Does the poet view man's parting from earth, that is, death, in a completely gloomy spirit? His conception of death as a "waking up" (prosnut'sja) argues against all notions of final closure in human destiny. Too, it is only in a religious sense that one can speak of death, mortality or parting from earth as a "waking up". The opening line of the poem would seem to contain an allusion to resurrection. The "lofty" and "high" (vysokoe) meaning that the poet attaches to parting may not only refer to man's final sleep (son) but also to his highest dream (son): the paradise of love, the paradise where the dream of love achieves its highest and eternal embodiment. In this interpretation the pathos of parting anticipates the pathos of the heavenly reunion.

In this connection, the final rhyming words of lines 1, 3 and 4 – "zna-čen'e", "mgnoven'e", and "probužden'e" deserve consideration. On the surface these words seem to sum up concisely a view of the poem's content as tragic. Yet the same sequence of words seem to reveal a subtext that argues against a tragic interpretation. In our sequence-seen-as subtext the word "mgnoven'e" (rooted in the verb "migat' ","mignut' " – to wink, to blink) is pivotal in place and meaning (as it is in the tragic interpretation of this same sequence). The awareness of the dream as a moment (a son – odno mgno-ven'e) here points *not* to the unhappy "awakening" in consciousness, but to awakening in the highest religious sense. "Mgnoven'e" in this interpretation is not only "moment", but movement, transition, as in the revelation of the most lofty religious dream. Thus we read in Corinthians I. 15:51–52: "Go-vorju vam tajnu: ne vse my umrem, no vse izmenimsja/Vdrug, *vo mgnoven'e oka,* pri poslednej trube; ibo vostrubit, i mertvye voskresnut netlennymi, a my izmenimsja" (my italics – RLJ). The poem's "lofty" Christian-religious subtext is unmistakeable. But in the poem as a whole is the poet really consoling himself with allusions to an afterlife, or is he speaking of the illusion not only of the dream of love and life, but also of the dream of immortality?

"A dolžen nakonec prosnut'sja čelovek". However one interprets the sequence "značen'e," "mgnoven'e," "probuzden'e," this final line strikes the reader with jarring force; it is terminal in position and in meaning. An unpleasant sense of the inexorable, of compulsion, of the idea of paying back a debt is carried by the word "dolžen." The moment of parting no longer lies in some unspecified time in the future (rano l', pozdno l'): the poet speaks of man waking up "at last" (nakonec). The end (konec) is at hand. In line 2 the poet alludes indirectly to man's lifespan: the maximum time one might love is for a lifetime, that is, a century (vek). Line 5 makes it clear that the worm of time is at work *in* man (čelo*vek*), that is, mortality is the very definition of man.

Thus to the ambiguous sequence "značen'e", "mgnoven'e", "probužden'e", with its hints at the overcoming of time and space, the poet opposes the unambiguous sequence "vek" – "čelovek", with its view of timebound man living out his earthly "moment" between two sleeps. In this perspective man's inevitable awakening from the dream of love and life preludes *not* resurrection and the kingdom of love, but a reentrance into the dreamless world of eternity: "son" without "son". Here, it would seem, is Tjutčev's "ešče chudšee".

The poem's allusions to two kinds of revelation, the one religious and optimistic in character, the other agnostic and pessimistic, coexist in the poem in a kind of creative tension. Yet the Christian "presence", though haunting, is passive; it does not fill the poem with a sense of promise; the unmistakeable and strange glow it gives to the poem seems only to illuminate the darker, more somber colors.

Yet Tjutčev's "even worse" is nonetheless a onesided and narrow appreciation of the poem. In the deepest sense "V razluke est' vysokoe značen'e" is not a pessimistic poem. Man's "moment" in the universe is seen as infinitesimal, transient, even tragic. Yet this moment as dream, illusion, poetry fills the universe. This paradox of man's presence is exemplified by the poet's extraordinary achievement in his microscopic poem: in a single "moment", in a flash of poetry, the poet reveals the landscape of the macrocosm – the infinity of man's universe and its endless dialectic of dream and reality, illusion and disillusionment, of contraction and expansion into and out of time. In this act of language, and in the vision it contains, man is neither earthbound nor timebound: he is the measure of his universe.

1. F. I. Tjutčev, *Sočinenija v dvuch tomach.* Tom II, Pis'ma (Moscow, 1984), p. 169.

Thomas Eekman

Turgenev and the Shorter Prose Forms

Few books in world literature have such a misleading title as Turgenev's *Zapiski ochotnika*. The actual hunting is restricted to just a few paragraphs, and usually the narrator, before he has caught even one woodcock, has arrived at some country house or somewhere else where he meets people, whose outward appearance and character he describes, whose life history he tells us and whose conversations he renders. No matter how important the function of nature is in his stories, as decoration and as a means to create the atmosphere – Turgenev is primarily a hunter of people, a fascinated observer of human characters, human passions, life vicissitudes, and the mutual relationships of men.

One peculiarity of the *Zapiski* is that they are all written in first person narration. This can be explained, at least partly, by Turgenev's wish to approach living reality as closely as possible, to strengthen the ties between literary imagination, fiction, and reality. Presumably the *Huntsman's Sketches* do contain Turgenev's own experiences, meetings, observations and contemplations. Telling a story in the "I"-form has the advantage of diminishing the distance between the author and the reader: the former takes the latter by the hand ("Dajte mne ruku, ljubeznyj čitatel', i poedemte vmeste so mnoj" – thus begins "Tat'jana Borisovna i ee plemjannik"), he turns directly to him, involves him in the events described; that immediate contact apparently was an attractive point for Turgenev. Especially when speaking of nature he likes to confide to the reader his enthusiasm and admiration, as in the concluding story "Les i step' ". And the "I" is the living tie that binds the stories together.

An additional reason that may induce an author to choose the first person narration is the urge to disclose his inner life, to communicate his intimate thoughts, to make confessions. That confessional character is traditionally inherent in much first person narration. In fact, every writer has a certain need to exhibit his inner I, to confess his intimate thoughts: without that need he would remain silent. And for testimonies about oneself "I"-narration seems the most natural, sincere and believable method.

However, in the *Zapiski ochotnika* the role of the "I" is different. This "I" never speaks about himself, he always encounters other people and directs our attention toward them; he rarely expresses his own feelings – only when talking about nature and in rare cases when people are concerned (at the end of "Svidanie" he remarks: ". . . no obraz bednoj Akuliny dolgo ne vychodil iz moej golovy . . ."). The narrator is the observer and recorder, the reporter who interviews others and who by his questions and remarks provokes other people to speak, to make their confessions and to expose their character. His words are, as a rule, neutral, informative. Sometimes he is simply the witness of events that happen to other people, or of their personal relations. Only in "Birjuk" he himself actively intervenes in the action; and in "Stu-čit!" (which was written much later than the original series) the narrator himself has an adventure; however, in this story, too, the attention is mainly directed towards other persons: the narrator's coachman, the alleged robbers they meet.

Yet Turgenev sometimes uses the "I"-procedure in a different way. In the story "Ermolaj i mel'ničicha" the landowner Zverkov tells the story of his maid Arina, whom he had refused permission to get married and whom he had chased away when it turned out that she was pregnant. Here it is not the narrator who is talking, but the landowner Zverkov whom he puts on the stage. This story acquires its bitter taste and is so impressive exactly because Turgenev does not retell the story, but we hear it directly from the mouth of the "I", a feudal lord who is not even aware of the injustice he and his wife have inflicted upon a subordinate.

A different case we find in "Uezdnyj lekar' ", in which the narrator plays again a very limited role – the pith of the story is the tale told by the doctor about a woman patient. It is not a tendentious story, but a love story, and one of an intimate, very personal and tragic character. Our huntsman did not experience the events himself, he is merely the man who takes notes; yet the story is in first person narration, and this way the intimate, confession-like character is reinforced.

The two latter stories belong to the type of frame stories, containing a story which is woven into another story and forming a more or less signifi-cant part of that framing story, or at least distracting our attention for some time from that story. This interpolation of secondary stories, figures, and descriptions, which break the strict, simple thread of the narrative, split it, stop it, deflect it and make it more colorful and diversified, is what is happening all the time in the *Zapiski*. In some instances, as in "Uezdnyj lekar' ", that inner story is so predominant that it acquires primary impor-tance and overgrows the frame. In "Petr Petrovič Karataev", too, the story this Karataev tells us forms the main part of the text – a story in which both the love element and the anti-feudal element play a role. In "Gamlet ščigrovskogo uezda" the reader is first, for six to seven pages, confronted with various types of landowners until finally the "Hamlet" enters the scene, whose narrative constitutes the kernel of the story; and here again, the inner story is in the first person.

Next to the 25 *Huntsman's Sketches*, Turgenev left us approximately 35

43

other stories and novellas of various form, size and character and from various periods in his literary career. To them belong "Ivan Kolosov", his very first writing to appear in print (1844), as well as the story with the ominous title "Konec", which he on his deathbed dictated to Pauline Viardot in French, German and Italian. As is well known, he changed the composition of the *Huntman's Sketches* several times. Among the stories that never figured among the *Zapiski* there are a few that would perfectly fit among them. They, too, deal with characters (both peasants and landowners), situations, relations and events in the Russian country: "Poezdka v Poles'e", for example, "Brigadir", or "Stepnoj korol' Lir", one of his most powerful stories. "Punin i Baburin" also portrays characters from the Russian countryside, but it exceeds the scope of the *Huntsman's Sketches*. The first chapter contains childhood reminiscences – of Turgenev himself, or so it seems. The second and third take place later in Moscow and St. Petersburg, where the "I" meets the same Punin and Baburin again (there is a fourth chapter, which is actually a short epilogue). On the other hand, "Konec" could as to its form, length, subject matter, atmosphere and style be one of the *Huntsman's Sketches*. Consequently, no sharp dividing line can be drawn between Turgenev's *Zapiski ochotnika* and his other shorter prose works. It may be mentioned here that, when size is the criterium, no clear dividing line can be drawn between the stories and novels either. There are stories of 10 to 16 pages, but "Vešnie vody" has 112 pages, whereas *Rudin* has only 102 pages.[1]

However, size is not the only or the most essential distinction that can be made between a short story or novella and a novel. As a rule, the novel is more elaborate in its structure, its theme and plot, as well as in its delineation of the hero's or heroes' character, often encompassing the whole life or a significant part of the life of one or more persons; whereas the novella does not admit deep psychological analysis and is mostly limited to one episode or moment in the hero's life. Goethe mentioned in his well known conversation with Eckermann "das Unerhörte" as the element characteristic of any novella.[2] In most definitions or discussions of the genre since then this occurrence of an unheard of, extraordinary event was put forward as a requirement of a good novella. Ludwig Tieck held that the novella "puts a big or small occurrence in the brightest possible light" and presents it as "extraordinary, perhaps unique"; the story should make "an unexpected turnabout", by which "it will impress itself the deeper in the reader's imagination".[3] Turgenev's older contemporary Nikolaj I. Nadeždin did not recognize this demand of the unusual central event: "The novella [povest'] is an episode from the limitless poem of human vicissitudes."[4]

However, contemporary theoreticians generally confirm that the novella "depicts a single event with the appurtenances necessary to understand it well".[5] "Thus one can recognize the novella by the fact that a chain of motifs leads to a central event, and then possibly away from it again";[6] "the occurrence that takes shape in it has the character of the surprising, the unexpected, the incalculable".[7] A crisis, a reversal of fortune, a conflict, a *pointe* is postulated by several writers on the subject.[8] Such a claim would not apply to some of Čechov's longer stories. But in Turgenev's case, the required central event or climax is usually there. It is reached when the "I" rushes to the place where he expects to find Asja, but she has disappeared; or when the "I" discovers the love affair between Zinaida and his father ("Pervaja ljubov' "); or when Fustov finally returns to the town to find out that Susanna has died ("Nesčastnaja"). In "Klara Milič" at least three such culmination points have been established.[9]

Such a climax is usually absent or much less dramatic in the *Huntsman's Sketches*. The novels do have a crisis, an apogee, or more than one. But what distinguishes Turgenev's novels thematically from the shorter forms is that the novels have two centers: the hero and society, with which he is in close contact and, at the same time, in conflict.[10] In the novels, the hero is socially involved, and in some cases even a social ideologist – whereas the novellas focus on the hero's personal emotional conflict, his love affair in the majority of cases; the reasons of his defeat are psychological, not social. This is a distinction in epic horizon between novel and novella; and here, too, Turgenev's novellas are closer to the typical romantic, traditional patterns.

In the light of this, we have to reconsider our above remark that the novella does not admit deeper psychological analysis and often deals with just one episode or critical point in the hero's life. Turgenev's shorter prose works are exactly characterized by their *not* being confined to just that: in them, by means of introductions, by inserting reminiscences or elaborations on the previous lives of the characters, and notably by adding an epilogue which gives glimpses of their later fortunes, he evokes a more or less complete picture of the main protagonists and their fate. And that is a feature which tends to efface the just established distinction between the novel and the novella.

In just seven out of the 25 *Huntsman's Sketches* is love introduced; rarely is a love affair the main theme of a story (as in "Uezdnyj lekar' "). In the novels love is, of course, a dominating element, except for *Otcy i deti*. In the novellas, too, love is a momentous factor in the life and the adventures of the heroes – with the exception of a story like "Mumu", where love appears only in an episode, and of two stories where love is absent: "Sobaka" and "Rasskaz otca Alekseja", both belonging to Turgenev's "mystic" or mysterious stories in which hallucinations are described.

Thus we see (in case we did not know yet) that love is Turgenev's stock theme, which he handles, elaborates and varies with consummate skill. It is his deeply felt, true to life depiction of the rising stream of love which becomes more and more powerful and carries the hero away, combined with his subtle evocation of atmosphere and fine character analysis that make these stories into such smart, moving, if not gripping, works of literature, even in our times, although the contemporary reader may be used to far more provocative, overtly erotic ways of dealing with the love theme.

Both on the *Huntsman's Sketches* and related stories and on the series primarily based upon the love motif Turgenev worked during his entire career as a writer. One similarity between the two groups of stories is that most of them are narrated in the first person. Typically, in the beginning of the love story a young man (a military man who arrives in a new garrison or a civil servant on a tour of duty, or simply a traveler) comes into contact with a milieu that is unknown to him, in a small provincial town, on an estate, sometimes in a foreign country, where the love adventure then develops. Recent occurrences or memories are never the subject matter; the narrator always goes back to his adolescence, or even his childhood – cf. stories like "Stepnoj korol' Lir", "Punin i Baburin", "Časy", "Son", in which he views the events with the candidness, the fresh and sharp observation of a boy. In those cases, however, the narrator himself is not taking part in the love relationship. More frequent are the stories in which the narrator is one of the partners, thinking melancholically back to an episode in his life, which, however, did not have a fatal result for him: he apparently recovered pretty soon from the shock and now he lives on; maybe he has had some other love adventures since then. "Vešnie vody" is an example: the memory which forms the contents of the story is evoked by a small garnet cross which the hero finds among love letters that came out of a drawer. That memory strikes him strongly, it is true – but apparently he had been able for years to repress it. The epigraph to the story is from an old romance, in which the moments of happiness are being compared to a swiftly fleeting brook in the spring. This mirrors the philosophy Turgenev seems to express. It is a philosophy of resignation, a consciousness that feelings and passions, happiness and sorrow are transient experiences which man is unable to change or to retain. Man, basically a weak, insecure and lonely being, is unable to master the forces of nature that work within him and upon him and set traps for him: he is "being lived" instead of actively shaping and directing his own life, until, before he realizes it, old age descends upon his head like snow (a favorite image of Turgenev), and solely the memory of so many missed opportunities remains.

A large part of these novellas employs the frame structure in some variety, although not all of them are *Rahmenerzählungen* in the strict, classical sense. From 1855 onward *all* of Turgenev's stories are provided with a frame, with two exceptions: "Prizraki" and "Klara Milič". But it is already present in his very first prose work, "Ivan Kolosov", in its most usual, conventional form: somewhere a small group of gentlemen is conversing, one of them takes the floor and obliges the company with his story; towards the end this company reappears for some concluding comments. In "Andrej Kolosov" we find this classical Turgenevian device in its most complete, most consistently sustained form. "Odin nebol'šoj, blednyj čeloveček" addresses a group of people at the fireside, suggesting that each of them in his turn will tell something about an unusual character. He is urged to begin himself, and thereupon we hear the story of Ivan Kolosov. This introduction occupies approximately a page; during the little gentleman's relation, at least in the beginning, the framing element is not forgotten: the listeners from time to time interrupt the narrator, he asks for a cigar, one of those present twice interrupts him with a quotation from Byron, the little gentleman repeatedly addresses his audience. Such interruptions occur less frequently once the story is well on its way, but even there they are not completely absent. When it is finished one of the listeners asks: "And what happened to Varja?" – "I don't know", answered the narrator. We all rose to our feet and went home." Thus the story is concluded by the embracing frame, albeit merely with a few short sentences. The idea that all in turn would tell a story about an unusual personality is not taken up any more. It might be pointed out that this firstling of Turgenev is actually a double first person story, because not only the inner story is told in the first person, but in the framing story, too, the "I" (supposedly the author) takes part ("ja tože byl v čisle sporivšich").

Two years later (still before his first *Huntsman's Sketch*) appeared "Tri portreta". This portrait story is a frame story in an even more extensive sense. It is this time a hunting company to which the "I" also belongs: a double first person narrative again. The actual central story begins after four pages. The narrator hardly plays a role in it: the main characters are his grandfather and some of his contemporaries; yet he throws in a remark from time to time and occasionally addresses his audience. At the end of the story, however, Turgenev fails to lead us back to the company of hunters under the three portraits: he leaves the frame open.

In the years that follow, Turgenev is very much occupied by his *Zapiski ochotnika*. But in 1850 two non *Zapiski* stories are created, and both are frame stories again, in which both the framing and the inner story are narrated in the first person; but the pattern is somewhat diversified. In "Dnevnik lišnego čeloveka" the hero, Čulkaturin, relates his love story, which is a story of the type Turgenev wrote more often, ending in a negative, unhappy way. Čulkaturin's superfluity is not socially indicative, but purely personal, it is a powerlessness, generated by his character, his nature, to gain the respect and concern of other people, and finally also the love of his chosen one: life goes on and gives him the cold shoulder, just like it does other figures from Turgenev's stories. The frame element consists merely of the fact that towards the end, after the last page of the diary, a "Note from the Editor" follows, which informs us that Čulkaturin did pass away the night after he wrote his last note.

The other story from 1850 (published only in 1856), "Perepiska", has the well known letter form, also used in "Faust" (1855). This time Turgenev has left out the frame altogether (about how the letters were found and published etc.). Yet the framing element is present: it is not a straight narrative, but a story couched within the framework of these nine letters, in which the letter-writer also communicates to his friend other things that have nothing to do with the actual story.

"Asja" (1857) does have the classical frame structure, although in a reduced form. It is again a story about somebody who is unsuccessful in the decisive moments of his life, who is worried and hampered by his own half-heartedness. He first makes some remarks about himself; then he starts his story. The first printing, in the *Sovremennik* of 1858, bears the subtitle "Rasskaz N. N.". But that is all that remained of the frame story idea. It looks like Turgenev got tired of coming out with that party of friends every time and starting the real story only after several introductory pages or paragraphs. It should be mentioned parenthetically that N. N.'s story contains a framed-in story, namely that which Asja's half-brother Gagin tells about her and himself; and in that story again the story is couched relating how Asja came into the world, as told by the man-servant.

The next novella, however, "Pervaja ljubov' ", written three years later (*Dvorjanskoe gnezdo* and *Nakanune* came in between), shows again the company of gentlemen, one of whom is talked into telling his love story, with a variation in that he does not start out immediately, but prefers first to write his account down and to read it at the company's next meeting. A concluding return to the company is again lacking. More traditional and complete in their frame structure are "Sobaka" (in which some persons of the listening company are described and called by their names, they repeatedly interrupt the narrator, a good-natured landowner from Kaluga, and come to the front again at the end to express their amazement at the inexplainable events) and "Istorija lejtenanta Ergunova", a story which is not told once, but which the lieutenant repeats each month for the same group of people ("we"). The "I" of the framing text retells Ergunov's tale, and therefore we find in this inner story, as an exception, not first, but third person narration. The actual story is, in this manner, three times removed from the reader.

Next came "Nesčastnaja", a frame story in its ideal form, so to speak. This time the framing story has just as much significance, content and dramatic climax as the framed one, with which it is organically connected. The inner story is placed approximately in the middle of the work (which is about 66 pages long) and constitutes more or less the clue to it. It was followed by Turgenev's most extensive novella, "Vešnie vody", which does contain love reminiscences and possesses the characteristics of a frame story, but is not written in the first person. Sanin lets the events pass his mind's eye; subsequently the external story is taken up again, we see him returning to the place where thirty years ago the described events took place. All subsequent novellas: "Son", "Otryvki iz vospominanij svoich i čužich" (consisting of two stories), "Pesn' toržestvujuščej ljubvi" and "Klara Milič" either are complete frame stories or at least contain some frame elements.

Now that we have ascertained how often Turgenev used these devices and procedures, we might ask *why* he did it. Every writer can have his own designs when using certain methods, or he can be led by certain motives without even being aware of them. As mentioned above, the "I"-procedure will lend a greater directness and verisimilitude to a story.[11] The effect seems to be that the author/narrator is drawn as closely as possible to the reader and the convincingness of the story is maximalized. The other device, the frame, has the opposite effect: that of removing the author from the reader, putting up a screen between them. It seems as if the author "pushes his responsibilities further and further away from himself", as Percy Lubbock put it: "this is not my story, says the author: you know nothing of me."[12]

Other reasons for using the frame structure include the author's wish to stylize, to embellish a story by providing it with an extra dimension; and his wish to write in the hero's own language, to render the speech of a person who does not use the regular literary language, but a dialect, an argot, children's language, or who speaks with a foreign accent. That is certainly a reason why Turgenev's contemporary Nikolaj Leskov so frequently used the device. In Turgenev's case this does not seem a strong motivation. It is true, the narrator of "Sobaka" has a parlance that is somewhat more juicy and jovial than Turgenev usually put into the mouths of his heroes from the landowning class; and the pope Aleksej, in "Rasskaz otca Alekseja", tells his story, as he announces in the framing text, in his own simple words. However, by and large all Turgenev's heroes talk just like Turgenev wrote: a grammatically and stylistically impeccable and well constructed Russian. Of course, where Turgenev introduces a peasant, he will let him speak in his own way; Hirschel in the story "Žid" speaks with Jewish particularities, and the words of Pantaleone in "Vešnie vody" are interspersed with Italian. But if we take the main characters, and particularly the narrators in his shorter prose, they express themselves, as a rule, in Turgenev's own language; their usage of language can therefore not have been a compelling reason to avail himself of the frame device.

More momentous than all this was, in all likelihood, the literary tradition of which he was part and which he followed. As was indicated above, Turgenev did not invent the novella-with-frame, it was widely used before him – in fact, the novella as a literary genre was born with the frame structure: generated by Boccaccio, further developed by Chaucer etc. In Germany, the habit of clothing a story (novella) in a frame was very general; only after Goethe this form became less stereotyped, but it was by no means totally abandoned. Theodor Storm wrote his "Immensee' and several other works as frame stories. Turgenev, during the years he lived in Germany, met Storm and read and admired his writings. Likewise, in France he knew and appreciated Prosper de Mérimée, whose novella "Carmen" had the frame structure. Even more important may have been the literary tradition in which Turgenev was brought up. It is characteristic that some of the most famous and influential love stories of the late 18th and early 19th centuries all had the frame form: "Manon Lescaut" by l'abbé Prévost, Goethe's "Leiden des jungen Werthers", Richardson's "Pamela" and "Clarissa Harlowe", Benjamin Constant's "Adolphe". Some of these consist of framed letters. "Adolphe", "une anecdote trouvée dans les papiers d'un inconnu", deeply impressed many Russians. By its theme (the tragedy of a love which extinguishes) and its atmosphere it is undoubtedly related to Turgenev's work and must have influenced him. In his dealing with the love theme, he continued preromantic and romantic traditions in form and fabula, spirit and style.

Aside from these international literary factors, however, there is the factor of personal disposition. Some writers are by nature more frank and unreserved, others more inhibited. Turgenev was not a person who would easily expose himself, either in daily life or as an author. Doesn't Henry James tell us that Turgenev would sometimes blush like a sixteen year old boy? From his correspondence, even with intimate friends, it also appears that he would be very careful not to exceed certain sexual and other decency norms. A certain prudery may well have contributed to his endeavor to erect screens between him and the reader. The class conventions and precepts in middle-19th century Russia were pretty rigorous: traditions, habits, decency rules played an important role in social life. And Turgenev was not a revolutionary in the realm of morals, not somebody to snap his fingers at all taboos. In European literature, certainly including Russian literature, it was not yet generally acceptable to delve deep into erotic questions in literary works, even though the romanticists had brought the individual emotional element and psychological analysis into the depiction of love.

If he nevertheless wanted to describe love, the most intimate human feelings, relations and situations, perhaps partly experienced by himself, he could do that no better than by writing in the first person and therewith stressing the personal and intimate character of the narritive, but at the same time, in order to avoid a shameful feeling and to keep a certain distance, by indicating that it was not he himself, but somebody totally different. This is no demonstrable truth, but a hypothesis which seems almost to force itself upon the reader of stories like "Asja" or "First Love". And it would at least to a certain extent explain the fact that Turgenev so strikingly often applied a definite pattern or scheme (that of the company and the narrator). One could object, of course, that there are a few frame stories in which love does not play a role ("Sobaka") or a very subordinate one ("Stepnoj korol' Lir"), so they would not require the frame. On the other hand, one might object, there are a few stories that do have the erotic element but are missing the encompassing frame (like "Zatiš'e" or "Klara Milič"), or that are framed love stories, but do not have the first person narration ("Vešnie vody"). But we do not propose an absolute rule, just a tendency; it would be strange and contradict Turgenev's many-sidedness if he would have moulded all his shorter prose works in exactly identical forms.

When the inner story is relatively slight or merges with the dominating frame, our hypothesis does not apply; the function of the inner story may then be to give a character some background, to clarify a situation or somebody's action, or sometimes just to vivify or retard the action. To heighten the interest, to make the story more colorful, Turgenev had, of course, more means at his disposal. One of his typical methods is to start out with an extensive description of the surroundings in which the action is going to take place, and subsequently of the dramatis personae – a description not always indispensable for our understanding of the course of events (in "Brigadir", for example). The counterpart of this lengthy, leisurely intro- duction is his urge to inform us about the lives of his protagonists after the story or novel is finished – as if he is unable to take leave of them, as if an urge for completeness makes it impossible for him to sudddenly leave them alone, without communicating anything about their further lot. Perhaps he was of the opinion that the reader, who was so intensively engaged in the lives of these heroes, has the right (and must have the desire) to learn about their later fortunes. "I konec?", sprosit, možet byt', neudovletvorennyj čitatel'. "A čto že stalos' potom s Lavreckim? S Lizoj?" – that's how he starts the brief epilogue to *Dvorjanskoe gnezdo,* and similar words are used in the epilogue to *Otcy i deti.* This phenomenon is, of course, not restricted to Turgenev – it has to do with the quiet flow and elaborateness of 18th–19th century prose and of life in general in those times. All Turgenev's novels (with the exception of *Nov')* possess – each in its own way – such a "perspectivistic" ending. But epilogues appear also in his shorter works. Strangely enough, he has one even in his very first play, "Neostorožnost' " (1843): it ends with a separate scene that takes place "ten years after", with its own decoration etc., in which only two short sentences are being pro- nounced. Virtually all his novellas are "epilogical". Even when a correspon- dence is rendered ("Perepiska", "Faust"), the last letter has a conclusive, more or less philosophical character. In "Tri vstreči" and "Jakov Pasynkov", one might say the whole last chapter serves as an epilogue. In "Bretter", which climaxes toward the end with a duel of the two male heroes (and a duel is a very common apogee in many stories), during which the *bretter* (fighter) kills the tragic hero Kister – Turgenev cannot refrain from adding a last sentence: "Maša . . . vse ešče živet" – a sentence which seems, at least to us, modern readers, an anticlimax after the dramatic finale and could better have been left out.

In short, frames and epilogues, together with nature descriptions and milieu evocations, personal portraits and biographies, interpolated addresses to the reader of a general, philosophical or contemplative nature, belong to Turgenev's stock of attributes which he used to build up and clothe the skeleton of his works and to make them more appealing, livelier and more personal.

NOTES

1. In the edition I. S. Turgenev, *Sobranie sočinenij*, 11 vols., Moskva: Pravda, 1949.
2. See Joseph Kunz, ed., *Novelle*. Darmstadt: Wissenschaftliche Buchgesellschaft, 1968, p. 4.
3. Quoted by Arnold Hirsch, *Der Gattungsbegriff "Novelle"*. Berlin: E. Ehering, 1928, p. 42.
4. Cf. G. B. Kurljandskaja, *Struktura povesti i romana I. S. Turgeneva 1850-ch godov*. Tula: Priokskoe kn. izdatel'stvo, 1977, p.3.
5. Hans Hermann Malmede, *Wege zur Novelle*, Theorie und Interpretation der Gattung Novelle . . . Stuttgart, 1966, p. 155.
6. Ibid.
7. Joseph Kunz, *op.cit.*, pp. 229–231.
8. Ibid., pp. 10–14.
9. Reinhold Trautmann, "Turgenjew als Novellist", a valuable text for this theme; in his *Turgenjew und Tschechow*, Leipzig: Volk und Buch Verlag, 1948, p. 21.
10. G. B. Kurljandskaja, *op.cit.*, pp. 229–231.
11. Cf. T. Eekman, "The 'Frame Story' in Russian Literature and A. P. Čechov", *Signs of Friendship*, To Honour A. G. F. van Holk . . ., ed. J. J. van Baak, Amsterdam: Rodopi, 1984, p. 404.
12. Percy Lubbock, *The Craft of Fiction*, New York: Jonathan Cape & Harrison Smith, 1931, p. 147.
13. Of course, not every reader is equally charmed by Turgenev's shorter prose works: Vladimir Nabokov thought that "As a story-teller, he is artificial and even lame . . . His literary genius falls short on the score of literary imagination." (In his essay "Turgenev", *Lectures on Russian Literature*, New York-London: Harcourt Brace Jovanovich, 1981, p. 70).

Geir Kjetsaa

The Stavrogin Lukewarmness

One of the most moving scenes in *The Possessed* takes place at the end of the novel when the runaway Stepan Trofimovič, now ill and miserable, turns to his Bible-seller companion Sof'ja Matveevna and asks her to read him a little more from the Bible, – "just the first thing you come across".[1] Following the habit of Dostoevskij, Sof'ja Matveevna opens the Bible at random and starts reading the message to the church of the Laodiceans (Revelation, III, 14 sq). Far from being a trained Bible-reader, Stepan Trofimovič is not able to recognize from where the passage is taken. Sof'ja Matveevna must help him: "It's from the Revelation." To which Stepan Trofimovič replies: *"Oh, je m'en souviens, oui, l'Apocalypse. Lisez, lisez!"*

In Dostoevskij's copy of *The New Testament* the following quotation is marked in pencil in the margin, with a stroke at the beginning and the end, obviously intended for use in the novel.[2] No wonder, for many readers will probably agree that the passage has the greatest importance for the understanding of the author's view of man's relationship to God.

"And unto the Angel of the church of the Laodiceans write: These things saith the Amen, the faithful and true witness, the beginning of the creation of God; I know thy works, that thou art neither cold nor hot; I would thou wert cold and hot. So then because thou art lukewarm, and neither cold nor hot, I will spew thee out of my mouth. Because thou sayest, I am rich, and increased with goods and have need of nothing: and thou knowest not that thou art wretched, and miserable, and poor, and blind, and naked".

"That too ... and that's in your book too!" Stepan Trofimovič cries "I never knew that grand passage! You hear, better be cold, better be cold than lukewarm, than *only* lukewarm. Oh, I'll prove it! Only don't leave me, don't leave me alone! We'll prove it, we'll prove it!"[3]

Regrettably, death prevented Stepan Trofimovič from giving his announced exegesis of the passage quoted. On the other hand, hundreds of commentators, from the Church Fathers to contemporary Professors of theology have been more than willing to shed light on the meaning of the terms involved, i.e., the key words "hot", "cold", and "lukewarm".

To some interpreters the terms are difficult and open to subjectivism of interpretation, especially the image of "lukewarmness". "L'Église de Laodi-cée est très sévèrement jugée," Pierre Prigent writes in his recent book on the Revelation. "Mais le reproche est exprimé en des images dont le

53

caractère général ne permet pas d'atteindre avec sûreté à une interprétation précise. Les commentateurs expliquent le texte en suivant les seules impulsions de leur propre sensibilité à l'image de la tiédeur".[4]

Most commentators have interpreted the terms as a piece of information to the Laodicean Church concerning its spiritual temperature. Thus "lukewarm" is said to denote a compromise between the fervent "heat" of a believer, and the indifferent "cold" of an unbeliever. The Greek word *chliarós* (lukewarm man) is the Christian who lacks zeal and fervor. Arethas, for instance, describes him as the man who "has participated in the Holy Spirit through baptism, but has quenched the Gift".[5] Again, Gregory the Great explains *chliarós* as "the man who has grown cool after his conversion; one cannot even have the hopes for him that one would entertain for a flagrant sinner."[6]

The Fathers' interpretation seems to be well in accordance with the one offered by the well-known contemporary theologian Jacques Ellul:

"Wir finden in diesem Brief die so häufig zitierte Formel von kalt, lau und heiss. Ich halte die Deutung für sehr einfach: Der Laue ist der Wunschlose, der den Mangel nicht empfindet, der nicht merkt, dass etwas fehlt, der nichts erstrebt, und darum auch nichts erhofft. Der Kalte ist der, dem viel fehlt und der das weiss, aber nichts erwartet, der sich im Wissen um sein Unvermögen und sein Scheitern auf sich selbst zurückgezogen hat. Der Heisse dagegen ist der, der handelt, der nach vorne ausgerichtet ist. Im Grunde sind sowohl heiss als auch kalt Aspekte dessen, was wir als Christen Hoffnung nennen. Der Laue, der mit den Gegebenheiten seines Lebens zufrieden ist, wird nichts unternehmen, um zu einem Wandel und zu Veränderung zu gelangen, denn alles scheint ihm recht zu sein, so wie es ist".[7]

According to the traditional explication, then, one is left with the following hierarchy in man's spiritual relationship to God: Nearest is the "hot", then comes the "cold", and last the "lukewarm". To quote a modern interpreter: "Any condition is better than nauseous lukewarmness".[8]

This hierarchy would also seem close to Dostoevskij, only that in his opinion both the "cold" and the "lukewarm" seem to have a higher status than with the theologians. "Dostoevskij", Vladimir Solov'ev writes, "is the preacher of the belief that no moral degradation, no moral meanness and vile act can suppress the spiritual strength of the human being; he is confident that the human soul is a part of the Divine Soul and can therefore revive from all meanness, from all abomination".[9]

Even so, highest on Dostoevskij's list is of course the spiritually "hot" persons, i.e. Christians as his own Sonja, Prince Myškin and Aleša. A little below them, but not very far, we find the spiritually "cold", the atheists – people like the early Raskol'nikov and Šatov, who, since they are not "lukewarm", have the possibility of joining the "hot" through suffering. At the bottom of his hierarchy, then, we find the "lukewarm" people, those who are indifferent and think they can manage perfectly well without God. For such people Dostoevskij leaves little hope but suicide, as demonstrated in the case of Stavrogin in *The Possessed*. However, at the same time this novel shows that even the lukewarm may be useful, at least through his negative example.

The fact that Dostoevskij has a higher opinion of the "cold" and even the "lukewarm" than most commentators seems to testify to his special brand of Christianity rather than to the view that he is wrong in his interpretation.

True, the implication that even the apathy of a pagan is preferable in God's sight to the half-heartedness of a Christian, is a doctrine that is difficult to defend from other passages of the Scripture. Indeed, one wonders why Christ would prefer the church to be "cold" rather than "lukewarm". On the other hand, Dostoevskij's view does seem to have a textual basis that is absent in the traditional commentaries on the passage. It would be natural to expect the text to read: "I would you were hot, or even cold", whereas, in fact, there is no "even", which means that "hot" and "cold" are to be taken as equally commendable alternatives. Moreover, on two out of three occasions in this context where the words "hot" and "cold" are coupled together, "cold" precedes "hot", as though it were the preferable condition.

However, a disturbing complication to both the traditional and the Dostoevskian interpretation of the passage is caused by the fact that the application of the epithets "hot" and "cold" to spiritual temperature, though natural to a modern reader, appears to be almost entirely foreign to the Ancient world. Thus *zetós* (hot) is normally applied to water, and figuratively to the passions of men, but there appears to be no example of its being applied to a person except here. The case is even more singular with *psychrós* (cold). It is much more widely used in the metaphorical sense than *zetós*, but this word, too, is extremely rarely applied to persons. The same holds true for the Biblical hapax *chliarós*. Indeed, this seems to be the only place in Greek literature where it is applied absolutely to persons. This should warn us against assuming that the Ancients used these words in the same metaphorical sense as we do.

Aware of the fact that the traditional interpretation of the passage finds little support in the known usage of the words concerned, several commentators have sought for other explanations. Thus an original approach is offered by the theologians who have turned to consider the local circumstances of Laodicea, and their possible bearing upon the meaning of the passage.

In Roman times Laodicea became the wealthiest city in Phrygia. Its major weakness was its lack of an adequate and convenient source for water, which had to be brought in from hot springs through a system of stone pipes. In stone pipes the water cooled slowly, and even after having flowed several miles it would still be warm when it reached the city. It has therefore been suggested that the "lukewarmness" of the Laodicean Church is an allusion to the poor quality of the city's water supply. On the other hand, the neighbouring city of Hierapolis was famous for its hot springs, which were much prized for their healing properties. Hence the mention of *zetós* would probably have reminded a Laodicean of the curative waters of the city's nearest neighbour. Colossae, of course, less than ten miles away, had a perfectly good supply of cold water, and the epithet *psychrós* may well refer to her.

If this reconstruction of the local situation be correct, Laodicea would have been notorious as a city which, for all its prosperity, could provide neither the refreshment of cold water for the weary, as, for example, its neighbour Colossae could, nor the healing properties of hot water for the sick, as its neighbour Hierapolis could. Its lukewarm water was useless for either purpose, and only fit to be "spewed out of the mouth". The Church in Laodicea would have been intended to see in itself a similar uselessness. It provided neither refreshment for the spiritually weary nor healing for the spiritually sick. It was totally ineffective, and thus distasteful to its Lord.

According to this interpretation, then, the Church is not being informed as to its spiritual *temperature;* rather it is being called to reflect on the barrenness of its *works.*

That "hot", "cold" and "lukewarm" are not to be taken as describing the spiritual fervor (or lack of it) of the people but rather as allusions to the local circumstances of Laodicea, was of course unknown to Dostoevskij. Nevertheless, he seems to have had a feeling that the force of the imagery derives from the function and utility of hot, cold and lukewarm water. Hot water heals, cold water refreshes, but lukewarm water is useless for either purpose, and can serve only as an emetic.

This, in my opinion, is exactly the role of Stavrogin. A man without convictions, without warmth, without enthusiasm, incapable of either loving or hating anyone or anything, he is, in his wordly indifference, not open either to faith ("hot") or to atheism ("cold"). From this morally "lukewarm" man who has completely lost contact with the people and his native earth, nothing new can ever come. He is consumed by boredom and his own superfluousness, "devoid of life",[10] reminding us of the saying that the opposite of love is not hatred, but indifference. Nevertheless, he is a great character, not only because he remains an enigma to us, but also because he has an important, albeit negative role to play in the exposure of the novel's message.

Stepan Trofimovič seems to have a feeling of this. Awakened by the angel's warning against lukewarmness, he suddenly wants Sof'ja Matveevna to read him the parable of the Gadarene swine, duly marked by the author in his copy of *The New Testament* for use in the novel, where it also serves as an epigraph to the entire chronicle. "You see, that's exactly like our Russia, those devils that come out of the sick man and enter into the swine," Stepan

Trofimovič explains afterwards. "They are all the sores, all the foul contagions, all the impurities, all the devils great and small that have multiplied in that great invalid, our beloved Russia, in the course of ages and ages. *Oui, cette Russie que j'aimais toujours.*"[11]

The function of the indifferent and complacent Stavrogin, then, is to serve as an instrument for the author's wish to free Russia from her demons. In the passage quoted from the Revelation we hear that Christ is about to spew out the Laodiceans because of their lukewarmness. In the novel Stavrogin, reminiscent of the lukewarm water in Laodicea, serves as an emetic making Russia spew out its demons. Apparently, this was also how the author felt when he explained the novel in his well-known letter to Apollon Majkov: "Russia has spewed out this trash with which it has been fed and, of course, in these spewed-out scoundrels there is nothing Russian left".[12]

So even the lukewarm Stavrogin has been useful: He has been instrumental in cleaning up Dostoevskij's "great invalid, our beloved Russia".

NOTES

1. Fyodor Dostoevsky, *The Possessed*. Translation from the Russian by Constance Garnett, London 1970, p. 594. The following quotations are taken from this edition.
2. See Geir Kjetsaa, *Dostoevsky and His New Testament*, Solum Forlag A. S.: Oslo/Humanities Press: Atlantic Highlands 1984 (= SLAVICA NORVEGICA III), p. 73.
3. *Op. cit.*, p. 594. In the latest English translation of the novel the use of "*only* warm" instead of "*only* lukewarm" (čem tol' ko teplogo) must be regarded as a sad misinterpretation. (*The Possessed*. A new translation by Andrew R. MacAndrew, New York: A Signet Classic, 1980, p. 669.)
4. Pierre Prigent, *L'Apocalypse de Saint Jean*, Lausanne 1981, p. 76. (= Commentaire du Nouveau Testament, XIV. Deuxième série.).
5. See M. J. S. Rudwick & E. M. B. Green, "The Laodicean Lukewarmness", *The Expository Times*, Vol. 69 (1957/58), p. 176.
6. *Ibid.*
7. Jacques Ellul, *Apokalypse. Die Offenbarung des Johannes – Enthüllung der Wirklichkeit*, Ins Dt. übertr. v. Jörg Meuth, Neukirchen-Vluyn: Neukirchener Verlag, 1981, p. 133.
8. George Eldon Ladd, *A Commentary on the Revelation of John*, Grand Rapids, Michigan, 1972, p. 65.
9. Geir Kjetsaa, "Neopublikovannaja reč' Vladimira Solov'eva o Fedore Dostoevskom", *Scando-Slavica*, tomus 31, 1985, p. 115. My translation, – G. K.
10. See William J. Leatherbarrow, *Fedor Dostoevsky*, Twayne Publishers: Boston 1981, p. 134.
11. *Op. cit.*, p. 596.
12. F. M. Dostoevskij, *Pis'ma*, II, 1867–1871, Moskva-Leningrad 1930, p. 291. Letter from 9/21 October 1870.

Victor Terras

On the Nature of Evil in *The Brothers Karamazov*

In a celebrated essay, "On the Knocking at the Gate in *Macbeth*" (1823), Thomas De Quincey explains the function of this particular detail in Act II, scenes ii and iii of the play. Macbeth and his wife have murdered their king and taken steps to blame the crime on two innocent servants. At this point a knocking is heard at the gate and repeated many times, until a porter finally opens the gate to Macduff and Lennox. De Quincey points out that the knocking announces a transition in the action, being a signal which "makes known audibly that the reaction has commenced, the human has made its reflux upon the fiendish: the pulses of life are beginning to beat again."[1] Reading the conclusion of Book XI, chap. ix of *The Brothers Karamazov,* one is instantly reminded of De Quincey's essay. Ivan Karamazov's tête-à-tête with the devil is terminated by a loud, persistent knocking heard at the window. Much as in *Macbeth,* the knocking continues for a while, growing louder and louder, so that no reader could possibly overlook it. Like in *Macbeth,* it signals a transition. The terrifying nightmare of Ivan's last interview with Smerdjakov and his encounter with the devil yield the stage to a normal human world. This juncture in the plot of *The Brothers Karamazov* draws attention to what may be a pervasive division in the text of the novel: while it generally proceeds on a mundane human level, it also has some scenes and episodes which are dominated by what De Quincey calls "the fiendish", and some which take us into a world of mystic visions. Here I shall deal with those in which the forces of evil seem to be palpably present.

The question of the nature of evil, always a concern in Dostoevskij, is posed more directly in *The Brothers Karamazov* than ever before. The key to the question is whether or not there is such a thing as transcendent evil. In essays published in the same volume in 1922, two Russian philosophers and Dostoevskij scholars take opposite views on this question. Nikolaj Losskij, while leaving his reader the option of believing in the existence of Satan, literally or merely as a symbol of quintessential evil, denies the very possibility of absolute evil:

> It takes little reasoning to arrive at the conclusion that the creature named by us 'Super-Satan' is an impossibility. Immediate hatred for God and the world created by Him would have to be also immediate hatred for one's

own being; but immediate denial of oneself is impossible; hatred for oneself always develops as a contingent phenomenon, e. g., as a result of dissatisfaction with one's being a coward or lacking wit, or being ugly, or not possessing imagination or any other real virtue.[2]

Losskij proceeds to prove his case by presenting many examples from Dostoevskij's works in which the evil actions or thoughts of a character are the result of empirical circumstances which are not *per se* evil, or are in fact good. Losskij also points out that in those instances where such a demonstration is impossible, nothing is known about the psychic condition or background of the evildoer, say, the Turkish soldier who kills a babe before its mother's eyes.

S. Askol'dov[3] sees two kinds of evil in Dostoevskij's world, and by implication in the world at large: empirical and transcendent. He also develops a dichotomy of personal and suprapersonal evil for both types. Empirical evil of the personal variety is "the very ordinary and infinitely varied evil of individual human passions, failings, vices and sins" (p. 20). Its suprapersonal equivalent is found in various social ills. Askol'dov suggests that the perpetrators of this kind of evil are in fact well understood and hence treated with some sympathy by Dostoevskij: "Even individuals who are drowning in their passions, such as Svidrigajlov and F. P. Karamazov, are without a doubt ethically and religiously forgiven by the author, after a fashion" (p. 21).

It is transcendent personal evil that most challenges Dostoevskij, according to Askol'dov. This kind of evil appears inexplicable to human reason and seems to enter the human soul from beyond its confines. It converts a human being, Stavrogin, into a destructive automaton, or causes another, Raskol'nikov, to become obsessed with a perverse and noxious idea. The manifestations of transcendent evil are inaccessible to psychological analysis. Characters such as Raskol'nikov, Versilov, and Ivan Karamazov are driven by a transcendent evil power. Askol'dov suggests that Dostoevskij is intent on showing that transcendent personal evil is a realization of transcendent suprapersonal evil, whose existence is hinted at in the visions of Raskol'nikov, Stavrogin, Versilov, and Ivan Karamazov. Akol'dov concedes that Dostoevskij never explicitly named or defined evil, but suggests that it is, in Dostoevskij's opinion, tantamount to "a replacement of otherwordly eternal values with empirical earthly ones: bread, power, luxury, technical civilization (miracle)" (p. 24). The name of transcendent evil, thus, seems to be "humanism".

The question whether or not transcendent evil appears as such in the composition of Dostoevskij's fiction is a real one, for it seems certain that he theoretically believed in a fundamental rift between the human spirit's striving for divine goodness, truth, and beauty – and man's earthly nature:

59

And thus on earth mankind strives toward an ideal *opposed* to his nature. When man has not fulfilled the law of striving towards the ideal, that is, has not *through love* sacrificed his *I* to people or to another person (Masha and I), he suffers and calls this state sin.[4]

In an often quoted passage of Father Zosima's exhortations, it is made clear that "we have been given a precious mystic sense of our living bond with the other world, with the higher heavenly world" and that "if that feeling grows weak or is destroyed in you . . . you will be indifferent to life and even grow to hate it."[5] Evil is thus defined as that certain heaviness which renders the human spirit earthbound and will not allow it to soar heavenward, quite in accord with Plato's myth in *Phaedrus*.

To what extent is this conception realized in the plot of *The Brothers Karamazov?* I shall recapitulate the plot of the novel, recalling the episodes in which evil that may be suspected to be of a transcendent nature makes an appearance.

In chap. iv of Book I Fedor Pavlovič mocks the traditional notion of hell and, having satisfied himself that there is no heaven or hell, gloats at the impunity with which he enjoys the fruits of sin. He thus attacks faith in divine justice *a tergo,* as it were.

In chap. i of Book II Fedor Pavlovič perversely recognizes in the harmless stranger Maksimov a double of "von Sohn", notorious victim of an obscene murder. Subsequent developments will show that Maksimov is in fact a double of Fedor Pavlovič and the latter himself a "von Sohn". In chap. ii Fedor Pavlovič half-cynically, half-contritely says: "I daresay it's a devil within me, albeit only a minor one" (p. 34), and further: "I am a lie, and the father of lies" (p. 37). Meanwhile, throughout his visit to the monastery, Fedor Pavlovič strikes the pose of a Voltairean humanist. In chap. vii we meet Rakitin, who seeks to deflate the significance of Father Zosima's prophetic bow before Dmitrij (p. 69). Throughout the novel, Rakitin, an avowed atheist and humanist, will act as the would-be corrupter of Aleša, Dmitrij, Grušen'ka, and even Kolja. In chap. viii we are surprised when Ivan brutally and without any reason pushes the pathetic Maksimov off the carriage Fedor Pavlovič had just invited him to mount. This is the first clear indication of Ivan's (another humanist's!) fall.

Book III develops the theme of evil on several fronts. In chap. ii we hear the somber story of the rape of Elizaveta, a *jurodivaja* and a ward of the community, and the uncanny circumstances of the birth of her son. There is a hint that the devil had a hand in it (p. 89). Subsequently we meet Smerdjakov, first as a child who "was very fond of hanging cats and burying them with great ceremony" (black mass! – p. 112) and then as a casuist who cynically mocks the Christian faith (pp. 115–120). Here, a detail of basic significance emerges: Smerdjakov's sharp mind is utterly mundane; it lacks the capacity for religious or even for aesthetic experience. Also in Book III, we see Dmitrij on the verge of mortal sin, as he threatens to kill his father and almost does. Dmitrij also produces the insight that a man "begins with the ideal of the Madonna and ends with the ideal of Sodom" (p. 97). Finally, we hear Ivan Karamazov's terrible words about the "two vipers" who "will devour each other" (p. 131).

Book IV begins with a chapter on Father Ferapont, an ascetic who sees devils in the flesh and in broad daylight. His case shows how a spiritual ideal is perverted by a crude materialist literalism. Chap. iv introduces a contrast between the tender familial piety which reigns in the Snegirev family and the terrible perversion of both father- and sonhood in the Karamazov family. Snegirev's nihilist daughter, though, views her father with a disdainful and contemptuous air, and he labels her attitude with a quote from Puškin's poem, "The Demon" (1823): "And in all nature there was nothing / He wished to bless, or rather in the feminine: that she wished to bless" (p. 184).

Book V has Smerdjakov curse his birth in chap. ii (p. 206). Chap. iv has Ivan "return his ticket" to God, because his earthly, "Euclidean" reason cannot accept this world of injustice and senseless suffering, never mind whatever ideal purpose may be concealed behind it all. In chap. v the Grand Inquisitor, or rather Ivan Karamazov, develops his atheist humanist philosophy which substitutes mundane utility ("bread"), power, and magic for faith and freedom. He credits the devil, "dread spirit of destruction and nonbeing", with being the source of this wisdom. Ivan also relates a medieval apocryph of the Virgin's descent to hell, where he is particularly impressed by the image of some sinners "whom even God Himself has forgotten" (p. 228). Chap. vi has Smerdjakov draw Ivan into the net of his diabolic plan, and the next chapter, "It's Always Worthwhile Speaking to a Clever Man", has him trapped. We have heard the expression "a clever man" before, from Fedor Pavlovič (in Book III, chap. viii, p. 121) and from the Grand Inquisitor (p. 242), and in both instances it refers to somebody who has satisfied himself that there is no God and uses this knowledge to his advantage. At this stage it is made explicit that Ivan is moved by a sinister force which he cannot resist.

Book VI contains the important passages on "contact with other worlds" and also Father Zosima's tract "On Hell and Hellfire". The latter maintains that hell "is the suffering of no longer being able to love." The damned are those who "cannot behold the living God without hatred, and they cry out that the God of life should be annihilated, that God should destroy Himself and His own creation" (p. 302). This position, which explicitly refutes Losskij's denial of the possibility of absolute evil, adds a basic point to the nature of the diabolic as presented in the preceding chapters: the damned not merely "return their ticket to God," because they believe, in their pride, that a godless humanist world will give a better life to most of mankind, but they actively and passionately hate God.

Book VII, chap. i, "The Odor of Corruption", brings back Father Ferapont, exultant over the early decomposition of Father Zosima's body: matter triumphing over spirit. Aleša succumbs to his grief and disappointment that no miracle has happened. He is now easy prey for the tempter Rakitin. Aleša joins his brother in refusing "to accept God's world" and momentarily embraces Rakitin's crudely materialist world. In chap. iii Grušen'ka tells the story of the wicked old woman in hell and the onion, affirming that God is infinitely merciful and that sinners are in hell by their own choice. Book VII ends in Aleša's blessed vision of Cana of Galilee, finishing his bondage to evil.

Book VIII has Dmitrij in despair and therefore once again on the verge of falling into mortal sin. In chap. iv, "In the Dark", it is only a miracle ("Whether it was someone's tears, or my mother prayed to God, or a good angel kissed me at that instant", p. 446) that prevents him from committing parricide. Chap. vi has the coachman Andrej describe a popular version of hell, populated by "all the mighty of the earth" (p. 389). Dmitrij is at this point ready to take his own life – the one sin which Father Zosima singles out as too terrible.

Book IX has Dmitrij undergo the trials of purgatory at the end of which he is reborn, fortified by his dream of the babe. He has now escaped the clutches of hell. Book X, "The Boys", features no palpable evil, though it shows how the roots of evil are planted early. Book XI, chap. iii, makes the latter point explicit, as fifteen-year-old Liza is shown having sadistic daydreams. Later in Book XI we learn that a morbid mutual attraction exists between her and Ivan Karamazov. In chap. iv Rakitin tries to tempt Dmitrij, but to no avail. Dmitrij observes: "And Rakitin does dislike God. Ough! Doesn't he dislike Him!" (p. 557). In chap. v Ivan hints at being visited by the devil (p. 570). Chaps. vi, vii, and viii have Ivan's three interviews with Smerdjakov, which progressively reveal the latter's diabolic nature, as well as the depth of Ivan's self-deception and the hollowness of his moral position. Chap. ix is Ivan's dialogue with the devil, which details the nature of evil embraced by Ivan: the devil, like the Grand Inquisitor, poses as a humanist to whom "nothing human is alien", but who cannot make himself join the "hosannah!" of the heavenly host. Throughout the scene an ambiguity persists as to whether the devil is merely Ivan's alter ego, as Ivan tries to convince himself, or a transcendent evil force. The dialogue with the devil ends with Aleša knocking on the window to bring the news of Smerdjakov's suicide.

Book XII takes us back into a world of mundane affairs. The trial demonstrates how a flagrant miscarriage of human justice serves God's designs. Mundane righteousness (an honest prosecutor and the evidence of an honest witness, Grigorij) causes an innocent man to be convicted of murder. Nobody in the courtroom, perhaps not even Aleša, is aware of God's truth taking its course or of the struggle in Dmitrij's soul.

From the above survey, which could be amplified and expanded, some principles are readily abstracted. Evil is consistently associated with a positivistic and humanist philosophy of life. It is also associated with atheism and a denial of all transcendent values. Atheism tends to turn into a virulent hatred of God and other transcendent ideas, such as "the people" or "Russia". In the case of Father Ferapont a materialist perversion of religion results in a passionate hatred of Father Zosima's serene spirituality. A proclivity to hatred of one's father and a contempt for fatherhood are a trait associated with evil.

An absence or loss of "contact with other worlds" is linked to evil, while the presence of such contact saves Dmitrij, a man drowning in sin. We meet individuals who are in the grip of evil in different conditions, ranging from self-satisfied smugness to suicidal despair. The circumstances under which we meet them extend from trivial everyday situations to the diabolically uncanny. Certainly there is empirical evil, a great deal of it, but there are also many allusions to as well as some explicit appearances of transcendent evil. Fedor Pavlovič is possessed, as he himself observes, by a "minor demon", who makes him do evil of a, one might say, disinterested nature. Ivan Fedorovič is attacked by evil on two fronts: his intellectual pride makes him a victim of a nobler demon in the disguise of the Grand Inquisitor, but the base corruption exuded by Smerdjakov causes his real downfall. Smerdjakov is unredeemed evil personified. Dostoevskij has made every effort to show that Smerdjakov is not merely a victim of his birth and infirmity, but like his master and probable father, possessed by an evil and unclean demon, one of a major calibre, moreover. Smerdjakov does evil for the sake of evil.

In *The Brothers Karamazov*, Dostoevskij has performed the *tour de force* of presenting as possessed by empirical and transcendent evil three characters who stand for the three types of suprapersonal evil which were his lifelong concern: the shallow libertinism of a Russian Voltairean, with contempt for the faith of the Russian people; the militant atheist positivism of an intellectual of the 1860s, likewise contemptuous of the traditions of the Russian people; the crude materialism of a semiliterate Russian of the lower classes, when he has lost his faith.

Dostoevskij has not committed himself to any unequivocal introduction of absolute, transcendent evil in the plot of *The Brothers Karamazov*. (The same is true of the mystic element.) He gives many details which a willing reader can readily understand as manifestations of transcendent evil, but there is always a way left open to give each episode a psychological or metaphoric, rather than a metaphysical interpretation. Hell, for example, is introduced in a variety of different contexts, all of which allow for a natural interpretation. The same goes for the devil. But the sheer mass of hints as well as outright facts builds up a powerful strain of experience that is of an existential order quite different from the mundane, so much so that it is not absurd to speak of intrusions of hellish forces into the world of the Karamazovs.

NOTES

1. Quoted from *Selections from De Quincey*, ed. Milton Haight Turk (Boston: Ginn and Company, 1902), p. 400.
2. N. Losskij, "O prirode sataninskoj (po Dostoevskomu)", *F. M. Dostoevskij: Stat'i i materialy*, ed. A. S. Dolinin (Peterburg: "Mysl'", 1922), p. 68.
3. S.Askol'dov, "Religiozno-ètičeskoe značenie Dostoevskogo," *F. M. Dostoevskij: Stat'i i materialy*, ed. A. S. Dolinin (Petersburg: "Mysl'", 1922), pp. 1–32.
4. Quoted from *The Unpublished Dostoevsky: Diaries and Notebooks 1860–1881* (Ann Arbor: Ardis, 1973), Vol. 1, p. 41.
5. Fyodor Dostoevsky, *The Brothers Karamazov*, ed. Ralph E. Matlaw (New York: W. W. Norton, 1976), p. 299. Further page references are to this edition.

Carl Stief

The Young Gor'kij and "The Exalting Delusion"

In 1958, Nils Åke Nilsson published his monograph *Ibsen in Russland*. Despite the appearance of more recent Soviet and Western European studies of the Russian fascination with the Norwegian writer, Nilsson's book remains the definitive work on Ibsen's reception by Russian theatergoers and readers.

Ibsen in Russland also examines Ibsen's influence on Gor'kij (see especially pp. 178–186). Nilsson focuses on the extent to which the question of "the vital lie" in *The Wild Duck* plays a role as one of the main themes of *The Lower Depths*. Apparently, this question was not explored in Gor'kij's first draft of the play from 1900. However, in the final draft, completed after *The Wild Duck* was staged at the Moscow Art Theater in 1901, the question of illusion and truth has become the very core of Gor'kij's play. Nilsson makes a convincing case for Ibsen's influence on Gorkij's play without, however, being able to prove it (pp. 185–86). Strangely enough, Gor'kij expressed his opinion on many of Ibsen's dramatic works, but was silent on *The Wild Duck*. Had this particular play perhaps touched a sensitive nerve in the Russian playwright?

Nilsson remarks on the importance of the question of mendacity/truth for Gor'kij: "Das war ein wichtiges und vielseitiges Problem. Es gibt mehrere Arten der Wahrheit, ebenso wie mehrere Arten der Lüge. Das wusste Gor'kij sehr wohl, denn das Problem war in seiner Dichtung nicht neu. Es hatte ihn schon früher beunruhigt, und er hatte es in mehreren Erzählungen behandelt, ohne eine bestimmte, endgültige Lösung geben zu können" (pp. 183–84). Nilsson then refers to the sketch "Ešče raz o čerte" and the allegory "O čiže, kotoryj lgal i o djatle-ljubitele istiny".

Why was Gor'kij so preoccupied with this problem? The following will attempt to give an answer.

During the famous Boldino Autumn in 1830, Puškin composed the poem "Geroj". Two lines of this poem have continued to influence the course of Russian literature.

T'my nizkich istin mne dorože
Nas vozvyšajuščij obman . . .
More than a myriad of low truths
I value the Delusion that exalts us (trans. Nabokov)

Puškin's aesthetic credo was summarized in these words. Poetry was not to be dragged down by mediocre pundits to their level of understanding, but was instead to elevate mankind into the divine sphere of beauty. It might be recalled that Puškin had no desire to see Byron on the chamberpot.[1]

These lines have not always been interpreted in this way. Dobroljubov accused Puškin of preferring delusion instead of low truths out of lethargy and a desire for spiritual peace of mind. By low truths Dobroljubov meant Russian reality, which Puškin in his ivory tower had supposedly kept at arm's length.[2]

Dostoevskij evidently disagreed. He understood the sense of Puškin's lines. In *A Raw Youth* (Part 1, chapter 10, first section), one of the Raw youth's friends quotes the provocative lines. The young man replies: "But that's true, you know. There's a sacred axiom in those two lines". The more level-headed friend rejoins: "I don't know. I can't undertake to decide whether those lines are true or not. Perhaps, as always, the truth lies in the mean: that is, that in one case truth is sacred and in another falsehood. The only thing I know for certain is that that idea will long remain one of the questions most disputed among men" (trans. Constace Garnett).

For the young Gor'kij, Puškin's lines caused a conflict in his mind. The question is whether he ever arrived at an unambiguous answer to the problems they raised. That he regarded the question as important is evident from the fact that it appears in his fiction as well as his articles. An example is the short story "Prochodimec" (1897–98), where the main protagonist takes a cynical view of mendacity, which he uses without remorse for his amusement and to make a living.

Gor'kij made his literary debut in 1892, and in the following years wrote the works which would pave the way for his unparalleled success: the vagabond stories. Vagabonds had been portrayed before, so it was not a question of the introduction of a new social class in Russian literature. Rather, Gor'kij's work caused a sensation because of its new tone. His vagabonds confronted an increasingly diluted realism bogged down in everyday trivialities and the resignation and defeatism pervading the intelligentsia. They transgressed all boundaries, took what they wanted and paid the price without complaint. They regarded the toil of the peasants and the constricted world of the townspeople with contempt. They were boisterously free and self-conscious. They were strong. Their attitude toward life impressed Gor'kij, who was apparently fascinated by hearty personalities. He saw in them characteristics he found more upright than the humility of the petit bourgeois or the thrift of the peasant. He portrayed the vagabonds with affectionate admiration and brought with them a salty breeze of the Black Sea and the wide horizon of the Southern Russian steppe into the stuffy drawing rooms of the 1890's.

However, there was no doubt that the reality described in these stories was a reality seen through the prism of Gor'kijs artistic temperament. In Gor'kij's portrayal, the wretched life of these nomads was suffused with a romantic aura.

What motivated this romantic vision, which Gor'kij sometimes acknowledged and sometimes denied? Many years later, he provided an answer in his article "Kak ja učilsja pisat' " (1928). He admitted that his partiality for vagabonds originated in a desire to depict unusual people. However, he was motivated even more by an urge to embellish his own tiresome, impoverished life by flights of imagination (vymyslom).[3]

In another article from his last years, "Besedy o remesle", written in 1930–31, Gor'kij recalls how embarassed he was when one of his political mentors pronounced final judgments on literature. These judgments followed a simple formula: if a work of literature depicted something as bad, it was true; if it depicted something as good, it was false. He added that he knew that the bad outweighed the good. More than that – good could not be found anywhere else but in books. However, Gor'kij disagrees with his mentor and gives as his reason the Puškin quote about an exalting delusion being worth more than a myriad of low truths.[4]

Thus, Gor'kij's vagabond romanticism initially originated as an urge to color his existence, to rise above the daily grind and extricate himself from the depressing hopelessness of life. He soon became aware that this urge brought him perilously close to delusion or mendacity. Already one year after his literary debut in 1893, he wrote the allegory "O čiže, kotoryj lgal i o djatle-ljubitele istiny", which Nilsson refers to (p. 184). The little siskin which with its song wanted to encourage other birds to search for the land of happiness, had to admit that it had lied. But the siskin excuses itself by saying that it only wanted to instill faith and hope in the other birds. That is why it lied. Maybe the woodpecker is right in its sober assessment of the facts: "What good is his truth, when it burdens us like a stone on our wings?"[5]

In thinking about the direction of his writing, Gor'kij grappled with the problem of truth/falsehood. Should he, in league with so many of his contemporaries, be content to depict the afflictions, despondency, and the resigned acceptance of the status quo? Or should he, by transgressing the confines of realism, offer encouragement? Not merely by adding cruder colors to his palette, but by choosing characters who overstepped acceptable norms and were larger than life.

Gor'kij described the desire to take refuge in a lie, when the truth became a burden like a stone on a wing, in stories such as "Boles' " (1897) and "Ešče raz o čerte" (1899), which Nilsson also refers to (p. 184). But what about the exalting delusion? Was it a means of escaping the pitiable state of not only Russian literature, but, as Gor'kij believed, of Russian life itself?

Gor'kij grappled with this problem throughout the 1890's. He wrote "true" stories such as "Skuki radi" (1897), as well as defiant paeans to the folly of the intrepid, which he interpreted as the wisdom of life – "Pesnja o Sokole" (1895).

The humorous story "Kak menja otbrili" (1896), with the wordplay on *otbrit'*, which means both to finish shaving and to rebuff, seems like a self-ironic parody of Gor'kij's preoccupation with the problem. When he asks his barber if he has read any of his work, the barber replies that he has stopped, because Gor'kij describes things as they are but is unable to invent (vydumy-vat') anything to take him away from the perpetual repetition of daily life. Gor'kij crawls along the earth and cannot rise above it. His writing is too straightforward.

The strength of the grip of illusion on Gor'kij can be seen in the verse written the same year, "Ballada o grafine Ellen de Kursi", where he declares outright:

O pravde krasivoj toskuja,
Tak žadno dušoj ee ždeš',
Čto ljubiš' bezumno, kak pravdu,
Toboj že roždennuju lož'.[6]

However, two years later (1898) Gor'kij seems to have reached some sort of solution in the short story "Čitatel'". Even though there is an undertone of hesitation in this story, it can nevertheless be interpreted as Gor'kij's credo, a declaration of the purpose of his writing.

The reader, like Puškin's "Geroj" friend, is the writer's alter ego. During an embarassing conversation with the writer, the reader asks some unpleas-ant questions: Why does he write, how does he feel about his work. They readily agree that the goal must be to "help man understand himself, strengthen his belief in himself, and develop his need for truth, struggle against triviality, know how to discover the good in man, arouse feelings of shame, anger, courage, do everything to make people noble, strong, to make them animate their lives with the sacred spirit of beauty".[7] Gor'kij thus acknowledges that literature has a didactic goal. Gor'kij and his contempo-raries saw this goal as a political one as well.

Instead of working towards these goals, the writer must admit that he has been dealing in trivialities and describing random facts. The reader re-proaches the writer, telling him that he serves up pitiful trifling truths, which confirm that man is dependent on outside circumstance. When man looks into a mirror and sees that he is evil, he has no chance of getting better. The reader therefore suggests: "Instead of giving us too many low truths, can't you just give us one little delusion which can exalt our soul?"[8]

Behind this question lies Gor'kij's faith in the endless possibilities for mankind and a conviction that by appealing to the good and rational in man, these possibilities can be nurtured. Neither the Marxist nor the natural science version of determinism, which dominated intellectual discourse during this time, could satisfy Gor'kij's temperament. His vagabond stories might well have expressed a good deal of escapism. Gor'kij now wanted his work to inflame the emotions, to make his readers realize that their lives were mere caricatures of what they could be, to enlist his readers in the struggle to change their lives. If a "small delusion" could further this goal, a writer should be allowed to use it. In the last decade of Gor'kij's life, this idea, expressed in different terms of course, contributed to the formulation of the programme for socialist realism.

At the turn of the century, Gor'kij sees Edmond Rostand's showpiece *Cyrano de Bergerac* at a theater in Nižnij Novgorod. He is so enthralled with the play that he immediately asks Čechov if he has seen it, adding in a less than tactful aside: "That's the way to live, not like Uncle Vanja and others of his ilk".[9] He writes a long review of the play, which he embraces wholeheartedly, presenting as it does an independent personality not rooted in his own epoch, with "the sun in his blood", an expression Gor'kij would later repeatedly return to. He remarks several times: "It's beautiful. But not very believable, of course". Or: "This is beautiful. But of course improbable, and a shame, by God, that it's improbable".[10]

Only a couple of weeks after the *Cyrano de Bergerac* review, Gor'kij reviews Čechov's "V ovrage". Now he is playing another tune: "There is nothing in Čechov's stories which can't be found in reality. The awesome power of his talent is precisely that he never invents anything, never depicts anything which doesn't exist, but might be good or perhaps desirable as well. He never embellishes his characters".[11]

However, after having read "Dama s sobačkoj" Gor'kij writes a letter to Čechov on 17 January, 1900, in which he congratulates him for having destroyed realism. He continues: "Yes, the time has come for heroics, everyone wants something stimulating, dazzling; something, you know, that doesn't resemble life, but is higher, better, more beautiful than life. It is absolutely necessary that contemporary literature start to beautify life a little. As soon as it does, life will be more beautiful. In other words, people will live at a faster pace, more energetically".Čechov refrained from comment on this tirade.[12]

Because the young Gor'kij regarded the problem of truth/falsehood, or to put it another way, illusion, existentially, Henrik Ibsen's *The Wild Duck* must have stirred something in him, causing him great anguish. This something was the question of what direction his writing should take, and the spirit that would bear it. The assumption might be made that the lucid and provoking way in which Ibsen had examined the question of mendacity caused Gor'kij to abandon his first draft of *The Lower Depths* and write the play we know today, where this question is the essence of the play. Is this his answer?

NOTES

1. Letter to P. A. Vjazemskij. November 1825. Michajlovskoe.
2. N. A. Dobroljubov. Polnoe sobranie sočinenij v 6 tomach. T. I, 1934. p. 320.
3. M. Gor'kij. Sobranie sočinenij v 30 tomach. T. 24. p. 498.
4. Ibid. T. 25. p. 334–5.
5. Ibid. T. I. p. 131.
6. Ibid. T. 2. pp. 472–3.
7. Ibid. T. 2. p. 195.
8. Ibid. T. 2. p. 201.
9. Ibid. T. 28. p. 118.
10. Ibid. T. 23. p. 307.
11. Ibid. T. 23. p. 314.
12. Ibid. T. 28. p. 113.

Vladimir Markov

Bal'mont and Karamzin:
Towards a "Sourceology" of Bal'mont's Poetry

The source of a poem is, naturally, an object of some interest for scholars. The sources that immediately come to mind are biographical events and literary texts. As practically everyone knows, "Ja pomnju čudnoe mgnoven'e" is based on Puškin's two meetings with Mme Kern. These biographical sources appear however in combination with another, less visible, literary one: Žukovskij's poetry. Puškin alters his friend's phrase, "genij čistyj krasoty", from "Lalla Ruk."

Such literary sources can be of a more extensive nature. A poem, a song, or a passage may induce a poet to rewrite it. In the old days, one of the most popular occupations was the paraphrasing (or "imitation") of biblical psalms. This resembles poetic translation where one translates not only from one language to another but also, occasionally, from one medium to another (as in Trediakovskij's *Tilemachida* or in the French tradition of rendering foreign verse as "prose poems").

A good theoretician can easily make a chart of source usage. He can also formulate the distinction among paraphrase, quotation, and echo, the two latter recently attracting more and more scholarly attention. In the past, quoting (as in the baroque) was a game, whereas paraphrasing bordered on an act of piety. Quotation continued throughout the nineteenth century (Vjazemskij's poetry is a good example), while paraphrasing moved towards extinction. In our century, quoting has grown both in quantity and in complexity (see, e.g., V. N. Toporov's study, *Achmatova i Blok*), but rewriting of other texts obviously has become a less than respectable business – with one exception. Who would expect a romantic impressionist and poetic butterfly like Konstantin Bal'mont to be the foremost practitioner of this activity? And yet, he was probably one of the most source-inspired poets in Russian literary history[1] (one more reason to consider him a neobaroque literary figure). In some of his books, everything seems to be retelling as in Žukovskij's poetry practically everything was translation.

In his very first book, *Sbornik stichotvorenij* (1890), Bal'mont gives more room to translations than to his original poems, and some of the translations are very free indeed (see, for example, the "Legenda", where he completely excised the gypsies from Jean Lahor's "Le Tsigane dans la lune"). In *Pod*

Severnym nebom (1894), one finds "Pesn' Judifi" that puts Bal'mont in the tradition of paraphrasing the Bible, a tradition that extends from Simeon of Polock and Lomonosov to Jazykov and beyond. In this poem, based on Chapter 16 of *The Book of Judith,* he takes much (and often verbatim) from the text of the Russian bible, occasionally distorting what he borrows and even adding elements from another source (the Psalter). The same combination of exactitude and freedom can be observed in the next book of Bal'- mont, *V bezbrežnosti* (1895), in "Na motiv Psalma XVIII-go" and "Na motiv Èkkleziasta".

In the February 1900 issue of *Žizn'*, Bal'mont published a cycle of eight poems entitled "Iz mira legend: Venok pesnopenij." The cycle begins with two prefatory poems[2] that emphasize one of the poet's favorite ideas – that his poetry is a later, and often a fuller and better, manifestation of the treasures of the past (as well as stresses the "antiphonal", responsive nature of his work). Of the six following poems, two elaborate the legends of antiquity on the enchanted and happy lands, and four deal with medieval Russian history. They are, in order, "Giperborei," "Strana Issedonov", "Ubijca Gleba i Borisa", "Opričniki", "V gluchie dni", and "Smert' Dimitrija Krasnogo". All six are based on Karamzin's *History of the Russian State.* When Bal'mont published his book, *Gorjaščie zdanija* (1900), he separated the "Russian" poems from the other two (placing the latter in the section, "Antifony") and, having bolstered the group with another poem, "Skify",[3] put them in the key section, "Otsvety zareva", that romanticizes violence, death, and evil. In this section, the poems form a hidden cycle (i.e., a cycle of poems not ostensibly presented as such).

"Giperborei," written in anapestic pentameter, immediately demonstrates a typical trait of Bal'mont's paraphrasing: it often takes its verse meter from the prose of the source,[4] as the following excerpt from Karamzin's Vol. I, Chapter 1 demonstrates:

Cvetuščee voobraženie grekov, ljubja prijatnye mečty, izobrelo giper- boreev, ljudej soveršenno dobrodetel'nych, živuščich dalee *na sever ot Ponta* Èvskinskogo, *za gorami Rifejskimi,* v sčastlivom spokojstvii, *v stranach mirnych* i veselych, gde buri i strasti neizvestny; gde smertnye pitajutsja sokom cvetov i rosoju, blaženstvujut neskol'ko vekov i, nasy- tjas' žizn'ju, *brosajutsja v volny morskie.*

As the underlined phrases indicate, Bal'mont heard the ternary cadence in "na sever ot Ponta" that immediately crystallizes into anapest with "za gorami Rifejskimi" (the beginning of the poem), while the end of the passage, the longest borrowed phrase – clearly an amphibrach – fits easily into the established anapestic meter. Perhaps the most interesting part of the process was the fact that Bal'mont, once anapest took root in his metrical imagination, also heard this meter in "v stranach mirnych" that, by itself, suggests trochee, but can also serve as a beginning of an anapestic line (which often has a non-metrical stress on the first syllable in anacrusis).

Bal'mont modified the rest of the Karamzin excerpt by using synonyms, changing grammar, and switching parts of speech while preserving original roots as we see in a comparison between the poet's and the historian's phrases:

Bal'mont	Karamzin
1. gde net ni vetróv, ni strastej	gde buri i strasti neizvestny
2. blažennych ljudej	blaženstvujut
3. I pitajutsja tol'ko cvetami i	pitajutsja sokom cvetov i
svežej rosoj	rosoju
4. pomnogu vekov	neskol'ko vekov
5. nasytivšis' žizn'ju	nasytjas' žiznju

Stanzas I and IV of Bal'mont's poem borrow heavily from Karamzin; II borrows only one line (quoted in full above, example 3); while in III, Karamzin is absent. In short, Bal'mont freely uses his source (as in his translations), and can easily be accused of "padding" by critics who misunderstand his poetic nature. In fact, for him such padding was natural; he was an "amplifying" poet[5] (as different from those who "compressed" like Annenskij who, incidentally, loved Bal'mont's work), demonstrating once more that what is a defect in one context, can be a virtue, or a legitimate stylistic device, in another as are the zatyčki (fillers) in folk poetry.

The same free handling appears even more striking in Bal'mont's other "legendary" poem, "Strana Issedonov", the only one that clearly points to Karamzin; it has an epigraph quoting him (again from Vol. I, Chapter 1) – "Sie prijatnoe basnoslovie . . ."[6] The quoted phrase, however, has nothing to do with the land of the Issedonians mentioned in the chapter and is even separated from the reference by two or three pages. Bal'mont bases his eight-stanza poem on one brief sentence in Karamzin: "Na vostok ot agrippeev (v velikoj Tatarii) žili issedony, kotorye skazyvali, čto nedaleko ot nich grify steregut zoloto". The first phrase gives Bal'mont his trochaic tetrameter, while he gets the phrases "v Tatariii velikoj", "žilo plemja issedonov", and "grify steregut", as well as the gold from Karamzin's text. But in contrast, Bal'mont's griffins guard the land, not the gold; his eight-month cold is a transformation of Karamzin's (or rather Herodotus') six-month sleep in the passage preceding the one quoted (again, having nothing to do with the Issedonians[7]); and the poem is mainly about a flying serpent that does not appear in Karamzin at all. Nor does Karamzin contain the petrified visitors, the inaccessibility of the land, nor the unchangeability of its population to each of which Bal'mont allots a stanza or nearly a stanza.

Lack of space prevents me from analyzing in detail the remaining "Karamzinian" poems of Bal'mont. One of them, "Skify",[8] is yet another poem based on Vol. I, Chapter 1 of the *History of the Russian State*. It freely borrows from Karamzin for Stanza I, but in II seems to suggest a first-hand acquaintance with Herodotus; the rest is pure Bal'mont, and this time the metrics do not derive from the source.

The "Russian" poems based on Karamzin, and in the book placed in reverse historical order, more or less continue this metrical independence.[9] Again, however, Bal'mont borrows, sometines generously, vocabulary and phraseology as in the Vološin-like "V gluchie dni" (based on Karamzin's vol. X, Chapter 21), where the repeated "Chleba!" seems to come from Musorgskij's *Boris Godunov*. The borrowing is minimal, however, in "Opričniki" (based loosely on Vol. IX, Chapter 3), where Bal'mont even substitutes "hot water" for the non-poetic "hot cabbage soup" with which Ivan the Terrible scalds his jester. "Smert' Dimitrija Krasnogo", in its "amplifying" loses much in comparison with Karamzin's terse report in Vol. V, Chapter 3, but, as in "V gluchie dni", verbal transplants are numerous, even if the metrical impulse only weakly comes from the source.

"Ubijca Gleba i Borisa", Bal'mont's last "Karamzinian" poem (and the only one not included in *Gorjaščie zdanija*) is in some respects unique. The poet reworks Karamzin's lengthy and detailed report in Vol. III, Chapter 1 with the utmost liberty. Omissions (as well as lyrical outbursts) abound; accents are placed differently, and textual transplants are reduced to a minimum. For a change, Bal'mont resorts to iambic tetrameter that helps make the poem, in comparison with the historical narrative, highly emotional and energetic. The poet barely touches on the murder of the saintly brothers by Svjatopolk the Accursed, and even deviates from both Karamzin and history. Bal'mont ignores the role of Jaroslav in subsequent events and noticeably concentrates on the much less important Svjatoslav. Karamzin has no bellringing nor involves Svjatopolk in making his sister a concubine of the Polish king. The end of the poem seems to derive more from Shakespeare's *Richard III* (incidentally, the source of an epigraph in *Gorjaščie zdanija*) than from Russian history: Bal'mont's Svjatopolk is haunted by the ghosts of those he killed; whereas in *The History* he is tormented by the fears of imagined foes who follow him. Perhaps the most interesting part of the poem is its epigraph from Puškin's "Ančar": "I umer bednyj rab u nog/ Nepobedimogo vladyki". Metrically, rhythmically, and phraseologically it seems to have affected the poem more strongly than Karamzin's story (cf. Bal'mont's "I umer on v stepjach čužich – XI, 3 and "Besčelovečnogo zlodeja: – VI, 4). The epigraph also creates an ironic contrast to the poem itself and possibly explains why Bal'mont separated this poem from the rest of the original Karamzin cycle as printed in the magazine and placed it, instead, in the "Soznanie" section of his next book of verse, *Budem kak solnce* (1903).

The role of printed sources grew in Bal'mont's subsequent books, especially in those written abroad during his first European exile of 1906–1913. He extensively used such well-known collections as Rybnikov's *Pesni*, Kireevskij's *Pesni*, and Sacharov's *Skazanija russkogo naroda*, and, to a lesser extent, Sobolevskij's *Velikorusskie narodnye pesni*. Individual poems are based on such different sources as W. Scott-Elliot's *The Story of Atlantis* or a Ukrainian folk-song in Vol. V of *Trudy ètnografičesko-statističeskoj èkspedicii v Zapadno-russkij kraj*. Entire verse collections by Bal'mont owe much to specific works: e.g., *Zelenyj vertograd* to V. Kel'siev's *Sbornik pravitel'stvennych svedenij o raskol'nikach*, Vol. 3 and *Chorovod vremen* to Ermolov's *Narodnaja sel'skochozjajstvennaja mudrost' v poslovicach, pogovorkach i primetach*. Several books of verse show that Bal'mont seldom parted with Afanas'ev's *Poètičeskie vozzrenija slavjan na prirodu*. Consequently, the "Karamzinian" poems illustrate only a small part of the poet's preoccupation with and use of source material.

NOTES

1. In this context even his numerous poems about painters of the past can be considered paraphrases – from one medium to another (see, for example, his poem on Sassoferrato's Madonna in *Tišina*).
2. "Prolog", which later lost its title and became the concluding poem in the section, "Antifony," in *Gorjaščie zdanija,* and "Osvoboždennye" which was saved by Bal'mont for *Budem kak solnce* (the "Soznanie" section), where it received a new title, "Namek".
3. "Skify" (see below) was previously printed in another, earlier issue (November 1899) of the same magazine as one of many poems under the title, "Lirika sovremennoj duši. Dnevnik poèta".
4. An interesting example is Bal'mont's poem, "Mirovoe pričastie" (from "Trojstvennost' dvuch" cycle in *Liturgija krasoty*). He heard Russian anapest in a phrase in a letter by Flaubert and used it, in the original French, both as the poem's first line and part of its epigraph.
5. Instances of amplification can be found in the verse of many other poets. See, e.g., in Pasternak:
   Ne spi, ne spi, chudožnik,
   Ne predavajsja snu.
6. The full sentence is "Nakonec, sie prijatnoe basnoslovie ustupilo mesto dejstvitel'nym istoričeskim poznanijam", and it immediately follows the passage on the Hyperboreans quoted above.
7. The "cold" is found in Karamzin, too, but it belongs to his interpretation of Herodotus.
8. Cf. not only Blok's well-known "Skify", but also Brjusov's poem in *Tertia vigilia* with the same title.
9. Unless one considers Bal'mont's pentameter, "Orly parili s krikom nad Moskvoj" (VI, 2) as metrically originating in Karamzin's "tetrameter", "Orly parili nad Moskvoju".

Анна Юнггрен

«Загадочное будничное слово» И. Анненского: архаизмы и галлицизмы

Редактор журнала «Аполлон» С. Маковский в своих воспоминаниях о современниках сделал несколько критических замечаний о языке поэзии И. Анненского:

> Больше чем кто-либо из русских поэтов, он любил неологизмы и галлицизмы [...] Галлицизмы, даже просто смелые заимствования французских слов представлялись ему неотъемлимым правом модернизма [...]
>
> Вкусу его вовсе не претили в самых задушевных строках такие обороты речи, как, например, «эмфаза слов» ... Или – такие любимые выражения, как – «мираж» («миражный рай»), «хлороз жасмина», «зигзаг полета», «кошмарный», «анкилозы», «симптомы» и несколько других [...] Нельзя их считать равноправными другим русским словам, органически связанным со всем строем русской речи [...] Анненский подчас ранил ухо своими галлицизмами, из какого-то непонятного озорства, из предвзятого франкоманства [...].
>
> Однако франкоманство не мешало И. Анненскому пользоваться словарем чисто народной речи ...[1]

Наблюдения С. Маковского – интересный лингвистический документ, говорящий о восприятии новых заимствований в поэтическом тексте. С момента, зафиксированного в воспоминаниях С. Маковского, (встреча С. Маковского с И. Анненским состоялась весной 1909г., т.е. в период создания журнала «Аполлон»), освоение иноязычия в русской поэзии идет двумя путями: в направлении интеграции заимствований у акмеистов,[2] и в направлении словотворчества «заумного» языка, часто имитирующего иноязычие.[3] Свидетельство С. Маковского относится к поворотному моменту в истории русской поэзии «серебряного века»: его наблюдения сделаны в преддверии 1910г., который Б. Эйхенбаум считал годом кризиса символизма[4] и на пороге перемен, уже намеченных в поэзии И. Анненского.

Отношение С. Маковского к «неологизмам» И. Анненского показательно как с точки зрения общеязыковой, так и с точки зрения поэтической «нормы». Так, с лингвистической точки зрения, можно сказать, что такие слова, как «зигзаг», или «кошмарный», постепенно вошедшие в основной фонд литературного языка, в тот момент еще не были усвоены. Кроме того, С. Маковский как редактор журнала «Аполлон» выступал в качестве арбитра поэтического слова и, с позиций аполлоновцев, с их пассеизмом и любовью к изящному, отвергал режущие слух «модернистические» заимствования И. Анненского. Не только «анкилозы» и «хлороз», но и «миражный» и «кошмарный» воспринимались как проявление «непонятного озорства» и «предвзятого франкоманства».

На заимствованиях, проникавших в тот период в изобилии в повседневный язык, лежит печать бытового вульгаризма. Так, директор императорских театров кн. С. Волконский в своей книге «Выразительное слово» призывает актеров следить за своей речью не только на сцене, но и в быту и предостерегает против таких слов, как «вираж», «ангар» и всех тому подобных слов, «приехавших к нам на автомобилях или прилетевших на аэропланах».[5] Пурист кн. С. Волконский составил список таких нерекомендуемых заимствований, в подавляющем большинстве галлицизмов, и объединил их в графе «Зачем?», а в графе «когда есть» привел список их русских эквивалентов. Так, по Волконскому, следует говорить не «дефект», а «изъян», не «вираж», а «поворот», не «ангар», а «сарай», не «pardon», а «виноват». Слова из «нерекомендованного» списка С. Волконского, «приехавшие на автомобилях или прилетевшие на аэропланах» были взяты на вооружение футуристами именно благодаря их лексической выделенности на нейтральном языковом фоне. Кроме того, чуждость внутренней формы слова ощущается как новизна, а непривычность звукового облика дает возможность прибегать к иностранному слову как к «звуковому жесту». Показательно, что С. Маковский смешивает «неологизмы» и «галлицизмы» у И. Анненского, отождествляя «новое» с «заимствованным». На самом деле, авторские неологизмы для И. Анненского не характерны[6] и ограничиваются вполне традиционными, идущими от Тютчева экспериментами с двусоставными прилагательными, типа «златошвейный», «зеленовейный», «темноризый», «пустоплясый», представленными, к тому же, в бóльшем объеме у «эллениста» Вяч. Иванова.[7] Такой авторский неологизм, как, например, «древожизненный» создает эффект архаизации, в то время как заимствование ощущается как современное, «модернистическое» слово. Не вступая на путь создания собственных неологизмов, И. Анненский в наброске статьи «Будущее поэзии» выделяет две группы лексики, которые могут служить ресурсами обновления поэтического словаря:

Необходимость слов *новых* [...] или *устарелых*. Скользить по словам, освобождаясь от тяжелых, пошлых мифологических метафор, ставших условными формулами. Пользуясь всеми средствами, сделать символ духовнее, объединить впечатленья от слов и от их значений. Поэт будет владеть искусством речи, он будет владеть историей своего языка и мифом преданий.[8]

Как «новые» слова, так и новые «устарелые» освобождают поэзию от стершихся образов.

Наряду с традиционными высокими поэтизмами («капище», «глагол»), И. Анненский прибегает к таким редким архаизмам, как «Триóдь», (служебник, собрание трехпесенных канонов), «оцéт» (уксус), «брáшно» (кушанье), – как правило, снижая их и растворяя в контексте стихотворения. Помимо слов, связанных с церковным обиходом, в поэтический оборот вводятся областные слова: «кирьгá» (кирка), «грáбарь» (землекоп), – а также аграрные, хозяйственные термины: «грудá» (мерзлые колеи по дороге), «жнивнúк» (сжатое поле), «крушúна» (хрупкое дерево).[9] Освоение старой, а также областной, народной лексики осознается И. Анненским как овладение «историей своего языка и мифом преданей», т.е. в ключе, уже предвещающем этимологические и диалектальные изыскания футуристов.[10] Овладение мифом идет в поэзии И. Анненского иными, чем у символистов, путями: через заимствованные или устарелые слова с конкретным значением, в отличие от книжного иноязычия и абстрактной лексики, как, например, у «мифотворца» Вяч. Иванова.

Иллюстрацией установки И. Анненского на введение архаизмов может служить история названия «Кипарисовый ларец». Первоначально И. Анненский собирался назвать свою книгу стихов «Из пещеры Полифема»,[11] затем эта античная метафора была отброшена, и первая книга стихов была названа «Тихие песни», вероятно, по строчке Верлена «Écoutez la chanson bien douce» (Sagesse, XVI), а вторая – «Вторая книга стихов. Из кипарисовой шкатулки»,[12] со сдвигом из античности в современность и с заменой «пещеры Полифема» на кипарисовую шкатулку, в которой И. Анненский хранил свои рукописи. Как и «Тихие песни», «Кипарисовая шкатулка» – название во вкусе французских модернистов, отождествлявших книгу с декоративным предметом (Ср. «Le Coffret de santal» Ш. Кро, «La Canne de jaspe» А. де Ренье, «L'Anneau d'améthyste» А. Франса и т.д.). Наконец, нейтральное слово «шкатулка», прямо называющее реалию, было архаизировано, поэтизировано благодаря замене на «ларец»; декадентское заглавие приобрело, тем самым, оттенок русской старины.

Если «устарелое» слово несет в себе прошлое культуры, то заимствования осуществляют экспансию в современную повседневность.

Коренная ошибка состоит в предположении, что красота слов служит для поэзии средством выражения движений духовного мира. Она – цель, как в живописи. Поэзия может быть самым смелым из искусств, для нее нет грязи, п⟨отому⟩ ч⟨то⟩ она превращает ее в алмазы.[13]

С. Маковский обращает внимание в своем рассказе на новые «непоэтические» – с точки зрения русской поэтической нормы – заимствования. Слова греческого происхождения: «эмфаза», «симптом», – несмотря на их интернациональность, воспринимаются им как галлицизмы. С. Маковский справедливо приписывает их появление в стихах И. Анненского влиянию французского модернизма.

Как продолжение пушкинской традиции в стихах И. Анненского появляются французские слова, обозначающие атрибуты туалета («трен»), прическу («эшафодаж»), названия модных цветов («платья pêche и mauve»). Далее, во вкусе «fin de siècle» И. Анненский обращается к «словарю болезни»: это физические и психические аномалии[14] («кошмар», «анкилозы», хлороз»), химические названия пахучих веществ и галлюциногенов («карболка», «фенол», «гашиш», «алкоголь»):

... Будь ты проклята, левкоем и фенолом
Равнодушно дышащая Дама!

(Баллада, 118)

Латинские и греческие названия цветов из орнаментального букета декадентов: «хризантемы», «азалии», «лилии», «центифоли» – не будучи, строго говоря, новыми заимствованиями, обновляются благодаря французской цветочно-декоративной моде конца века. Так, стихотворение И. Анненского «Падение лилий» называлось первоначально по-французски – «La Chûte des lys».[16] «Трилистники» также можно представить себе как перевод латинского «trifolium». К «trifolium» этимологически восходит французское слове «trèfle», в значении «трефа». Параллелизм «трилистник» – «trèfle», поддерживаемый также темой карт в стихах И. Анненского, позволяет сделать предположение о том, что прообразом «Трилистников» могли быть два прозаических триптиха А. де Ренье «Le Trèfle noir» и «Le Trèfle blanc».[17]

«Устарелое», т. е. полузабытое слово, и «новое», т.е. не вполне усвоенное, – выделяются на фоне привычной поэтической лексики и благодаря общей для них «отмеченности» могут создавать единый, стилистически гомогенный контекст, связывающий родное и иноязычное:

Отрадна тень, пока *крушин*
Вливает кровь в *хлороз жасмина* ...

(Nox vitae, 123)

Ядром заимствований у И. Анненского можно считать термины: это яркие воплощения «нового» слова, выделяющиеся на фоне нейтральной лексики как из-за чуждости их морфологии, так и из-за своей «непоэтичной» семантики. Экспрессивные возможности терминов использовались французскими модернистами; этот прием представлен в своем крайнем воплощении в творчестве Ж. Лафорга. (М. Волошин находил сходство между поэзией И. Анненского и Ж. Лафорга; в стихах И. Анненского ему слышалось «salto mortale à la Laforgue»). Слова из «словаря болезни» превращаются в средство изображения «тоски повседневности» (Ah, que la vie est quotidienne!»).[19] Стихотворения сборника «L'Imitation de Notre-Dame la Lune» имитируют и пародируют литургию. Из-за связи термина со сферой низкого, телесного, «Жалобы» – так называются стихотворения сборника – достигают накала инвективы, опережая образные выпады имажинистов:

> Tu ne sais que la fleur des *sanglantes chimies;*
> Et perces nos rideaux, nous offrant le lotus
> Qui *constipe* les plus larges *polygamies*
> Tout net, de l'*excrément logique* des *foetus.*

(La Lune est stérile, 203)

Следуя французским образцам, И. Анненский вводит в поэтический оборот такие слова, как «хлороз», «алкоголь», «гашиш», «анкилозы». Так, «хлороз жасмина» из цитировавшегося выше стихотворения «Nox vitae» – рефлекс бодлеровской рифмы «хлорозы» – «розы»:

> Je laisse à Gavarni, poète des *chloroses*
> Son troupeau gazouillant de beautés d'hôpital.
> Car je ne puis trouver parmi ces pâles *roses*
> Une fleur qui ressemble à mon rouge idéal.

(L'Idéal, 1286)[20]

«Алкоголь» и «гашиш» также можно возвести к Ш. Бодлеру:

> Как в *кошмаре,* то и дело:
> «*Алкоголь или гашиш?*»

(Трактир жизни, 76)

> Поймешь ты сладостный *гашиш* . . .

(Тоска, 93)

Ср. «Les Paradis artificiels» Ш. Бодлера с подзаголовком «Opium et haschisch», состоит из двух частей, «Le Poème de haschisch» и «Un Mangeur d'opium»; обе поэмы рассказывают об «искусственном рае» – эйфории курильщика наркотиков:

> Parmi les drogues les plus propres à créer ce que je nomme L'Idéal artificiel [...] les deux plus énergique substances [...] sont *le haschisch* et *l'opium.*
>
> (Le Goût de L'Infini, 133)[21]

> L'auteur veut avant tout venger *l'opium* de certaines calomnies [...] Il établit ensuite une comparaison entre les effets de *l'alcool* et ceux de *l'opium,* et il définit très-nettement la différance ...
>
> (Voluptés de l'opium, 197)

Слово «анкилоз», по-видимому, заимствовано И. Анненским из словаря А. де Ренье. У И. Анненского это слово встречается в своем терминологическом значении «утолщение, сращение суставов»:

> И с *анкилозами* на пальцах две руки
> Безвольно отданы камина жгучей ласке.
>
> (На полотне, 194)

У А. де Ренье это слово встречается в виде авторского неологизма «ankyloser», которое употребляется как в своей связи с термином, так и в переносном значении:

> L'infirmité qui *ankylosait* le corps entier ...
>
> (Jours heureux)[22]

> Ma solitude *s'ankylosa* de silence et de regret ...
>
> (Contes à soi-même)[23]

Терминологизмы – лингвистический аналог излюбленной декадентами «причудливой вещи».[24] Отталкиваясь от натурализма Э. Золя, французский модернизм создает эстетику искусственного: в центре ее, в отличие от парнасцев, – не прекрасный, а странный, «придуманный» артефакт.[25]

В отличие от латинской и греческой лексики, хорошо усвоенной французким классицизмом, термины не унаследованы от античности, а изобретены. Это сконструированные слова в духе модного «византиниз-ма».[26]

По своей семантике медицинская и химическая терминология отвеча-ет интересу декадентов к аномалиям (болезням, лжи, состояниям «ис-кусственного» опьянения наркотиками) и духу эмансипации от «Иде-ала» (Ср. в «Art poétique» П. Верлена: «Prends l'éloquence et tords-lui son cou!»).

Любовь французских декадентов к именам пахучих веществ предо-пределена поэтикой синэстезии. Поэтические манифесты родоначаль-ников модернизма, «Correspondances» Ш. Бодлера и «Voyelles» А. Рем-бо, утверждают не столько концепцию двоемирия, сколько соответст-вие между зрительным, слуховым, ольфакторым ассоциативными ряда-ми – и словом («Les parfums, les couleurs et les sons se répondent»:

> Il est des parfums frais comme des chairs d'enfants,
> Doux comme des hautbois, verts comme les prairies,
> – Et d'autres, *corrompus, riches et triomphants,*
>
> Ayant l'expansion des choses infinies,
> Comme *l'ambre, le musc, le benjoin et l'encens*
> Qui chantent les transports de l'esprit et des sens.

> (Correspondances, 1577)

«Ассоциативный символист»[27] И. Анненский также прибегает к синэс-тезиям. (Ср., например, «Невозможно», написанное в подражание «Vo-yelles» А. Рембо, связывающее звуки слова и цвет, «Офорт», объединя-ющий звук и зрительный образ, «Аромат лилеи мне тяжел», где сочета-ются цвет и запах.) Названия искусственных веществ с «ядовитыми» запахами: «карболка», «фенол», – входят у И. Анненского в пары с именами цветов, образуя «опьяняющие» составы («хлороз жасмина») или «запахи смерти». Так, «левкой и фенол» заменяет в позднейших редакциях «Баллады» «карболку и фенол» черновика:

> О проклятая, суконная, фенолом
> И карболкой надушившаяся Дама![28]

Поэтическая практика французских модернистов переходит от синэс-тезий к изобретенным, вымышленным словам. Синэстезия выделяет ассоциативный ореол слова, а не его прямое значение, указывая, тем самым, путь к созданию слов, освобожденных от своего обыденного смысла, уводящих за пределы повседневности («les transports de l'esprit et des sens»). Декадентские «дедушки» футуристической «зауми» – слова-синэстезии. Вот несколько примеров искусственных экзотизмов Р. де Гурмона:

> Quelles réalités me donneront *les saveurs* que je rêve à ce fruit de l'Inde et des songes, *le myrobolan,* – ou les *couleurs royales* que je pare *l'omphax,* en ses lointaines gloires?
> Quelle *musique* est comparable à *la sonorité pure des mots obscurs, ô cyclamor?* Et quelle odeur à tes émanations vierges, ô sanguisorbe?

> (L'Ivresse verbale)[29]

«Ядовитые» и «пахучие» терминологизмы И. Анненского связаны с поэтикой синэстезий и выступают в качестве проводника французского «неопрециозного» словотворчества. Прием И. Анненского вводить устарелое слово или галлицизм разветвился в дальнейшем на футуристическую «заумь» и на акмеистическое «воспоминание» о чужеязычном слове. Эллинистические «блаженные слова» О. Мандельштама[30] обнаруживают, при ближайшем рассмотрении, родство с французским «византинизмом». Экзотическое иноязычие также представлено в обеих парадигмах, футуристической и акмеистической: «Зангези» В. Хлебникова соответствует «Жирафу» Н. Гумилева.

Лексически маркированные слова (архаизмы) и морфологически и лексически маркированные (термины) дополнительно подчеркиваются как у И. Анненского, так и у французов, рифмованной позицией. Греческое или латинское слово, традиционно ученое, высокое, сталкивается у модернистов с бытовой французской лексикой:
Ср.: у Верлена в «Офортах»:

> Moi, j'allais, rêvant du divin Platon
>   Et de *Phidias,*
> Et de Salamine et de Marathon,
> Sous l'oeil clignotant des bleus becs de gaz.

> (Croquis Parisien)[32]

Терминологизмы легко проникают во французскую поэзию благодаря формальному сходству с высокой иноязычной лексикой и создают эффект «кривого зеркала», пародируя и снижая традиционные поэтизмы («chloroses – roses») или литургийную латынь:

> Ces malédictions, ces blasphèmes, ces plaintes,
> Ces extases, ces cris, ces pleurs, ces *Te Deum,*
> Sont un écho redit par mille labyrinthes;
> C'est pour les cœurs mortels un divin *opium.*

> (Les phares, 1367)

И. Анненский заимствует этот формальный прием у французов и рифмует иноязычное слово с родным: «гашиш – не спешишь», «декорум – с укором», «дни – агоний». Однако термины, вырванные из системы французской лексики, меняют свой стилистический потенциал. Вместо конфронтации стилей достигается эффект отчуждения бытового слова, далее развивающийся в футуристический «звуковой жест», как например, у раннего Пастернака в рифмах; «бацилл – резцы», «в дифтерите – отворить ей», «заслезил – жалюзи».

Искусственные и причудливые терминологизмы укоренены в быт и воплощают по своей языковой форме парадокс «загадочного будничного слова». Кроме того, связанные со смысловой сферой болезни и смерти, термины «страшны». Описание поэтического слова, которое И. Анненский противопоставляет «словесному культу» символистов, совпадает с перечнем лингвистических черт термина:

> ...за последнее время и у нас – ух – как много этих, которые нянчатся со словом и, пожалуй, готовы говорить об *его культе*. Но они не понимают, что самое *страшное* и *властное* слово, т.е. самое *загадочное,* – может быть, именно слово *будничное*.[32]

Поэтические инновации И. Анненского, устарелые русские слова и галлицизмы, не покрывают области «загадочного будничного слова» и не исчерпывают обыденной лексики в его поэзии. Однако именно эти группы слов отчуждают «страшную» повседневность, обладающую магической властью над человеческим сознанием. Терминологизмы, в которых ощутима генетическая связь с эстетикой искусственного слова-символа у французских декадентов, выдвигаются на фоне устаревающего «слова» русского символизма как предвестники нового поэтического языка.

1. С. Маковский, *Портреты современников,* Нью-Йорк, 1955, с 261–263.
2. Об эволюционном характере акмеизма см.: Б. Эйхенбаум, *Анна Ахматова,* Пб. 1923, с. 24.
3. См., напр.: N. Å. Nilsson, «A. Kručenych's Poem «dyr, bul, ščyl», *Scando-Slavica,* t. 24, 1979, с. 139–148.
4. Б. Эйхенбаум, там же, с. 7.
5. Кн. С. Волконский, *Выразительное слово,* СПб. 1913, с. 206–207.
6. О поэтическом словаре И. Анненского, см.: А. Федоров, *Иннокентий Анненский. Личность и творчество,* Л. 1984, с. 128–130.
7. Ср., напр., такие эпитеты, как «скрежетопильный», «звонкогремучий», «среброзаркий» в стихотворении «Цикады»: Вяч. Иванов, *Стихотворения и поэмы,* Л. 1978, с. 87.
8. Цит. по: И. Ф. Анненский. *Избранное,* М. (в печати).

9. Значения этих слов даются по: Вл. Даль, *Толковый словарь живого великорусского языка*, М. 1956.

10. Ср., напр., «этимологии» В. Хлебникова: В. В. Хлебников, «Наша основа», *Собрание сочинений, Slavische Propyläen*, т. 3, с. 27.

11. Титульный лист в: ЦГАЛИ, ф. 6, оп. 1, ед.хр. 27.

12. ЦГАЛИ, ф. 6, оп. 1, ед.хр. 17.

13. И. Анненский, «Будущее поэзии», *Избранное*.

14. Ср., напр., сборник стихов М. Роллина: Maurice Rollinat, Les Névroses, Р. 1883.

15. Здесь и в дальнейшем стихи И. Анненского цит. по: Иннокентий Анненский *Стихотворения и трагедии*, Л. 1959.

16. ЦГАЛИ, ф. 6, оп. ед.хр. 27 (2).

17. См.: H. de Régnier, *Le Trèfle blanc*, Р. 1899, а также *Le Trèfle noir*, Р. 1895.

18. Лавров А. В., Тименчик Р. Д., «Иннокентий Анненский в неизданных воспоминаниях», *Памятники культуры. Новые открытия. Ежегодник 1981*, М. 1983, с. 71.

19. Здесь и в дальнейшем цит. по: Jules Laforgue, *Poésies complètes*, Р. 1894.

20. Здесь и в дальнейшем стихи С. Бодлера цит. по: Charles Baudelaire, *Œuvres complètes*, ed. Yves Florenne, 1966, т. 1.

21. Здесь и в дальнейшем проза Ш. Бодлера цит. по: Charles Baudelaire, *Œuvres complètes*, t. 3.

22. H. de Régnier, *Le Trèfle blanc*, с. 19.

23. H. de Régnier, *La Canne de jaspe*, Р. 1897, с. 271.

24. См. описание таких причудливых предметов у: J.-K. Huysmans, *A Rebours*, с. 55.

25. Ср. определение эстетики французского символизма у Р. де Гурмона: «Que veut dire *Symbolisme?* Si l'on s'en tient au sens étroit et étymologique, presque rien; si l'on passe outre, cela peut vouloir dire: individualisme en littérature, liberté de l'art, abandon des formules enseignées, tendances vers ce qui est nouveau, étrange et même bizarre; cela peut vouloir dire aussi: idéalisme, dédain de l'anecdote sociale, antinaturalisme . . .»: R. de Gourmont, *Le Livre des masques*, Р. 1986, с. 8.

26. О «неологизмах» поздней латыни см.: J.-K. Huysmans, op.cit., 43; примеры «прециозных» словообразований в греческом стиле см.: Philippe Jullian, «Dreamers of Decadence», L. 1975, с. 35–36.

27. Вяч. Иванов, «О поэзии И. Ф. Анненского», *Аполлон* 1910 N° 4 (Slavistic Printings and Reprintings, The Hague 1971, с. 16).

28. ЦГАЛИ, ф. 6, оп. 1, ед.хр. 17.

29. R. de Gourmont, *Le Chemin de velours*, Р. 1902, с. 227–228.

30. О. Мандельштам, «Я научился вам, блаженные слова» («Соломинка», 2), *Стихотворения*, Л. 1974, с. 100.

31. Цит. по: Paul Verlaine, *Œuvres complètes*, Р. 1900, с. 18.

32. И. Ф. Анненский, «Письма к М. А. Волошину», публ. А. В. Лаврова и Р. Д. Тименчика, *Ежегодник рукописного отдела Пушкинского дома на 1976г*, Л. 1978, с. 247.

Per-Arne Bodin

The Sleeping Demiurge: An Analysis of Boris Pasternak's Poem "Durnoj son"

In Boris Pasternak's second collection of poetry, *Poverch bar'erov* (1917), we find three poems written in succession under the influence of the outbreak of the First World War in 1914: "Durnoj son", "Artillerist stoit u kormila", and "Osen'. Otvykli ot molnij". "Durnoj son", which will be discussed in this article, was revised in 1928 by the poet for republication in *Poverch bar'erov. Stichi raznych let* (1929) and I shall mainly refer to this later text in my analysis on the assumption that it is clearer and more complete, but consideration will naturally also be given to the 1914 version.[1] The 1928 text reads as follows:

ДУРНОЙ СОН

1. Прислушайся к вьюге, сквозь десны процеженной,
   Прислушайся к голой побежке бесснежья.
   Разбиться им не обо что, и заносы
   Чугунною цепью проносятся поннзу
   Полями, по чересполосице, в поезде,
   По воздуху, по снегу, в отзывах ветра,
   Сквозь сосны, сквозь дыры заборов безгвоздых,
   Сквозь доски, сквозь десны безносых трущоб.

2. Полями, по воздуху, сквозь околесицу,
   Приснившуюся небесному постнику.
   Он видит: попадали зубы из челюсти,
   И шамкают за́мки, поместия с пришептом,
   Все вышиблено, ни единого в целости,
   И постнику тошно от стука костей.

3. От зубьев пилотов, от флотских трезубцев,
   От красных зазубрин карпатскнх зубцов.
   Он двинуться хочет, не может проснуться,
   Не может, засунутый в сон на засов.

4. И видит еще. Как назем огородника,
   Всю землю сравняли с землей на Стоходе.
   Не верит, чтоб выси зевнулось когда-нибудь
   Во всю ее бездну, и на небо выплыл,
   Как колокол на перекладине дали,
   Серебряный слиток глотательной впадины,
   Язык и глагол ее, – месяц небесный,
   Нет, косноязычный, гундосый и сиплый,
   Он с кровью заглочен хрящами развалин.
   Сунь руку в крутящийся щебень метели, –
   Он на руку вывалится из расселины
   Мясистой култышкою, мышцей бесцельной
   На жиле, картечиной напрочь отстреленной.
   Его отожгло, как отеклую тыкву.
   Он прыгнул с гряды за ограду. Он в рытвине,
   Он сорван был битвой и, битвой подхлеснутый,
   Как шар, откатился в канаву с откоса
   Сквозь сосны, сквозь дыры заборов безгвоздых,
   Сквозь доски, сквозь десны безносых трущоб.

5. Прислушайся к гулу раздолий неезженных,
   Прислушайся к бешеной их перебежке.
   Расскальзывающаяся артиллерия
   Тарелями ластится к отзывам вегра.
   К кому присоседиться, верстамн меряя,
   Слова гололеднцы, мглы и лафетов?
   И сказка ползет, и клочки околесицы,
   Мелькая бинтами в желтке ксероформа,
   Уносятся с поезда в поле. Уносятся
   Платформами по снегу в ночь к семафорам.

6. Сопят тормоза санитарного поезда.
   И снится, и снится небесному постнику . . .

The poem consists of six segments varying in length from two to nineteen lines. The metre is amphibrack with several omitted stresses, a rarity in trisyllabic metres, and therefore the poem has been given attention by specialists on Russian verse.[2] The poem has only a few rhymes, and all these elements together create a rather free structure in "Durnoj son".

The poem is somewhat enigmatic with a mystical protagonist, the "heavenly ascetic", "nebesnyj postnik", and an imagery which is sometimes difficult to visualize. The poem depicts, however, a landscape of war in winter with storm winds, the thunder of the artillery and a hospital train rushing through this landscape at enormous speed. The time is thus the first winter of the war. The place name in the text, the River Stochod, is anomalous in this context, referring to the military operations of 1916. But this word is a change and a specification in the revised version since the original poem only used the word "zdes'".[3]

The poem can be devided into three parts. The first, comprising the first segment, describes the landscape of war by following the wind which blows through it. The poem begins with the imperative "prislušajsja", a call to listen to the sounds of the wind and the war, an almost prophetic invocation (cf. the use of the word "slušajte" in the prophetic books of the Bible: "slušajte i vnimajte, plemena" (Is. 34:1)).

The second part (segments 2–4) depicts the landscape of war, but now as a nightmare seen by the protagonist of the poem. The third part (segments 5–6) also begins with the imperative "prislušajsja", as an echo of the first part. Here the wind is described again, together with the protagonist and the hospital train.

The storm wind blowing through the landscape thus becomes a key concept in the poem with a series of words describing it: "v'juga", "pobežka bessnež'ja", "otzyvy vetra", "ščeben' meteli". The snow storm is used as a symbol of the devastating forces of war:

Sun' ruku v krutjaščijsja ščeben' meteli.

The snowflakes are interchanged with the rubble from the ruins of demolished buildings. The notion of snowstorm earlier used in 20th century Russian poetry by Aleksandr Blok to describe the forces of passion ("Snežnaja maska") is here lowered stylistically to depict the realities of war.

The landscape of war is seen by the protagonist in his dream, but at the same time the text suggests that the earth itself is a part of him. This is realized by means of a series of parallels and metaphors equating the earth with a head. The teeth of the protagonist are put in the same line as the teeth of the Carpathian Mountains, the marine symbol of the trident, the silhouette of a castle ("šamkajut zamki") and so on (segment 2). The protagonist is dreaming that his teeth are falling out, which in Russian folklore is a presage of death, linking the poem even more with death and destruction.[4] This makes the title of the poem clear: the dream is not only a nightmare but it also represents a bad omen ("durnaja primeta") both for the protagonist and for the earth.

The slums through which the wind is blowing are compared to gums in a mouth:

Skvoz' doski, skvoz' desny beznosych truščob.

This also implies that the wind is the breath of the protagonist. The adjective "beznosyj", "noseless" is in Russian an epithet for the death which refers to the appearance of a skull, as in these lines from Puškin's poem: "Kogda za gorodom, zadumčiv, ja brožu":

Na mesto prazdnych urn i melkich piramid,
Beznosych geniev, rastrepannych charit
Stoit široko dub nad važnymi grobami,
Kolebljas' i šumja ...

The word "beznosyj" also suggests that the topography of the poem is a
landscape of death. The word can perhaps also be linked with the disease of
syphilis (cf. Achmatova's "Tot gorod, mnoj ljubimyj s detstva": "Skripač
beznosyj zaigral") which goes very well with the theme of inarticulate sounds
in the poem.

In the fourth stanza the sky is compared with a mouth, a comparison easy
to apprehend in the Russian language because of the similarity or almost
indenticalness between the words "nebo" meaning heaven and sky, and
"nëbo", meaning palate. The word "zevnulos'", used here to mean "open"
or "clear up", has the proper meaning of "yawn", an image which also
contributes to the mouth-metaphor in the poem.

The moon is first compared to the mouth's silver ingot and a bell, a
comparison which is immediately retracted and replaced by the expressionistic image of the moon as a tongue which has been cut off in the war and
which rolls out into the landscape:

On na ruku vyvalitsja iz rasseliny
Mjasistoj kultyškoju, myšcej bescel'noj

The concrete level of this extremely complex metaphor is perhaps a juxtaposition of the visual image of the moon moving on the horizon and the
acoustic impression of the echo of the artillery thunder spreading out over
the landscape. The shift between the refuted and the realized metaphor is
realized with the help of the double meaning of the word "jazyk" denoting
both the tongue of a bell and the tongue in a mouth.

All these metaphors are connected with Russian folk beliefs, for example
to compare the moon to silver and according to Afanas'ev there is a Russian
saying that someone has cut a piece from the moon when it is not full.[5]

The sounds of the war are also continuosly equated with the sleeping
protagonist by applying the sounds of a body to the realities of war. The
castles are muttering ("šamkajut"), the brakes of the hospital trains are
panting ("sopjat"), the bones are rattling ("stuk kostej"). The last example
is perhaps a description of the sounds from the artillery. Thus two rows of
sounds are united in the metaphor of the tongue.

The horror scene in the middle of the poem has the flow of an English
Gothic novel with the mountains, the castle, the terrible protagonist and the
suggested danse-macabre ("stuk kostej"). The horrors described seem to be
strengthened by the use of negatively charged images that one would expect

to be positive. We have already seen that the moon is first compared with a bell and its beautiful sound, but this image is immediately replaced with a comparison between the moon and a severed tongue. The words "nazem ogorodnika", "the gardener's manure" has the potential of developing into a metaphor of dying and revival but this is only realized in the parallel of the gardener's leveling out a mound of earth in the same way as the war is leveling out everything on earth and turning everything into ruins: and there is no thought of something growing up out of the manure.

The word "skazka" is also negatively charged, it is not a fairy tale with a happy ending, but a tale full of horrors. The fairy tale motif of a round object on the loose rolling through the landscape (for example the bun in the popular tale "Kolobok") is here transformed into the frightful description of the severed tongue rolling through the landscape:

> On prygnul s grjady za ogradu. On v rytvine,
> On sorvan byl bitvoj i, bitvoj podchlesnutyj, . . .

Pasternak did use the word "skazka" later on in his poem about the Second World War, "Strašnaja skazka", but without the expressionistic overtones of "Durnoj son".

It would be possible to see all the negations in the poem as a sort of immanent protest against the horrors of war; "ni", "ne", "net" and words containing a negation like: "bessnež'e", "beznosyj", "bezgvozdyj", "neezženyj", "bezdna". I would even like to suggest that the words "nebesnyj" and "nebo" in this context of negations take on a negative ring as though they were compounds of the words "ne" and "bez", a sort of poetic etymologization of these words.

Against the background of these atrocities the poet asks himself:

> K komu prisosedit'sja, verstami merjaja,
> Slova gololedicy, mgly i lafetov?

Now it is no longer the tongue or the moon rolling through the landscape, but words, and the question is how these words will find someone to approach. This can be decoded as a question of who will write about the new realities of war when the sound of the silver bell has been interchanged with the inarticulate sounds of war. The poem itself has the same inarticulate sounds as is heard on earth, with all its š-, ž-, and č-sounds, with the lack of symmetry and smooth rhythm. The poetry itself has lost its beautiful silver tone in the war. The poem can therefore implicitly be seen as a refutation of the symbolists' beautiful verses set agianst the background of war. A new time demands a new poetry and a new poet.

Who then is the protagonist in the poem? We know that the war is his nightmare, that he has cosmic dimensions and that he is called "nebesnyj postnik", a heavenly ascetic, which was capitalized in the original version of the poem. "Postnik" is a Russian word for the Greek ascetic, used to describe saints and monks who fast extremely severely. Dostojevskij, for example uses this word to describe the antagonist of Father Zosima in his novel *Brat'ja Karamazovy,* Father Therapont, who has a very narrow and fanatical view of Orthodoxy.[6] All these clues lead us to think that here we have a sort of god image, or rather a sort of demiurge. It is a terrible caricature of an orthodox conception of God, it is a God who cannot do anything against the evils of war, and who is only concerned with his own ascetic trials far from the suffering man. The word "postnik" becomes a terrible sarcasm in light of the description of all the bloodiness in the poem. I see the poem as an answer to all the cheap nationalistic-religious rhetoric at the beginning of the war, about the Orthodox God who will help the Russians to victory: "Spasi Bože ljudi Tvoja". This God will not help the people, on the contrary, he is asleep.

The words we expect to hear from God ought to be like the ring of a silver bell and have the same sonority as the Church Slavonic word "glagol":

> Jazyk i glagol ee, mesjac nebesnyj.

But what we hear instead in the time of war can be compared to a tongueless mumbling: "kosnojazyčnyj", "gundosyj", "siplyj", which are indirectly connected with the sleeping protagonist in the poem, words suggesting an idiot's or a syphilitic's way of talking.

The poem is a reproach against a God who is far from mankind; the heights do not open up. He is not almighty, he has no power at all:

> On dvinut'sja chočet, ne možet prosnut'sja.
> Ne možet, zasunutyj v son na zasov.

But as we have seen, he is not only asleep, perhaps it is also suggested in the poem that he is dying. This is a sharp contrast to the Christian idea of death and resurrection. In the hymns of the Orthodox Church the word "sleep" is indeed also used in reference to Christ in the grave, for example in this well known hymn from the Easter service:

> Plotiju usnuv, jako mertv Tsarju i Gospodi,
> tridneven voskresl esi,
> Adama vozdvig ot tli, i uprazdniv smert':
> pascha netlenija, mira spasenie.[7]

God is asleep in this hymn but the result will not only be his own awakening but also the Resurrection of all men. In "Durnoj son" God is asleep and men – the injured in the trains who are only indirectly described in the poem – are also sleeping in delirium and perhaps both the demiurge and men are going to die. The poem is a description of an anti-Easter in autumn with a dying God and dying men. It is a poem related to the trend of "bogoborčestvo" in Russian literature from the beginning of this century, for example Sologub and Majakovskij.

In the original version of the poem from 1914, we have one more aspect of this discussion about the relation between God and man:

> Kak v nebo posmel on igrat', čelovek?

When there is no God, or when God has no power, man takes on the role of God, and the evil will of man creates war. This is a Dostojevskian thought and the reproach against the sleeping God has the same intensity as Ivan's accusation against God in *Brat'ja Karamazovy*. This verse line is certainly a direct influence from Dostojevskij and his discussion of the difference between "Bogočelovek", God who becomes man, and "čelovekobog", man who turns himself into a god.

Yet another line in the original version of the poem continues this Dostojevskian motif:

> Net grjad, čto ruki igroka by izbegli.

"Grjada", a garden bed, is here a variant of "nazem ogorodnika" in the 1928 poem and the word "player" refers to men who play heaven, that is who have made themselves into gods. Man has not been able to keep his hands away from anything and has turned everything on earth into ruins.

The name of the river Stochod in the 1928 version means that Pasternak here puts the poem in relation to the military operations on that river in 1916, but the poem still has much of the flavour of the first autumn of the war in 1914. At that time Pasternak lived in the town of Aleksin on the River Oka, where he could see the trains with soldiers leaving for the front and the hospital trains returning with the injured:

> Tem vremenem, kak ona (Rossija) myslila vagonami, v vagonach ètich dni i noči spešno s pesnjami vyvozili krupnye partii svežego korennogo naselenija v obmen na porčenoe, vozvraščavšeesja sanitarnymi poez-dami.[8]

Some of these impressions certainly served as components in the conception of the poem "Durnoj son".

The train is also depicted in the third poem about war in *Poverch Bar'erov*

"Osen'. Otvykli ot molnij", here seen as a train overcrowded with people at the beginning of the war. This poem was cut by the military censors when first published, so that only the first stanza was left:

> Osen'. Otvykli ot molnij.
> Idut slepye doždi.
> Osen'. Poezda perepolneny –
> Dajte projti! Vse pozadi.[9]

The manuscript of this poem has also been lost, but even this single stanza shows points of connection with the poem analyzed here: the train motif, the gloomy landscape and the overall pessimistic tone.

The train motif, which mainly represented technical progress in Russian literature from the end of the 19th century, here has taken on the connotation of the devastating forces of modern technology. We find another similar use of the train motif in Aleksandr Blok's poem "Petrogradskoe nebo mutilos' doždem" from the first of September 1914, which depicts the soldiers travelling to the front by train and the indifference of the steel colossus of the train to all human sufferings and feelings.

The poem "Artillerist stoit u kormila", the second poem of war in *Poverch bar'erov,* depicts an artilleryman standing on a warship waiting to hear a word from the captain. As I have shown in an earlier analysis, the artilleryman represents the late tsar and the captain is an encoded godimage.[10] The artilleryman awaits a word of guidance but the only thing he hears is the sounds of war ("golosom peresochšej gaubicy"). God's word is here, as in "Durnoj son", called by the Church Slavonic "glagol". Both "Durnoj son" and "Artillerist" are poems about a nonintervening god during the war, a reproach of a powerless god who does not take care of his creatures.

Pasternak returns to the search of God in his poems written between 1946 and 1953 which are included in the last poetic chapter of his novel *Doktor Živago.* The difference in outlook can be illustrated by comparing "Durnoj son" with the poem "Na strastnoj" from 1946, a poem which describes the celebrations of Christ's Passion and Resurrection in the Russian Orthodox Church. There are many common traits between the two poems, it is winter and the earth is sleeping:

> I esli zemlja mogla,
> Ona by Paschu prospala
> Pod čtenie psaltyri.

The battle going on in "Na strastnoj" is not a war but a battle between life and death, between spring and winter. Even the church bell motif returns here, but now there is a hope of resurrection, a real hope to hear the word of God, to hear the "glagol":

No v polnoč' smolknut tvar' i plot',
Zaslyšav sluch vesennij,
Čto tol'ko-tol'ko raspogod',
Smert' možno budet poborot'
Usil'em vozkresen'ja.[11]

The imagery in thus almost the same but here all the negations have turned into affirmations. The First World War led Pasternak away from a Christian tradition, the Second World War meant, on the contrary, a rapprochement to Christian values for the Russian poet.

Knowing Boris Pasternak's interest for Rainer Maria Rilke it is of a certain importance to compare "Durnoj son" with Rilke's series of tales "Geschichten vom lieben Gott" which was published for the first time in 1900. These stories deal with the relation between God and man and especially the first two of them ("Das Märchen von den Händen Gottes" and "Der fremde Mann") have many points of contact with Pasternak's poem. These two stories are a sort of paraphrase of the Biblical story of creation and incarnation in a conscious naive style. Rilke depicts a God who loses control over his creatures, he can not help a little bird which has got lost, he can not see what happens on the earth because of the clouds, man escapes from the hands of God the day of creation before God has had the possibility of inspecting him. In Rilke's text we have the same personification of God as in "Durnoj son" though without the expressionistic details. God's hands fall off and go down to the earth, first the right and then the left goes down to see what has happened:

In dem selben Augenblicke begann Gottes linke Hand, die vor seinem offenen Blute lag, unruhig zu werden, und mit einem Mal verliess sie, ehe Gott es verhindern konnte, ihren Platz und irrte wie wahnsinnig zwischen den Sternen umher ...

The result of this is that God begins to bleed:

Die ganze Erde aber war rot vom Blute Gottes, und man konnte nicht erkennen, was darunter geschah.

God can not longer see what is happening on earth and is almost dying:

Damals wäre Gott fast gestorben.[12]

94

This is a parallel to the tongue image and the description of the sleeping God in "Durnoj son". Both texts depict a God with no power over his creatures.

Rilke and Pasternak also use the same designation of genre for their texts – "Märchen" respectively "skazka". All these details together convince me that here we have a case of direct influence from Rilke on Pasternak, or to express it better perhaps, Rilke's stories are a sort of starting point or raw material for Pasternak's poem. But the somewhat idyllic tone in the German text has changed to an overall picture of horrors in "Durnoj son". The motif of the helpless God has changed in character under the influence of the First World War.

"Durnoj son" takes up the existential question of the relation between God and man with an almost Dostojevskian frenzy. The answer which is given is a negative one – God is sleeping and perhaps even dying. This question will, however, be posed again some thirty years later in *Doktor Živago*, both in the novel as such and in the poems, and then be given another, more positive answer.[13]

NOTES

1. The poems are quoted from: Boris Pasternak, *Izbrannoe v dvuch tomach, tom pervyj.* Moskva 1985, pp. 40–42.
2. M. Gasparov, *Sovremennyj russkij stich,* Moskva 1974, pp. 151–153.
3. The original poem is published in Pasternak, *op.cit.* pp. 474—475.
4. See for example Dostojevskij's use of this motif in *Besy* in a passage describing the death of Stepan Stavrogin: "On uverjal ee tože, čto vidit vo sne kakuju-to raskrytuju čeljust' s zubami i čto emu èto očen' protivno", third part, seventh chapter, II.
5. A. Afanas'ev, *Poètičeskie vozzrenija slavjan na prirodu,* t. 1, Moskva 1865, pp. 189–190.
6. Fedor Dostojevskij, *Brat'ja Karamazovy,* third part, seventh book, II.
7. Vo svjatuju i velikuju nedelju Paschi, na utreni, kanon, èksapostilarij.
8. Pasternak, *op.cit.,* tom vtoroj, p. 210.
9. *Ibid.,* p. 361.
10. Per-Arne Bodin, "God, Tsar and Man. Boris Pasternak's Poem *Artillerist*", *Scottish Slavonic Review,* no. 6, Spring 1986, pp. 69–80.
11. Boris Pasternak, *Doktor Živago.* Milano 1957, pp. 533–535.
12. Rainer Maria Rilke, "Geschichten vom lieben Gott", in: *Sämtliche Werke,* vierter Band, Frankfurt 1961, p. 301.
13. This poem has been somewhat discussed earlier by D. Segal in his article "Zametki o zjužetnosti v liričeskoj poèzii Pasternaka", *Slavica Hierosolymitana,* vol. III, Jerusalem 1978, pp. 282–301. Segal is mainly interested in the differences between the two versions of the poem.

Peter Alberg Jensen

Boris Pasternak's "Opredelenie poėzii"

ОПРЕДЕЛЕНЬЕ ПОЭЗИИ

I.   Это – круто налившийся свист,
Это – щелканье сдавленных льдинок,
Это – ночь, леденящая лист,
Это – двух соловьев поединок.

II.   Это – сладкий, заглохший горох,
Это – слезы вселенной в лопатках,
Это – с пультов и с флейт – Figaro
Низвергается градом на грядку.

III.   Все, что ночи так важно сыскать
На глубоких купаленных доньях,
И звезду донести до садка,
На трепещущих, мокрых ладонях.

IV.   Площе досок в воде – духота.
Небосвод завалился ольхою.
Этим звездам к лицу-б хохотать,
Ан вселенная – место глухое.[1]

Boris Pasternak's "Opredelenie poėzii" from "Sestra moja žizn'" (1922) has a peculiar chameleon-like quality: the sentences in which the poet defines poetry seem to be new and familiar at one and the same time.

On closer inspection the new turns out to be the sentences taken in isolation, whereas the impression of déja vu derives from relations between them. It is as if Pasternak has taken a number of conventional phrases apart and put their elements together in a new way. The device is signalled through a chiastic figure in the first Stanza, lines 1 and 3, *nalivšijsja svist – ...ledenjaščaja list,* in which the "reverse" combinations, 'ledenjaščij [dušu] svist' and 'nalivšijsja list', are closer at hand in ordinary usage. Similarly both *svist* (I.1) and *ščelkan'e* (I.2) often appear together with *solov'ev,* from which they have been "separated" here.

Once we start looking for them, other "displacements" of this kind readily present themselves. Participles of three verbs that often appear in figurative descriptions of certain sounds, i.e., of the semantic sphere represented by

svist, have been separated from it and qualify something else:
- 'sdavlennyj' (I.2) is common about voice and voice-products meaning 'priglušennyj', e.g., 'sdavlennyj golos'; here it is used literally to describe 'l'dinki';
- 'zaglochšij' (II.1) as an adjective means 'zapuščennyj'; but in the sound-dominated context of the poem the primary meaning of the verb 'zagloch-nut'' is strongly activized, the more so because of 'gluchoe' in IV.4;
- 'trepeščuščij' (III.4) – 'trepetat'' is also conventional about sounds or voice in the meaning "preryvisto, nerovno zvučat' v vozduche",[2] but here it qualifies 'ladoni'.

Clearly this is a matter of principle in our poem. The text presents a series of more or less unusual word combinations that serve as concrete, once-only descriptions; but in their close vicinity we recognize conventional "partners" of the words used, partners from more or less figurative phrases.

These displacements are not simple, but, on the contrary, complex and difficult to disentangle. A case in point is the already mentioned *trepešču-ščich* in III.4. The verb 'trepetat'' is used regularly not only about sounds, but also about sources of light, meaning "mercat', nerovno goret'",[3] and accordingly also about *stars;* and we do have stars here, both in the very same clause (III.3) and in the following stanza, but they appear in new connections. Another conventional partner of 'trepetat'' or 'trepeščuščij' is 'list', which we have in Stanza I. Furthermore, the same verb may occur in phrases such as 'trepetat' smechom',[4] so that it anticipates the *chochotat'* of Stanza IV; another conventional combination is 'trepetat' cholodom', which relates the *trepeščuščich* in III.4 to *ledenjaščaja* in I.3. As we see, *trepešču-ščich* is the centre of a network; the poem contains many words which serve as traditional partners of 'trepetat'', but the verb has been detached from them and reserved for a concrete connection.

A closer look at Stanza II reveals several minor networks:
- 'sladkij' is commonly used about sounds and therefore has close relations with *svist* and *ščelkan'e* in Stanza I and with 'flejta' in II,3;
- 'slezy' is readily associated with the 'nalit'sja' of I.1 (e.g., 'glaza nalilis' slezami') as well as with 'chochotat'' in IV.3, cf. 'chochotat' do slez';[5]
- 'goroch' in II.1 is intimately connected with *gradom na grjadku*, not only phonetically, but also because of the idiomatic metaphor 'gorošiny grada'; the word 'grad' in its turn is conventionally linked with attributes such as 'ledenjaščij' (I.3) as well as with 'ščelkanie'/'ščelkat'' (1.2, cf. 'grad ščel-kaet');
- 'lopatki' in II.2 is used in a special meaning which Pasternak later specified in a footnote,[6] but as a diminutive of 'lopata' the word fits well into the sphere of 'ogorod' that is established in the stanza.

In Stanza III *donesti* is connected with *zvezdu*, which is arrestingly new. However, the verb 'donesti'/'donosit'' is traditionally used about sounds, e.g., 'veter dones zvuki . . . perestrelki';[7] thus it is connected with the sound-sphere of the poem, the more so because the word 'zvuk' is anagrammatical-ly present in the line: I ZVezdU donesti do sadKa. Through contrast the verb also connects with the theme of 'gluchota' in the following stanza.

Here, the line *Nebosvod zavalilsja ol'choju* claims attention. Its verb appears with a new and surprising agent, which makes the whole construc-tion ambiguous.[8] Close by we have a word with which the verb 'zavalit'' is often combined, namely 'doski' (cf. 'dvor zavalen doskami'). Phonetically 'zavalit'sja' is very close to 'zalivat'sja/'zalit'sja', which conventionally ap-pears with laughter, 'smech' or 'chochot'; thus the verb anticipates the theme of 'chochot' in the next line.

To date "Opredelenie poèzii" has been viewed mainly in terms of its statement, and the consensus is that Pasternak defines poetry as *nature*[9] or as "nature's rival".[10] Now we have seen that to a high degree the poem is also a verbal demonstration: it is a displacement-show, and as such seems a fine illustration of Pasternak's often quoted definition from "Ochrannaja gra-mota":

> Наставленное на действительность, смещаемую чувством, искусство есть запись этого смещенья. Оно его списывает с натуры. Как же смещается натура? Подробности выигрывают в яркости, проигрывая в самостоятельности значенья. Каждую можно за-менить другою. Любая драгоценна. Любая на выбор годится в свидетельства состоянья, которым охвачена вся переместившаяся действительность.[11]

In "Opredelenie poèzii", then, Pasternak practices 'smeščen'e natury', or establishes his 'peremestivšajasja dejstvitel'nost'' in a strikingly *literal* way: the words seem to have moved a few places down the line, away from their habitual lodgings; or, as one might put it in Russian, "peremestivšimsja veščam sootvetstvujut peremestivšiesja slova".

It is a commonplace of Pasternak criticism to say that the poet modifies ordinary usage.[12] But it has passed without notice that in the poem entitled "Definition of Poetry" the device is exposed to a degree which makes the text a literal demonstration of the claim quoted above that "Každuju možno zamenit' drugoju". As has been noted by Ju. Lotman (ibid.), the technique is meaningful in itself: if on the level of language any feature can take the place of any other, this implies the postulate that in spite of conventional semantic differentiation everything has an equal share in an all-important unity.

Many of the phrases the elements of which have been displaced are more or less "dead" images. Pasternak dissects them and reuses the "limbs" in concrete description. The effect is double: not only is the concrete description arresting, but the dissection also makes the dead verbal tissue stir again. There is a fine tension in the poem between its series of new once-only descriptions and the variegated phraseology that has been "awakened" through dismemberment.

Thus, it is insufficient to say that Pasternak breaks up the conventional verbal framework; he coins his concrete description *from among the fragments* of this framework, in such a way that all the words seem to be reaching out towards one another. This effect can also be likened to that of a photographic double exposure, in which the dismembered phrases can be glimpsed beneath the surface of the actual wording.[13] Pasternak unites by separating; the principle we have seen at work in "Opredelenie poėzii" could be aptly defined in Russian as 'raz"edinitel'no-soedinitel'nyj'. And in fact the poet presented this very principle in the title poem of the collection "Sestra moja žizn'": "Bessporno, bessporno *smešon tvoj rezon,* / Čto v grozu *lilovy* glaza i *gazony,* / I *pachnet* syroj *rezedoj gorizont.*" (Italics added, here and elsewhere.) One "funny" thing about the poet's "rezon" is that the predicates *lilovy* and *pachnet rezedoj* have changed their places (cf. "každuju možno zamenit' drugoju"); Pasternak separates 'lilac' from 'horizon' and 'smells . . .' from 'lawns', and by interchanging them he posits a new essential unity to the things.[14]

From description to discussion

As stated above, the syntactical and phraseological principle of "Opredelenie poėzii" has direct bearings on its content, and if we turn to other levels of the poem we shall see that the text actually *says* the same as it *does*: through apparent distinction of particulars it arrives at a more general statement, which is announced when in III.1 the word *Vse* takes the place that initially belonged to *Ėto*. Let us examine this development in a little more detail.

On the levels of syntax, meter, rhythm, and rhyme "Opredelenie poėzii" displays, to begin with, a spectacular regularity. Its anapestic tetrameter is strictly adhered to in the first half of the poem; the rhyme alternates between masculine and feminine (aBaB), and the number of syllables in each line is fixed in all four stanzas (9-10-9-10).

Syntactically Stanzas I–II present seven juxtaposed noun phrases, each introduced by the anaphorical *Ėto,* and the first six of them contain a neat syntactico-rhythmical pattern, with the main word shifting from final position in the "outer" lines 1 and 4 to an initial position in the "inner" lines 2 and 3:

I. Ėto – . . . . . . *list,*
    Ėto – *ščelkan'e* . . . . .,
    Ėto – *noč'*, ... ,
    Ėto – . . . . *poedinok.*

II. Ėto – . . . . . *goroch,*
    Ėto – *slezy* . . . .,

In the last two lines of the second stanza, however, this pattern is disturbed in several ways. Firstly, the sentence here occupies two lines; secondly, the main word *Figaro* is at the end of the line and not, as was to be expected, at its beginning (below *slezy*); thirdly, the sentence is of a new kind, namely a verb phrase with *nizvergaetsja* as the first finite verb form in the poem.

The change in II.3–4 is sustained on the level of orchestration as well.[15] Stanza I is dominated by 's', 'š', and 'šč', by 'l' and by 'd':

Ėto – kru*t*o naLivŠijSja SviS*t*
Ėto – ŠČe*l*kan'e SDavLennych L'Dinok
Ėto – noč', LeDenjaŠČaja Lis*t*
Ėto – Dvuch SoLov'ev poeDinok

The same orchestration prevails until line II.3, the last word of which *Figaro* launches the new dominants 'g' and 'r':

FiGaRo / nizveRGaetsja GRadom na GRjad*k*u

On closer inspection we see that 'g' and 'r' were introduced by 'GoRoch' in II.1 and were in part prepared by '*k*Ruto' in I.1.[16]

The rhymed words also display a sudden irregularity in II.3–4. In Stanza I the rhyme is patently regular, whereas in II.3–4 the conformity is challenged by *goroch – Figaro* and *lopatkach – grjadku.*

Last, but not least, the impression of a change in II.3–4 is enhanced by the fact that the clause does not quite fit into the definition scheme. Until now we have had no difficulty in reading the lines as definitions that refer through *Ėto* to the *'poėzija'* of the title, but II.3–4 seem to challenge this reading; all the preceding definitions have been noun phrases, whereas here poetry is defined by a verb phrase: (Poėzija) ėto . . . Figaro nizvergaetsja . . .

There are thus good grounds for seeing these lines as a turning-point in the poem. They break the syntactico-rhythmical pattern; they launch a new consonantal orchestration; they take liberties with the rhyme; and they more or less disregard the pattern imposed on them by the construction with 'Ėto –'. Clearly lines II.3–4 mark a breakthrough in the text.

A breakthrough of what? The definitions presented in Stanzas I–II imply that poetry is dynamics and energy. Although the first six lines are noun phrases, they contain an inherent tension, most importantly a tension between *sound* and *silence*. Both a sudden whistle, a crackle, and the song of nightingales are characterized by discontinuity; they are sounds on the verge of silence. There is also tension between "sound-verses" such as these and the silence stated in, for instance, 'sweet smothered peas'. And this tension between silence and sound is also clearly expressed by the features observed on the phonological leve, i.e., by the dominance of the plosives 'd', 'g'. Furthermore, confined in the noun phrases there is considerable energy; in the participles *nalivšijsja, sdavlennych,* and in the noun *poedinok* there is compressed action, and *ledenjaščaja* used with a direct object is indeed very active. Thus, II.3–4 give expression to a breakthrough of accumulated tension: sound bursts forth as music (Figaro), the phrase frees itself from limitations in rhythm, rhyme, and space and jumps on to the next line, exposing the very dynamic verb *nizvergaetsja* in the front place that had seemed predestined for another schematic *Èto*.

This turning-point in the poem is, as already mentioned, markedly expressed by the word *Vse* that begins Stanza III. After the list of particulars the way has been opened for a more general statement, and actually the second part of the poem differs from the first in important respects. The construction with 'èto' is left out, and the question arises whether it still underlies each of the subsequent clauses, or only some of them, or none at all. Looking for guidance, we notice that the syntactical constructions vary in character and length, in contrast to the stanzas analysed above. But along with this formal variety and complication we also notice a growing coherence in subject-matter;[17] Stanzas III and IV can be read as a description of a coherent situation, or at least of a specific setting, namely a night-scene by a pond or river.

Stanza III is syntactically ambiguous. Firstly, we cannot decide whether the definition scheme 'poèzija, èto' underlies only the two first lines, or both this segment and the next one III.3–4. Secondly, who or what is the zero subject of the infinitive *zvezdu donesti* – is it the night (in continuation of III.1–2) or a person, i.e., the poet? A clear answer to this question cannot be found either, the text simply does not tell us. We must conclude that the poem *does not want* us to know anything specific about agents here – the verbs are not finite, the agents in oblique case or zero. Something is going on, but who or what is acting is deliberately veiled.

The last stanza poses its own problems. Lines IV.2 and IV.3 will not lend themselves to a reading with an underlying 'poèzija, èto'. Because of the finite verb in line 2 and the irrealis in line 3 these segments cannot be part of definitions, since both imply a distance between something actual and something else;[18] in IV.2 somebody *narrates* about, and in IV.3 *comments* on, an actual situation. At this point we must conclude that in its last two stanzas our poem develops into something quite different from what it was at first. And this new 'smeščenie' is sustained on the rhythmical level as well. Not only *Vse* in III.1, but also *Plošče* in IV.1 and last, but not least, *An* in the concluding line of the poem must be partly stressed and thereby modify the hitherto rigid metrical pattern. How, then, are these stanzas to be understood?

In III.1 the night is said to be looking for something. This is a common image in Pasternak, who varied it from his early verses on to the famous lines in "Gamlet": "Na menja nastavlen sumrak noči / Tysjač'ju binoklej na osi". In fragments of an early poem we find the searching or looking night connected with water: "Gde sumrak skorbnoj capleju večernej / Vyklevyval zrački zari v vode".[19] In our poem, however, the image is less concrete and less visual. The light of darkness is doing something not on the surface of the water, but at the bottom. We need not concretize the image. It is more important to realize that on a certain level of generalization, this segment and the following one about the carrying of a star state the same thing, namely that nature is minding its own business, and that this business is the *establishing of connections* – the finding of something, bringing a star where it was not before. And in both cases water is essential as the element which makes possible the connection, or the diffusion.

With this notion we move to the last stanza. *Plošče dosok v vode – duchota*; it still is not clear whether 'poèzija, èto' is implicit here. I think it is not and read the line as a description of the more concrete, actual setting on which the poet then comments in the two subsequent segments. But how is this description to be interpreted? Qualified as 'flatter than boards in water' the *duchota* can mean absolute contact, or total contiguity. This reading allows us to take the line as a continuation of the preceding ones, as a brief description of a case in point, i.e., of nature's "business", the establishment and minding of pervasive connections. And this reading can point the way to an understanding of the following segment – *Nebo zavalilsja ol'choju.* The image can be understood as a view of the sky reflected in a pond surrounded by trees. This means that the sky is *in* the water, and I would argue that this interpretation is suggested by the very word 'nebo-s-vod'. All is there at once, in one instant of time and space.

The final lines are a commentary: "It would suit these stars to guffaw". The question arises, why? According to what expectations or norms? And why *chochot?* The notion of 'chochot' is not in any way contained within the sound-sphere defined as poetry earlier in the poem; it seems alien here. Therefore it is not surprising that the poem concludes by rejecting the standards implied in this line. And now an addressee of the commentary is signalled: *An vselennaja – mesto gluchoe* cannot but recall the final lines of V. Majakovskij's "Oblako v štanach":

Èj, vy!
Nebo!

Snimite šljapu!
Ja idu!

Glucho.
Vselennaja spit,
položiv na lapu
s kleščami *zvezd* ogromnoe ucho.

Pasternak's concluding remark makes almost explicit a dimension of the poem that has been more implicit until now – a discussion with Futurist poetry.[20] This takes us to the last point of my commentary, namely the literary context of "Opredelenie poėzii".

From discussion to polemics

There are several words in the poem which serve as more or less specific references to Futurism. The first ones are *kruto . . . svist,* which in the sense of 'whistle through one's fingers' may recall the Futurists' rude manners and the public's reactions to them. Point four in "Poščečina obščestvennomu vkusu" reads: "Stojat' na glybe slova "my" sredi *morja svista* i negodovanija". More specifically the group Pasternak adhered to, "Centrifuga", associated its own name with 'svist'. This is apparent from the verse-manifesto "Turbopėan":

Zavertelas' CENTRIFUGA,
Raspustila kolesa:
Oglušitel'nye svisty
Blesk parjaščich spletnych ruk!
(. . .)
O, protki čudesij tugo
Bezpristrastij ljubosot,
Preblaženstvuj CENTRIFUGA,
V *osvistelyj* krugolet.[21]

And a sentence in a letter from Pasternak to S. Bobrov refers to these particular lines and shows that to Pasternak himself 'svist' was associated with the appearance of Futurism: "*Svist Centrifugi* dejstvitel'no oglušitelen".[22]

As to the word 'flejta' (II.3), D. Plank rightly suggested that here "there are echoes of Majakovskij's backbone-flute".[23] 'Flejta' was a marked word in Futurist poetry; Majakovskij had already used it in his metapoetical poem "A vy mogli by", B. Livšic's and N. Aseev's first collections contained it in their titles, etc.[24]

But the most direct reference by a single word to Futurism is, of course, contained in *sadka* in III.3: *I zvezdu donesti do sadka*. The publication in 1910 of the first volume "Sadok sudej" marked the appearance of the Russian Futurists as a group,[25] and according to "Ochrannaja gramota" Pasternak's first encounter with Futurism and with Majakovskij was associated with "Sadok sudej".[26] The word 'sadok' is rare in poetic usage, so that here it cannot but serve as a signpost directing our attention to Futurism.

Following this sign we notice that the images in which it appears may recall the imagery in specific texts by Majakovskij and Chlebnikov. The 'zvezda' in III.3 is readily associated with a little fish: it is something to be found in the water, and it is carried in wet trembling hands from one reservoir to another (from the river or lake to the sadok, in its own right a new 'smeščenie'). In "Čelovek" Majakovskij had stated that his birth, in contrast to Christ's, had not been marked by the appearance of a star, which leads him to repeat the question he had already posed in "Poslušajte!", namely what are the stars there for? This argument is followed by an image of *fishing* (an allusion to Puškin's "Skazka o rybake i rybke") introduced by the imperative of the verb 'sudit'' (cf. "Sadok *sudej*"):

> *Zvezda* – mol –
> len' sijat' naprasno vam!
> Esli ne
> čelovеč'ego roždenija den',
> to čёrta l',
> zvezda,
> togda ešče
> prazdnovat'?!
>
> *Sudíte:*
> govorjaščuju *rybёšku*
> *vyudim* nitjami nevoda
> i poem,
> poem zolotuju,
> vospevaem rybač'ju udal'.[27]

Could this not be the star-fish that one must *donesti do sadka* in Pasternak's poem? As to the *ladonjach* in III.4 we find a similar image in Chlebnikov's poem "Krymskoe", which was published in the second volume of "Sadok sudej":

> *Beregu*
> *Svoich rybok*
> *V ladonjach*
> Soslonennych.[28]

Thus, the imagery around the key-word *sadka* in Pasternak's third stanza seems to allude to passages such as these in Majakovskij and Chlebnikov.

However, the relationship between "Opredelenie poėzii" and Futurist poetics turns out to be a complex matter, which deserves a special study.[29] I must limit myself to a few remarks. The poem both approaches Futurist poetics and distances itself from them. The principle of 'smeščenie', which we have described above, is essentially Futurist. The same applies to the orchestration with its plosive dominants 'd', 'gr'/'kr', announced already in *kruto*,[30] or with the demonstrative exposure of 'cho' in the last stanza (prepared by *zaglochšij goroch* in II.1); networks such as *zaglochšij – glubokich – gluchoe*, the paronomasia in *sladkij – sadka – dosok*, the resounding three times 'don' in Stanza III (*don'jach – donesti – ladonjach*) – all this is Futurist 'facture'.

At the same time, on the other hand, the poem opposes itself to Futurism, more specifically to its Urbanist wing, or to Majakovskij.

It does so in its choice of subject-matter, which resembles the stuff of traditional nature lyrics: nature, nightingales, garden, music, reflections at a nightly river – this is very far from Majakovskij's "hell of a city" ("adišče goroda"). It does so also in its metrical and syntactical regularity. After all the authors of "Sadok sudej" had declared: "Nami sokrušeny ritmy. (. . .) My perestali iskat' razmery v učebnikach".[31] Obviously Pasternak *did* look up his tetrameter and follows it with demonstrative piety. Correspondingly, the declaration in "Sadok sudej" to the effect that "My rasšatali sintaksis" (ibid.) is met here by Pasternak's rigid scheme of definition.

Furthermore, and most importantly, the entire verbal stance of Pasternak's text is markedly different from that of a Majakovskij poem. The third person pronoun 'ėto' takes the place which in most poetry prior to Pasternak belongs to the lyrical 'I' (cf., for instance, K. Bal'mont's "Ja – izyskannost' russkoj medlitel'noj reči . . .", "Ves' – vesna", "Vozglas voli"). 'Poėzija' in Pasternak's text has taken the place of 'poėt' in Majakovskij; the scheme 'poėzija – čto' is opposed to Majakovskij's formular 'Ja – vaš poėt'. Indeed, the 'Ja' of the poet, which in Majakovskij is overwhelming, is totally absent here in Pasternak. And in contrast to Majakovskij, who is constantly addressing somebody, be it the crowd, or the earth ("Zemlja! . ."), or God, in "Opredelenie poėzii" *no-one says anything*; there is neither an 'I' nor a 'you', and a communicative stance is not detectable until the last stanza. The contrast between *sladkij zaglochšij goroch* and Majakovskij's "Poslušajte!. ." is remarkable. Poetry according to Pasternak is an 'it', i.e., something going on in life, and not what a poet says, even less so the poet himself.

It is these implicit polemics with Majakovskij and *his* Futurism which become more explicit in the last stanza of "Opredelenie poėzii". After the clear signal of 'sadok' in Stanza III, Pasternak develops the reference through the theme of 'chochot' in IV. 'Laughter' was, of course, a hallmark in "Hylaean" Futurism, prominent as it was in Chlebnikov, Kamenskij and Majakovskij. Through repetition of the syllable 'cho' Pasternak makes the whole stanza laugh; thereafter he ironically refers to norms according to which the stars should laugh, but only in order to dismiss such expectations in his last line. The wise-after-the-event *An* introduces a conclusion which now looks like a direct comment on Majakovskij's attempts at a dialogue with the universe.[32]

Pasternak's "Definition of Poetry", however, goes beyond its own narrow context. By means of allusion, concrete classical texts are brought into the poem and broaden its meaning, and, conversely, the poem and its polemics are projected onto the poetic tradition.

The insistent use of 'ėto' in initial position recalls Afanasij Fet's poem "Ėto utro, radost' ėta ...":

> Ėto utro, radost' ėta,
> Ėta mošč', i dnja i sveta,
>   Ėtot sinij *svod,*
> Ėtot krik i verenicy,
> Ėti stai, ėti pticy,
>   Ėtot govor vod,
>
> Ėti ivy i berezy,
> Ėti kapli – ėti *slezy,*
>   Ėtot puch – ne *list,*
> Ėti gory, ėti doly,
> Ėti moški, ėti pčely,
>   Ėtot zyk i *svist,*
>
> Ėti zori bez zatmen'ja,
> Ėtot vzdoch nočnoj selen'ja,
>   Ėta *noč' bez sna,*
> Ėta mgla i *žar* posteli,
> Ėta *drob'* i ėti *treli,*
>   Ėto *vse* – vesna.[33]

Although the syntactical function of 'ėto' is not the same in Fet's poem as in Pasternak's, the unusual foregrounding of the word cannot but link the two poems together.[34] The construction is clearly the same in both texts – a series of juxtaposed particulars leads on to a 'vsë' – and the linkage between them is strengthened by correspondences of subject matter: *sinij svod, vody, slezy, list, svist, noč' bez sna, žar, drob', treli* – all this corresponds to items in Pasternak's poem.

Among these correspondences, however, the rhyme *list – svist* is of special

106

interest, since it points back to an important subtext, Puškin's humorous "Istorija stichotvorca":

Vnimaet on privyčnym uchom
    Svist;
Maraet on edinym duchom
    List;
Potom vsemu terzaet svetu
    Sluch;
Potom pečataet – i v Letu
    Buch![35]

Pasternak introduces his poem with the very rhyme that Puškin presented as a mark of bad versemaking, and thereby includes Puškin's definition of a bad poet into his definition of poetry. But relations between the two texts are more intricate than that. The sound-sphere which pervades Pasternak's poem from beginning to end, is also prominent in Puškin (cf. *vnimaet ... uchom svist, terzaet sluch*); the sound-combination 'ucho' from Puškin's *uchom – duchom* reappears in Pasternak's last stanza, *duchota – gluchoe*.

What is more, Pasternak's poem can be read as a transformation of Puškin's "story": Stanzas I–II exemplify the sphere of sound and music within which Puškin operates in the first three lines; and Pasternak's Stanzas III–IV can be seen as a playful elaboration on Puškin's reminder of the bad poet's fate, death by drowning in the river Lethe. Stanza III describes swimming and diving for fish (if we associate *zvezdu* in III.3 with a fish), and, taken line by line, Stanza IV can be read as the last perceptions of a drowning person, i.e., the lack of air (*v vode – duchota*), a glimpse of the sky from below the water, the lack of reaction from above.

Pasternak's use of Puškin's "Istorija stichotvorca" provides new instances of 'smeščenie', namely in genre and in time; Puškin's "low" text is incorporated into a "high" philosophical poem, and the distance in time between them amounts to one hundred years (Puškin's poem is dated 1818). But what led Pasternak to combine Puškin's 'stichotvorec' with a discussion of Futurist poetics? Although the poem by A. Fet quoted above with the rhyme *list – svist* may be part of the answer, the impulse may also derive from a more direct context. After the Cubo-Futurists in their loudest manifesto had proposed to throw Puškin overboard from the steamship of modern times, Puškin, as well as the concept 'stichotvorec', had become topical in the discussions about Futurism. The "Centrifuga" defended Puškin, and when S. Bobrov in 1916 published a separate volume with the articles in which the defence had been formulated, the book bore the title *Zapiski stichotvorca*. An apposite example of how readily Puškin and the Puškinian 'stichotvorec' came to be associated with the Futurists is furnished by A. Blok's "Iz 'Žizni moego prijatelja'" from the 1915 anthology "Strelec":

Žizn' prochodila kak vsegda:
V sumasšestvii tichom.
Vse govorili krugom
O boleznjach, vračach i lekarstvach.
O službe rasskazyval drug.
Drugoj – o Christe,
O gazetach – četvertyj.
Chlebnikov i Majakovskij
Nabavili cenu na knigi
(Tak čto prikasčik u Vol'fa
Ne mog ich prodat' bez ulybki).
Dva *stichotvorca* (*poklonniki Puškina*)
Knižki prislali
S množestvom rifm i razmerov.
(...)
On s večera krepko usnul
I prosnulsja v drugoj strane.
Ni cholod utra,
Ni slovo druga,
Ni damskie rozy,
Ni *manifest futurista,*
Ni *stichi puškin'janca,*
Ni laj sobačij,
Ni grochot teležnyj, –
Ničto, ničto
V mir vozvratit' ne moglo ...[36]

Thus, there was nothing far-fetched about Pasternak's association of Puškin and 'stichotvorec' with Futurism. The connection had been there from the very beginning of the polemics of which his poem forms a part.

"Opredelenie poėzii" is a complex poem, and the above remarks are far from being an exhaustive analysis. Nevertheless I hope that they can contribute to an unravelling of its complexities. As we have seen, the definition encompasses several layers of the text. On the level of phraseology it presents a "displacement-show", thereby demonstrating that, as it were, anything can go with anything; on the level of content it states the same experience of pervasive connections in life, this unity being life itself, and the presentation of it – poetry. I have argued that in both form and content the poem establishes a metapoetical discussion for and against Futurist poetics, and that, through a built-in reference to Puškin's "Istorija stichotvorca",

Pasternak endows his definition with a far-reaching *double entendre*. It reaches back into Greek mythology and reminds us that the bad poet is doomed to perish in the waters of Lethe. Both this "backward" orientation of the reminder and the issue at stake, i.e, the question *which poets* will end up in which waters, are polemically aimed at the Cubo-Futurists, who in their eagerness to dispose of the classics may have cared too little about whether they could swim themselves. To call a short poem "Definition of Poetry" may seem rather audacious. But the more we look into the present poem, the more it seems to qualify for its title.

NOTES

1. Boris Pasternak, *Sestra moja žizn'*, Berlin-Peterburg-Moskva 1923, p. 47.
2. Cf. *Slovar' sovremennogo russkogo literaturnogo jazyka,* t. 15, M. – L. 1963, col. 899.
3. Ibid.
4. Ibid.
5. Ibid., t. 17, M. – L. 1965, col. 429.
6. "V dannom slučae slovo 'lopatki' označaet stručki gorocha", B. Pasternak, *Stichotvorenija i poèmy,* M. – L. 1965, p. 126.
7. Cf. *Slovar' sovremennogo russkogo literaturnogo jazyka,* t. 3, M. – L. 1954, col. 979.
8. The ambiguity derives from the instrumental *ol'choju*: is it an *instrumentalis comparationis* (= 'the sky has fallen like an alder') or *instrumenti* (= 'the sky has been filled with alder')? On Pasternak's use of the instrumental in "Sestra moja žizn'", see Krystyna Pomorska, *Themes and Variations in Pasternak's Poetics,* Lisse 1975, pp. 17–19.
9. Cf. Bodo Zelinsky, "Selbstdefinitionen der Poesie bei Pasternak", Zeitschrift für slavische Philologie, Band XXXVIII, 1975, pp. 268–278.
10. Cf. Dale L. Plank, "Dictation from Nature", in his *Pasternak's Lyric*: A Study of Sound and Imagery, The Hague – Paris 1966, p. 52. Plank draws attention to a number of the displacements mentioned above, but he regards them in the light of the broader concept 'ambiguity', and his commentary takes a different direction from mine.
11. B. Pasternak, *Proza 1915–1958.* Povesti, rasskazy, avtobiografičeskie proizvedenija, Ann Arbor 1961, p. 243.
12. See, for instance, Ju. M. Lotman, "Stichotvorenija rannego Pasternaka i nekotorye voprosy strukturnogo izučenija teksta", *Trudy po znakovym sistemam,* IV, Tartu 1969, p. 223 ff.
13. This makes the poem an exposition of its own verbal genesis and an illustration of other often quoted lines from "Ochrannaja gramota". "... lučšie proizvedenija mira, povestvuja o nairazličnejšem, na samom dele rasskazyvajut o svoem roždenii", *Proza 1915–1958,* p. 241.
14. For a detailed analysis of this poem, see Fiona Björling, "Aspects of Poetic Syntax: Analysis of the Poem "Sestra moja – žizn' i segodnja v razlive" by Boris Pasternak", Nils Åke Nilsson (Ed.), *Boris Pasternak.* Essays, Stockholm 1976, pp. 162–179.
15. Cf. Plank, op. cit., p. 49.
16. As far as the level of the vowels is concerned, a change also occurs in Stanzas I–II, although here it takes place between the stanzas and not in II.3–4. Stanza I is dominated by the 'i' which we have in all stressed final positions, whereas in II an alternation occurs between 'o' and 'a'. This alternation was introduced in I (*ščëlkan'e sdavlennych, noč' ledenjaščaja*), but from II it takes over the rhymed words, so that all rhymed stressed vowels from now on alternate between 'a' and 'o'.
17. There is a progressive development through the poem in this respect: the four segments in I appear to be disconnected examples – a duel of nightingales is not likely to occur in icy nights, etc.; the three examples furnished by II appear to be taken from the same setting,

namely a summerly 'ogorod'; finally this growth in situational coherence results in the two last stanzas' dealing with one identifiable situation.

18. In *zavalilsja* it is a distance in time, the verb has perfect meaning; in the irrealis it is, of course, a distance in attitude.

19. Cf. E. V. Pasternak (Ed.), "Pervye opyty Borisa Pasternaka", *Trudy po znakovym sistemam*, IV, 1969, p. 271.

20. Possibly Majakovskij's concluding image can solve the riddle of Pasternak's *Nebosvod zavalilsja ol'choju*. The enormous ear of the universe *s kleščami zvezd* can be associated with 'ol'cha', alder, for two reasons: firstly, the alder is known to be a favourite *habitat* of ticks; secondly, in Majakovskij's image the 'ticks of the stars' have replaced 'ear-rings', 'serёžki' (as an "adornment" of the ear), but the Russian 'serёžki' also means 'catkins', the flowers of certain trees, among them the alder. Thus, 'ucho s kleščami zvezd' → 'ol'chovye serёžki'. (This reading was suggested by Igor' Smirnov.) Accordingly, *nebosvod zavalilsja* in Pasternak can be a paraphrase of Majakovskij's *Vselennaja spit*, in which case the whole line reads like a humorous restatement of Majakovskij's image, i.e., the sky has "crashed" like (or *as*?) an alder.

21. Cf. V. Markov (Ed.), *Manifesty i programmy russkich futuristov*, München 1967, p. 109.

22. Cf. L. Flejšman, *Stat'i o Pasternake*, Bremen 1977, p. 79.

23. Cf. Plank, op. cit., p. 49.

24. B. Livšic, *Flejta Marsija* (1911), N. Aseev, *Nočnaja flejta* (1914).

25. Cf. V. Markov, *Russian Futurism. A History*, Berkeley – Los Angeles 1968, p. 8.

26. B. Pasternak, *Proza 1915–1958*, p. 269.

27. V. Majakovskij, *Polnoe sobr. soč. v trinadcati tomach*, t. 1, M. 1955, p. 247.

28. *Sadok sudej 2*, M. 1913, p. 32.

29. On Pasternak and Futurism, see Krystyna Pomorska, *Themes and Variations in Pasternak's Poetics*, Lisse 1975, Ch. I; L. Fleišman, *Stat'i o Pasternake*, Bremen 1977, and the same, "Fragmenty 'futurističeskoj' biografii Pasternaka", *Slavica Hierosolymitana*, Vol. IV, 1979, pp. 79–113; on Pasternak's polemics with Majakovskij in the poem "Ljubimaja – žut'!..", see I. P. Smirnov, *Poroždenie interteksta* (Èlementy intertekstual'nogo analiza s primerami iz tvorčestva B. L. Pasternaka), Wien 1985 (Wiener slawistischer Almanach. Sonderband 17), pp. 50 ff.

30. Cf. Krystyna Pomorska, op. cit., p. 14.

31. V. Markov (Ed.), *Manifesty i programmy . . .*, p. 19.

32. On the relation between "I" and "You" in Majakovskij's poetry, see Peter Ulf Møller, "Addressing the Second Person: The Life of a Central Priёm in Majakovskij's Poetry", K. Heltberg et al. (Eds.), *We and They*: National Identity as a Theme in Slavic Cultures, Copenhagen 1984 (= Copenhagen University. Institute of Slavonic Studies. Studier 11), pp. 147–157.

33. A. Fet, *Lirika*, M. 1965, p. 128.

34. Apparently Fet is the only poet before Pasternak who used 'èto' in a similar way several times. Another example, which I owe to Erik Egeberg, is the final stanza of the poem "Net, lučše golosom, laskatel'no obyčnym . . .":

> Ved' èto – prach svjatoj zatichšego stradan'ja!
> Ved' èto – milye počivšie serdca!
> Ved' èto – strastnye, blažennye rydan'ja!
> Ved' èto – ternii koljučego venca!

(*Polnoe sobr. stichotvorenij A. A. Feta*, t. 1, S. Ptb. 1912, p. 115.)

35. A. Puškin, *Polnoe sobr. soč. v desjati tomach*, t. 1, M. – L. 1950, p. 393. I owe this reference to Boris Gasparov; I also want to thank Anna Ljunggren, Michail Safonov, and Savely Senderovich for valuable remarks to an early version of this article.

36. *Strelec*. Sbornik pervyj, Petrograd 1915, pp. 54–55.

Jerzy Faryno

«Золотистого меда струя . . .» Мандельштама

Основной смысловой ход стихотворения «Золотистого меда струя из бутылки текла . . .» (1917; Мандельштам 1967, 1, с. 63–64) покоится на принципе постепенного выявления присутствия эллинского начала в обыденной современности. На композиционном уровне он осуществляется при помощи чередования, так сказать, описательных и рефлективных строф. Описательные вводят в текст некоторую реальную ситуацию: «Здесь», «в [. . .] Тавриде» (I) → «сад», «виноград» (III) → «в комнате», «в [. . .] доме» (V) с отчетливой последовательностью пространственной устремленности ‚вовнутрь‘, ‚в дом‘. Рефлективные имеют характер проникновения в глубинный исконный смысл этой реальности: панорамирующая картина Тавриды с признаками локуса повышенного ранга (II) → восприятие виноградника в категориях эллинского опыта (IV) → опознание ‚дома‘ в терминах мифа о Пенелопе и Одиссее (V, т.е. стихи 19–20, и VI) с не менее отчетливой темпоральной устремленностью ‚вспять‘, ‚в реальность мифа‘. При этом ‚рефлексия‘ здесь не произвольна, она не привносится сюда извне, а естественно мотивируется собственными фактурно-вещественными свойствами ‚реальной‘ Тавриды, что и обеспечивает всему тексту характер сплошного семантического образования (ср. образцовый в последнем отношении анализ данного стихотворения в: Сегал 1968 или 1970):

I.   Золотистого меда струя из бутылки текла   (1)
      Так тягуче и долго, что молвить хозяйка успела: (2)
      Здесь, в печальной Тавриде, куда нас судьба занесла, (3)
      Мы совсем не скучаем – и через плечо поглядела.   (4)

II.   Всюду Бахуса службы, как будто на свете одни   (5)
      Сторожа и собаки – идешь, никого не заметишь – (6)
      Как тяжелые бочки, спокойные катятся дни: (7)
      Далеко в шалаше голоса – не поймешь, не ответишь. (8)

III.   После чаю мы вышли в огромный коричневый сад, (9)
      Как ресницы на окнах опущены темные шторы, (10)
      Мимо белых колонн мы пошли посмотреть виноград, (11)
      Где воздушным стеклом обливаются сонные горы. (12)

IV.	Я сказал: виноград как старинная битва живет,	(13)
	Где курчавые всадники бьются в кудрявом порядке.	(14)
	В каменистой Тавриде наука Эллады – и вот	(15)
	Золотых десятин благородные, ржавые грядки.	(16)

V.	Ну, а в комнате белой как прялка стоит тишина.	(17)
	Пахнет уксусом, краской и свежим вином из подвала.	(18)
	Помнишь, в греческом доме: любимая всеми жена –	(19)
	Не Елена – другая – как долго она вышивала?	(20)

VI.	Золотое руно, где же ты, золотое руно?	(21)
	Всю дорогу шумели морские тяжелые волны,	(22)
	И покинув корабль, натрудивший в морях полотно,	(23)
	Одиссей возвратился, пространством и временем полный.	(24)

Первая пара строф сосредоточена на категориях времени и пространства. Время здесь длительно, бесконечно, однообразно и спокойно («тягуче и долго», «спокойные катятся дни»). Бесконечно и пространство: «идешь, никого не заметишь», «далеко», «не поймешь, не ответишь». И время и пространство производят тут впечатление незаполненных: первое бессобытийно («в печальной Тавриде»; ,оправдательное‘ «Мы совсем не скучаем»; бесконфликтность наливания меда и речи «хозяйки» – «молвить хозяйка успела»; «спокойные катятся дни»), второе же – просторно, безлюдно и как будто некоммуникабельно («не поймешь, не ответишь»; глагол «молвить», предполагающий скорее автокоммуникацию, чем инициирование разговора, – коммуникация же осуществляется на другом уровне, при помощи взгляда: «через плечо поглядела», т.е. на уровне соприсутствия или соучастия). Бессобытийность оборачивается беспечностью, несуетностью, самобытностью: «Как будто на свете одни Сторожа и собаки» – признак доверчивости, признак отсутствия деления на ,своего‘ и ,чужого‘, на ,дружелюбного‘ и ,враждебного‘. Такие категории в этом мире отсутствуют. О том же свидетельствуют и слова "Далеко в шалаше голоса". Это не столько ,некоммуникабельность‘, сколько ,ненадобность в присмотре‘. Такой же смысл стоит и за образом отворачивающейся при наливании меда хозяйки «через плечо поглядела»: в данном мире каждый процесс протекает согласно своему характеру и не требует вмешательств или ,ухода‘. ,Время‘ с его плотностью и тягучестью просто ,есть‘, оно – форма существования мира, а не форма ,изживания‘ мира. Примечательно при этом, что на фоне ,пустого‘ и как бы ,дематериализованного‘ пространства время здесь, наоборот, материализовано и уравнено с бытовыми предметами (повторяя смысл ,длительности‘ слова «долго» слово «тягуче» получает временной характер и объединяет в одно целое «струю меда» и ,время‘;

откровенно временны́е «дни» определены здесь как хозяйственные «тяжелые бочки»).

Вторая строфа уточняет сущность времени и пространства. «Всюду Бахуса службы» – особое время – пространство (по терминологии Бахтина – хронотоп): п р а з д н и к, р и т у а л. Праздничность знаменует собой специальное время, момент приобщения уровня бытового к уровню космическому, вечному (отсюда, видимо, и темпоральная замедленность, ‚тягучесть‘ в мире Тавриды). Обстоятельство «Всюду» соотносится с пространством. «Бахус», в свою очередь, квалифицирует этот хронотоп как мифический, снимает с него характер обыденности. «Дни» «Как тяжелые бочки» в контексте «Бахуса» получают смысл ‚бочек, наполненных вином или медом‘. В результате данное время-пространство оказывается вином-медом, т. е. божественным напитком, т.е. субстанцией вечной жизни и мудрости.

Как ‚праздник‘ («службы»), так и ‚напиток‘, и прежде всего – «мед» – ‚вино‘, предполагают состояние инобытия. Именование Тавриды «печальной», локусом «судьбы», мотив ‚оглядки‘ («‚Здесь, в п е ч а л ь н о й Тавриде, куда нас с у д ь б а з а н е с л а, Мы совсем н е с к у ч а е м‘, – и ч е р е з п л е ч о п о г л я д е л а»), – все это соотносит мир Тавриды если и не с миром потусторонним, то во всяком случае с миром инобытия, миром, который, как обычно у Мандельштама, имеет характер идиллии, эллинской домашности и уюта.

Впечатление просторного, несуетного, едва ли не ‚пустого‘ пространства сохраняется и в третьей строфе, хотя оно и претерпевает здесь некую материализацию. «Огромный сад» определен как «коричневый». Выбран цвет, который ассоциируется обычно с густотой, плотностью, осязаемостью, землей. При этом он явственно перекликается с «медом» и «чаем» по цвету, что имеет и обратное воздействие – «сад» в таком контексте способен ослабить свою статичность или ‚жесткость‘ в сторону аналогичной, как в случае «меда», ‚густоты-тягучести‘. Дальше появляется стих «Где воздушным стеклом обливаются сонные горы», который эту ‚размягченность‘ пространства утверждает окончательно, сохраняя одновременно и его ‚легкость‘ («воздушным»), и его ‚прозрачность‘ («стеклом»), и его ‚инобытийность‘ («Как ресницы на окнах опущены темные шторы» и «сонные горы» с общим для них признаком пребывания в некоем онейрическом состоянии), и, не исключено, что также и ‚временну́ю тягучесть‘, если «темные» и «сонные» читать как варианты «тяжелых бочек» = «дней», т. е. ‚замедленности‘.

Смысл длительности, несуетности, покоя и просторности возобновляется в пятой строфе – уже в локусе «комната» и «дом»: «как прялка стоит тишина», «как долго она вышивала?» Возобновляется здесь и смысл праздничности, обогащенный ‚светлостью‘ и ‚чистотой‘: «в комнате белой», «стоит тишина», «Пахнет уксусом, краской и свежим вином из подвала» (ср. раньше упоминаемые «Бахуса службы», «тяжелые бочки», «спокойные катятся дни»). С одной существенной разницей. Прежняя ‚густота-тягучесть‘ трансформируется здесь в ‚легкость‘ и ‚духовность‘: «Золотистого меда струя […] текла Так тягуче и долго» → «воздушным стеклом обливаются сонные горы» → «в комнате белой […] стоит тишина. […] Пахнет уксусом, краской и свежим вином», где даже по природе ‚густая‘ краска превращена в пневматическую струю («Пахнет […] краской»). Признак ‚духовности‘ просматривается также и в упоминаниях «прялки» и «вышиванья». С одной стороны, они вводят ассоциацию с ремеслом-искусством. С другой, будучи женскими домашними занятиями, вводят представление об искусстве ‚домашнего очага‘ и даже шире – об ‚искусстве жизни‘. Последнее свободно прочитывается в перекличке «прялки» с упоминавшейся в третьем стихе «судьбой» и в отсылке в стихе двадцатом к мифу о Пенелопе: и ‚пряденье‘ и ‚вышиванье‘ активизируют здесь, таким образом, свою древнюю связь с ‚испытывающей судьбой‘ и с достойным ее исполнением (ср. слова хозяйки «Здесь, в п е ч а л ь н о й Тавриде, к у д а н а с с у д ь б а з а н е с л а, Мы совсем н е с к у ч а е м» и «Помнишь, […] к а к д о л г о о н а в ы ш и в а л а?»).

Заключительный же стих текста (24) время и пространство истолковывает как ‚груз‘ = «золотое руно»: «Одиссей возвратился, пространством и временем полный».

Один из наиболее активных признаков, которые единят весь мир данного стихотворения в одно нечленимое целое, – пластичность и гибкость очертаний его компонентов: «меда струя» (1), «бутылка» (1), «судьба занесла» (3), «через плечо поглядела» (4), «бочки» (7), «катятся дни» (7), «ресницы» (10), «Мимо белых колонн» (11), «виноград» (11, 13), «воздушным стеклом обливаются сонные горы» (12), «курчавые всадники бьются в кудрявом порядке» (14), «прялка» (17), «вышивала» (20), «золотое руно» (21), «тяжелые волны» (22), «корабль» (23), «полотно» (23) и «возвратился» и «полный» (24). В рефлективных строфах признак этот эксплицируется как ‚курчавость-кудрявость‘, но не хаотическая, а упорядоченная, не стихийная, а ‚культурная‘ («в кудрявом порядке»; «вышивала») и кульминирует в понятии «золотое руно», с которого в свою очередь снимается предметно-вещественный статус. «Руном» оказывается как весь этот мир (‚время-пространство‘), так и накопленный человеком ‚опыт‘ (23–24: «натрудивший в морях полотно, Одиссей возвратился, пространством и временем полный». При этом небезынтересно подчеркнуть, что «руно» как таковое – не предел семантической эволюции текста, что оно тут же переименовывается в ‚возвращение‘ и ‚полноту‘, получившие фактическую финальную позицию в стихотворении.

Другой, не менее активный и не менее всеобщий, признак этого мира

114

– цветовой: «Золотистого меда струя» (1), «После чаю» (9), «коричневый сад» (9), «темные шторы» (10), «Золотых десятин благородные, ржавые грядки» (16), «Золотое руно, где же ты, золотое руно?» (21); «мимо белых колонн», (11), «воздушным стеклом» (12), «в комнате белой» (17).

«Коричневый» перекликается с «медом», «чаем», «темными шторами» и «ржавыми грядками», благодаря чему устанавливается родство внешнего пространства («грядки»), пространства, окружающего дом («сад»), и внутреннего («шторы») и ,домашнего' («мед», «чай»). Цвет «штор» – «темный» – не противоречит к тому и ,прозрачности' «воздушного стекла»: «шторы» истолкованы тут в категориях онейрической углубленности вовнутрь («Как ресницы на окнах опущены темные шторы») и утяжеленности («опущены»), в категориях, которые присущи и внешнему пространству – «горам»: они также онеричны («сонные») и ,утяжелены' («воздушным стеклом обливаются»). Кроме того не бесследна здесь и перекличка «на окнах» и «стеклом» (которое подразумевалось также и в «бутылке»), «ресницы» и одушевляющее «обливаются», чем и мотивируется потом переход к «Виноград [...] живет» (13) и возврат к «дому» (строфа V).

,Ржавь' «грядок» передает в свою очередь ,потемнение золота' и подчеркивает их старинность («Виноград как старинная битва живет»).

,Ржавый' цвет «грядок» – ,земли' в соприсутствии «коричневого (сада)» ассоциируется с ,кирпичным' цветом, характерным для эллинского искусства. Поэтому стих «Виноград как старинная битва живет» содержит в себе отсылку к греческому изобразительному искусству вообще и к греческой вазописи в частности. С этой точки зрения «виноград» и «грядки» оказываются эквивалентны искусству: они такое же ,хранилище' былого опыта, как искусство является ,хранилищем-передатчиком' былых событий («как старинная битва ж и в е т» – «всадники б ь ю т с я в к у д р я в о м п о р я д к е», где «порядок» можно понимать как ,осмысленность' и ,упорядоченность' искусством, → «В каменистой Тавриде н а у к а Э л л а д ы – и вот [...] г р я д к и», где в свою очередь «грядки» срифмованы с «порядком» и повторяют звуковой состав слова «виноград»). Более того, характер искусства – зрелищно-изобразительного – сообщается «винограду» и «грядкам» стихами 11–12, в особенности словами «мы пошли п о с м о т р е т ь виноград» и упоминанием о «воздушном стекле», ситуирующим «виноград» как бы в ином измерении.

При более внимательном взгляде оказывается, что цветовая последовательность претерпевает в стихотворении своеобразную трансформацию, что о цвете как таковом правомерно говорить лишь по отношению к первым трем строфам: сначала идет как бы сгущение и темнение цветообозначений – «золотистого меда струя» (1), → «чай» и «коричневый сад» (9) → «темные шторы» (10), после чего внезапно появляется белый цвет, который тут же превращается в прозрачность и как бы исчезает: «Мимо белых колонн» (11) → «воздушным стеклом» (12), причем прозрачность дополнительно подчеркивается ‚зримостью‘ («мы пошли п о с м о т р е т ь» – 11), контрастирующей с предыдущим ‚потемнением‘ (особенно в случае именования сада «коричневым»). Возобновление «золотого» в стихе 16 – это уже не столько цветохарактеристика, сколько переход на иное, повышенное, качество: «Золотых десятин благородные, ржавые грядки» (16), притом недвусмысленно соотнесенное с ‚духовностью‘ («благородные»), которая окончательно оформится как духовное начало в «комнате б е л о й» (см. выше) и в понятии «золотое руно» (21) с его последующей экспликацией (в 22–24).

Такое чередование «золотого» и «белого» и такая эволюция от цветообозначения к одухотворенности вполне последовательны. В древней цветосимволике белый рассматривался не как эквивалент серебра, а как эквивалент золота, и наравне с ним соотносился с высшим духовным началом (см. статью Colour (Positive/Negative) в: Cirlot 1981, p. 58).

Отнюдь не маловажно, что мотив виноградника локализован в тексте между двумя упоминаниями белого, сначала как цветообозначения, а потом как качественной характеристики. «Белые колонны» занимают тут место входа в виноградник: «мы вышли в огромный коричневий сад, [...] Мимо белых колонн мы пошли посмотреть виноград» (9–11). Этим самым в «колоннах» активизируется, с одной стороны, их древний смысл входа в ‚небесный мир‘, а с другой – смысл ‚мировой оси‘ и ‚стабильности мироздания‘, единства его противоположных начал, ‚всеведения‘ (см. статью Column в: Cirlot 1981, pp. 60–61). «Воздушное стекло» «гор» – не что иное, как тот же ‚белый‘ цвет, знаменующий собой сферу вечного света – ‚мудрости‘ (этот смысл гор обнаруживается, например, в частом назывании их ‚белыми‘ – см. статью Colour (Positive/Negative) в: Cirlot 1981, p. 58).

При таком взгляде «наука Эллады» (15) – только экспликация неявно присутствовавшей ‚мудрости‘ в упомянутых в предшествующей строфе «колонн» и «гор» («белых«, ‚стеклянных‘) и в инициальном «меде» (1), который в той же символической системе связывается с категориями ‚знания‘, ‚мудрости‘ и ‚вечного возрождения‘ (см. статью Honey в: Cirlot 1981, p. 150). «Старинная битва» и «живет» – экспликация ‚вечности‘, с одной стороны, а с другой, – экспликация равновесия между земным и небесным, материальным и духовным, равновесия, которое в менее очевидной форме подсказывалось «колоннами», и, кроме того, оппозицией ‚земного‘ («коричневый сад») и ‚небесного‘ («мимо белых колонн»), ‚материального‘ и ‚духовного‘ («коричневый» – как цвет земли, «белый» как символ духовности). Дальше эта оппозиция получает вид «битвы». Причем «битва» мыслится здесь не как сражение войск, а как ,сражение' между инертной, безжизненной, стихийной материей («каменистая Таврида», раньше – в 3 – именуемая «печальной») и облагораживающей и ,упорядочивающей' ее и дающей ей жизнь ,мыслью' («наука Эллады»; рифма «в кудрявом порядке – ржавые грядки»). Результат – не ,победа', а гармонический синтез обоих начал: «Золотых десятин благородные, ржавые грядки», где «золотой» и «ржавый» не противопоставлены друг другу, а приведены во взаимосоответствие, и где абстрактные «десятины» реализованы в виде материально существующих плодоносных «грядок» (выбор определения «ржавые» призван, по-видимому, поддержать их ,реальность').

Открывшаяся «Я» ,истина' о Тавриде принципиально меняет и образ «дома»: это ,дом в доме', то есть и дом таврический, и его эллинская сущность («в комнате белой» и «Помнишь, в греческом доме»).

,Белизна' «комнаты», повторяя смыслы «белых колонн», вводит еще представление о чистоте, о духовности жизни, об искусстве жить и строить свою судьбу («прялка», «вышивала»). Противопоставление «Елене» «другой», т. е. подразумеваемой Пенелопы, имеет в виду не внешнюю красоту и не раздор, а красоту внутреннюю, духовную, чистоту, гармонию, верность, культ устойчивого домашнего очага («стоит тишина», «Помнишь, [...] как долго она вышивала?»).

Все эти смыслы объединяются в последней строфе под именем «золотое руно», где эпитет «золотое» кумулирует и цветовые и ценностные аспекты мира, а «руно» – фактурные и формообразующие, с доминацией признака ,плодородия'. Последних три стиха (22–24) вносят смысл ,накопления', ,обогащения', но не материального, а духовного. ,Накопления' как поддержки и хранения ,опыта'. Он наблюдался уже в предыдущих строфах в виде мотива ,одно в другом' и мотива ,хранилище' (о выскокой значимости этого мотива в поэтике Мандельштама см. в: Faryno 1985; а в поэтике Ахматовой в: Седакова 1984): «меда струя из бутылки текла» (1), «Здесь, в печальной Тавриде, куда нас судьба занесла, Мы» (3–4), «Как тяжелые бочки, [...] дни» (7), «в шалаше» (8), «мы вышли в [...] сад» (9), «виноград, Где [...] горы» (11–12), «Виноград [...], Где курчавые всадники» (13–14), «в кудрявом порядке» (14), «В каменистой Тавриде наука Эллады» (15), «в комнате» (17), «Пахнет [...] вином из подвала» (18), «в греческом доме» (19), «в морях» (23) и «полный» (24). При этом ,одно в другом' реализуется по принципу постепенного проникновения в сущность, в первооснову данного мира, с одной стороны, а с другой – по принципу сюжетного ,вхождения' в этот иной мир: «куда нас судьба занесла» (3) → «идешь» (6) → «мы вышли в [...] сад» (9) → «мы пошли посмотреть виноград» (11), заканчивающееся ,мнемоническим вхождением': «Помнишь, в греческом доме» (19), которое примечательно тем, что оно не только уводит вглубь времен, но и наоборот, актуализирует прошлое в настоящем, выводит из глубины времен в актуальную реальность, тем, что предполагает наличие прошлого в пределах жизни одного человека, т.е. ,вспоминающего‘, так как нельзя «помнить» не пережитого, не испытанного (о структуре «памяти» см. в: Faryno 1985a), и тем, что, обращенное к некоему ,ты‘, имеет характер объединяющего говорящего и слушающего, т.е. строит определенную ,общность‘. Одновременно, как уже отмечалось выше, это есть и вхождение в ,потустороннее‘, в ,инобытие‘ (мотив ,оглядки‘, ,праздничности-опьянения‘, ,сна‘, выхода в сад и за его пределы «Мимо белых колонн»). Он свое окончательное истолкование получает в последних трех стихах текста.

Одиссей возвращается домой после долгих и трудных испытаний: «В с ю д о р о г у ш у м е л и морские т я ж е л ы е волны» (22), «корабль, н а т р у д и в ш и й в морях полотно [= паруса]» (23). Его ,добыча‘ – «пространство и время» (24). Легко заметить, что тут подразумевается ,умудренность‘, ,проникновение в суть бытия‘ и что это и есть «золотое руно». Но это не всё. «Дорога», дважды упомянутое море («морские [...] волны», «в морях»), «корабль», подмена парусов «полотном», шум («шумели» в противовес предшествующей «тишине» в 17), иное «тяжелые» (противостоящие «тяжелым», но «спокойным» «бочкам»-«дням» в 7 «шумели морские тяжелые волны» в 22), открытость, стихийность вместо облагораживающей замкнутости и организованности-упорядоченности («мед» в «бутылке», «дни» как ,мед-вино‘ в «бочках», «вино» в «подвале», «бьются в кудрявом порядке», «Золотых десятин благородные, ржавые грядки» и т.д.) – все это атрибуты и признаки потустороннего, загробного, чреватого смертью локуса. ,Возвращение‘, по той же античной мифосимволической системе, соотносится с ,преодолением смерти‘, с ,воскресением‘, с возвращением из царства мертвых. «Золотое руно» Одиссея получает тут, таким образом, смысл преодоления ,смерти‘, косного, нетворческого, стихийного начала материального мира. Добытое им «пространство и время» – это облагороженная, оформленная трудом, в «мед», «вино», «сад», «грядки», «печальная» и «каменистая» Таврида. ,Волнистость‘ и ,тяжесть‘ «морских волн» преобразованы в «кудрявый порядок» и в «тяжелые бочки», с одной стороны, а с другой – в бессмертный божественный («Бахуса») напиток, в «тягучую» «Золотистого меда струю» (ср. семантические рамки стихотворения: «из бутылки» и «полный»). Здесь, как видно, мы вплотную подошли к Мандельштамовской концепции эллинского быта-бытия (которую прекрасно раскрывает Сегал 1968 и 1970) и к Мандельштамовской концепции искусства. Последняя в данном стихотворении раскрывается, однако, лишь частично и требует привлечения более широкого авторского контекста. Поэтому предложенные наблюдения уместно закончить отсылкой к разборам хотя бы таких его вещей как «Есть

118

иволги в лесах . . .», «Бессонница . . .», «Возьми на радость . . .» и особенно «Адмиралтейство» в книге: Nilsson 1974.

В заключение желательно остановиться еще на одном вопросе – на вопросе местоименных употреблений.

Произносимые «хозяйкой» «нас» и «мы» (3–4) эксклюзивны – не включают в себя подразумеваемое ‚я‘ текста. Правда, ‚я‘ здесь соприсутствует с «мы», о чем свидетельствует глагол контакта «поглядела» (4), но тем не менее остается за пределами таврической общности «мы».

Во второй строфе это ‚я‘ обретает уже некие очертания, хотя и здесь остается и не эксплицированным, и даже не личным: «идешь, никого не заметишь» (6), «не поймешь, не ответишь» относятся к ‚любому‘, ‚всякому‘. Но здесь играет роль уже не только физическое присутствие этого ‚любого‘ в данном мире, но и принципиальная его ‚не-чуждость‘ этому миру (об отсутствии категорий ‚свой – чужой‘ в мире Тавриды см. выше).

В третьей строфе появляются уже два местоимения «мы». На этот раз они произносятся подразумеваемым ‚я‘ и инклюзивны: имеют в виду ‚я‘ и ‚хозяев‘. В данном случае ‚я‘ уже почти эксплицитно и включено в таврическую ‚общность‘. О включенности свидетельствует как «после чаю», предполагающее более тесное знакомство, так и «мы пошли посмотреть виноград» (11), которое, в свою очередь, свидетельствует о ‚доверительности‘ ‚хозяев‘: ‚гостю‘ показывается ‚гордость дома‘, его ‚святая святых‘ («виноград» и все его текстовые коннотации); более того, совместное ‚обозрение‘, как правило, призвано сплотить ‚обозревающих‘, создать общий, объединяющий ‚опыт‘ или ‘переживание‘. Такая разница между «мы вышли в [. . .] сад» (9) и «мы пошли посмотреть виноград» (через стих, т.е. в 11) для данного текста закономерна – ср. аналогичные столкновения имеющие целью подчеркнуть градацию по ‚рангу‘ в 14: «к у р ч а в ы е всадники бьются в к у д р я в о м порядке», в 16: «З о л о т ы х д е с я т и н благородные, р ж а в ы е грядки», в 17 и 19: «Ну, а в к о м н а т е» и «в греческом д о м е», в 22 и 23: «шумели м о р с к и е тяжелые волны» и «натрудивший в м о р я х полотно» и образующее рамку всего текста «З о л о т и с т о г о м е д а струя» (1) и «З о л о т о е руно, где же ты, з о л о т о е руно?» (21). Всякий раз, как видно, градация устремлена к полюсу ‚духовное‘.

Четвертая строфа начинается с эксплицированного «Я»: «Я сказал» (13). Данная эксплицитность, несомненно, – знак оформления неявного до сих пор ‚я‘ в ‚личность‘. Но это не любая личность, а ‚понимающая‘, ‚узнающая‘ или ‚опознающая‘, которой доступна сущность «винограда», а этим самым и жизни: «Я сказал: виноград к а к с т а р и н н а я б и т в а (тут налицо ‚опознание‘) живет, Где курчавые всадники б ь ю т с я (иное ‚биться‘, чем в «битва») в кудрявом порядке » (опознание ‚системности' или ‚упорядочивания хаоса'). Такую же роль играет и слово «сказал»: все предшествующие сравнения, хотя и усложнялись, но оставались как бы на уровне самого предметного мира («Как тяжелые бочки, спокойные катятся дни» – 7, «Как ресницы на окнах опущены темные шторы» – 10), т.е. были не высказаны, не оформлены в текст. Высказывание, ‚текст' появляется лишь теперь и совпадает с организованной ‚текстовой' природой мира данной строфы. Тем не менее некоторая дистанция между «Я» и миром сохраняется, поскольку ‚текстовость' мира опознается при помощи ‚посредника', т.е. иного текста – «как старинная битва» с прозрачной отсылкой к эллинскому изобразительному искусству.

‚Текст-посредник' снимается в очередной строфе. Глагол «Помнишь» подключает говорящего (‚я') к древнему миру, приобщает его к нему как ‚помнящего', т.е. участвовавшего в том древнем мире или бывшего ‚свидетелем' тех событий. Появляющееся здесь подразумеваемое ‚ты' (тоже, предположительно, ‚помнящее') имеет уже другую задачу: снимает с памяти ее индивидуальный характер и сообщает ей общекультурный, общечеловеческий (поскольку ‚ты' здесь а-индивидуально и может относиться к любому, в том числе и к читателю).

Риторический вопрос «Золотое руно, где же ты, золотое руно?» (21) с эксплицитным «ты» (вместо объектного ‚оно') ставит теперь уже ‚всякого' ‚я' (так как вопрос задается абстрактно) перед фундаментальной экзистенциальной проблемой. А ее решение – названный в финале по имени «Одиссей» и все общекультурные коннотации, связанные с данным мифом.

В результате здесь наблюдается крайне интересная картина. Согласно отмеченной в начале особенности чередования описательных и рефлективных строф и согласно устремленности вычленяемых признаков мира текста от конкретного к абстрактному, т.е. ‚духовному', текстовое ‚я' тоже устремляется от полюса единичного, личностного к полюсу ‚обобщенного'. А чередование подразумеваемых форм ‚я' и ‚ты' размывает в свою очередь границу между этими ‚я' и ‚ты': ‚ты' с одинаковым успехом тут может читаться и как ‚ты' и как тот же ‚я'. А это ведет к окончательному эффекту внеличностного, интерсубъективного, общечеловеческого ‚я'.

Варшава, 25–29 июня 1985.

Литература

Cirlot, J. E., 1981. A Dictionary of Symbols. Second Edition. Translated from the Spanish by Jack Sage. Foreword by Herbert Read. Philosophical Library, New York.
Faryno, J., 1985. Blaženo nasljedstvo Mandeljštama: «Na sanjkama, prostrim slamom ...». «Književna smotra», br. 57/58, Zagreb.

Faryno, J., 1985a. «Я помню (чудное мгновенье . . .)» и «Я (слово . . .) позабыл». «Wiener Slawistischer Almanach», Band 16, Wien.

Мандельштам, Осип, 1967. Собрание сочинений в трех томах, том первый: Стихотворения. Издание второе, дополненное и пересмотренное. Inter-Language Literary Associates, Washington-München.

Nilsson, N. Å., 1974. Osip Mandel'štam: Five Poems. Almqvist-Wiksell International, Stockholm.

Сегал, Д. М., 1968. Наблюдения над семантической структурой поэтического произведения. «International Journal of Slavic Linguistics and Poetics», XI, Mouton, The Hague.

Сегал, Д. М., 1970. Семантическая структура одного стихотворения Мандельштама. (В:) Signe. Langue. Culture. The Hague-Paris.

Седакова, О. А., 1984. Шкатулка с зеркалом. Об одном глубинном мотиве А. А. Ахматовой. (В:) Труды по знаковым системам, т. XVII: Структура диалога как принцип работы семиотического механизма. Тарту.

Kiril Taranovsky

Two Notes on Mandel'štam's "Hayloft" Poems

1. *Mandel'štam and Pasternak*

During the last two decades it has been shown that quotations and reminiscences from Russian poets, who were contemporaries of Mandel'štam, have played a very significant role in Mandel'štam's own poetry. Strangely enough, subtexts taken from the Symbolists (Bal'mont, Blok, Belyj, Vjačeslav Ivanov, Annenskij et al.) are more numerous and important than those from his fellow Acmeists (primarily Gumilev and Achmatova). Still the most surprising is the fact that the poetry of Boris Pasternak did not affect Mandel'štam's poetry to a greater degree, despite Mandel'štam's enthusiastic welcome of *Sestra moja žizn'*. This book seemingly contains only one poem, "Step'" ("The Steppe"), which Mandel'štam used as a subtext for one of his famous "twin-poems" from 1922.

According to the anonymous author of the excellent study "Zametki o peresečenii biografij Osipa Mandel'štama i Borisa Pasternaka"[1], the Mandel'štams and the Pasternaks met for the first time in the spring of 1922 and became friends very quickly. Pasternak's book *Sestra moja žizn'* was published that same spring and Mandel'štam was probably one of the first to receive a copy from the author.[2] Mandel'štam's twin-poems "Ja ne znaju s kakich por" and "Ja po lesenke pristavnoj" were published in November 1922 with a common title "Senoval" ("The Hayloft"); for the sake of brevity we will refer to them further as the first and second "Hayloft". It is highly probable that the poems were written in the summer or fall of 1922, that is, after the poet read Pasternak's "Step'".

As I have discussed elsewhere, Pasternak's "Step'" and Mandel'štam's "Hayloft" have a common predecessor, A. Fet's famous poem, "Na stoge sena noč'ju južnoj".[3] Besides this, some crucial images from Pasternak's "Step'" (written in 1917) were further developed in his poem "Belye stichi" (written in 1918, but published for the first time in 1924). Thus, the relationships among all these texts are quite complicated.

A very original and unusual image of cosmic dust is shared by both Pasternak texts and by the second "Hayloft". In "Step'" it appears in the central part of the poem (quatrains IV–VI):

IV Ne *stog* li v tumane? Kto pojmet?
    Ne naš li *omet?* Dochodim. – On.
    – Našli! On samyj i est'. – Omet,
    Tuman i *step'* s četyrech storon.

V   I Mlečnyj Put' storonoj *vedet*
    Na *Kerč', kak šljach, skotom propylen.*
    Zajti za chaty, i duch zajmet:
    Otkryt, otkryt s četyrech storon.

VI Tuman snotvoren, kovyl', kak med.
    Kovyl' vsem Mlečnym Putem rassoren.
    Tuman razojdetsja, i *noč'* obojmet
    Omet i step' s četyrech storon.

This landscape is even further elaborated in "Belye stichi":

1. Iz vsech kartin, čto pamjat' sberegla,
2. Pripomnilas' odna: *nočnoe pole.*
3. Kazalos', *v zvezdy, slovno za čulok*
4. *Mjakina zabiraetsja i kolet.*
5. *Glaza,* kazalos', *Mlečnyj Put' pylit.*
6. Kazalos', *noč'* vstaet bez sil *s ometa*
7. *I sor so zvezd smetaet. Step' neslas'*
8. *Rekoj bezbrežnoj k morju, i so step'ju*
9. *Neslis' stoga i so stogami – noč'.*

In these two quotations there are many word-signals common to both texts,
such as: *stog, omet, step', noč', Mlečnyj Put', zvezdy* (cf. in "Step'" quatrains VII and VIII), and several striking parallelisms, for example: (1)
"*Kovyl' vsem Mlečnym Putem rassoren*"/ "*I [noč] sor so zvezd smetaet*", (2)
"*Mlečnyj Put'*... skotom *propylen*"/"*Mlečnyj Put' pylit*", (3) *Mlečnyj Put'*...
vedet na *Kerč'* (that is: to the seashore)/"*Step' neslas'*... *k morju*". Moreover, there are also a few parallelisms between the fragment from "Belye
stichi" and the stanzas from "Step'", which we did not quote. Lines 3–4
from the fragment of "Belye stichi" echo, as it were, the following lines from
"Step'": "Tuman otovsjudu nas morem obstig/*V volčcach voločas' za čul-
kami*" (st. III) and *"Volčcy po Čulkam Torčali"* (st. IX). In the line from
"Step'" "Zakroj *ich*, ljubimaja, *zaporošit*" (st. X) "eyes" are only metoni-
mically indicated by the pronoun "them"; in "Belye stichi", however,
"eyes" are mentioned explicitly: "Glaza, kazalos', Mlečnyj Put' pylit".[4]
    In Mandel'štam's second "Hayloft" the image of cosmic dust already
appears in the first stanza:

I Ja po lesenke pristavnoj
   Lez na vskločennyj senoval, –
   Ja dyšal zvezd mlečnych truchoj,
   Koltunom prostranstva dyšal.

As we see, here the hayloft (*senoval*) takes the place of the hayrick (*omet*) from "Step'". But the realistic picture of the first two lines is distorted in the second part of the quatrain: the hay in the hayloft becomes "the matted hair [plica] of space" and the haydust in the air seems to be coming from "the milky stars" (*"zvezd mlečnych trucha"*). The latter exactly corresponds to the dust of "feather grass" in "Step'" (st. V) which is "strewn over the whole Milky Way" (*"Kovyl' vsem Mlečnym Putem rassoren"*). We have to admit that Mandel'štam's *"trucha zvezd"* is very close to *"sor so zvezd"* from "Belye stichi". We do not know whether Mandel'štam had the opportunity to hear this poem from Pasternak or to read it in manuscript. In any case, these two phrases could have been developed independently, from the image of feather grass in the line from "Step'" quoted above.

In the fourth stanza of Mandel'štam's second poem the hayloft acquires cosmic dimensions and becomes an eschatological threat:

IV Rasprjažennyj ogromnyj voz
   Poperek vselennoj torčit.
   Senovala drevnij chaos
   Zaščekočet, zaporošit.

To be sure, *voz* is a dialect form for the constellation *Ursa major,* while *zaščekotat'* and *zaporošit'* are perfective verbs with the emphasis on the end of the action. Thus, the last two lines of the fourth stanza have the following meaning: "The ancient chaos of the hayloft will tickle [us] to death and cover (bury) [us] with haydust." As for the "ancient chaos", it is an obvious reminiscence of Tjutčev's lines: "O, strašnych pesen sich ne poj/*Pro drevnij chaos, pro rodimyj*" ("O čem ty voeš', vetr nočnoj?").

One final remark: the verb "zaporošit'" is rather rare in the Russian literary language. Pasternak also used it in the last stanza of his "Step'". The appearance of this word in Mandel'štam's second "Hayloft" is, perhaps, the most convincing proof that Mandel'štam's poem is affected by Pasternak's.

2. *Mandel'štam, Verlaine and Horace.*

There is in the first "Hayloft" a puzzling image of a "sack in which carraway seeds are sewn up" (*"mešok, v kotorom tmin zašit"*). As I have shown[5], the *sack* is connected with the semantic field *Poetry* (in *Egipetskaja marka* and *Razgovor o Dante*), while the *carraway* borders on the semantic field *I, my life:* it becomes an allusion to the poet's Jewish ancestry and, possibly, to the recollections of his childhood. Cf. "the cloying Jewish air" ("pritornyj evrejskij vozduch") in Mandel'štam's grandfather's house (in *Šum vremeni*) and the "native carraway smell" (rodimyj tminnyj zapach" in *Egipetskaja marka*). While accepting my explanation, Levinton and Timenčik[6] broached a second chain of connotations leading to the semantic field *"Poetry"*. They assume that Mandel'štam's *tmin* is connected also with Verlaine's *thym* from the last stanza of his famous "Art poétique", both in the French original and in the Russian translations:

(1) "Art poétique":

Que ton vers soit la bonne aventure
Éparse au vent crispé du matin
Qui va fleurant *la menthe* et *le thym*. . .
Et tout la reste est littérature.

(2) Annenskij's unfinished translation:

Kak veter utrennij v sijanii dolin,
Pachnet on *mjatoju*, krylom zadenet *tmin*.
Vse pročee – izjaščnaja slovesnost'.

(3) Brjusov's translation (1919):

Tvoj stich nesetsja vdol' poljan
I *mjatoju* i *tminom* p'jan.

To be sure, French *thym* (English *thyme*) is not *carraway* (Fr. *cumin*), and should be translated in Russian as *timian* or *čebrec*. Levinton and Timenčik convincingly demonstrate how this switch of terms in the Russian translations might have occurred.[7] In their discussion they go even further and suggest several other subtexts from the "Art poétique" in the first "Hayloft":

The ringing of the dry grass ("Suchon'kich trav zvon"/"Travy suchorukij avon") – contaminates in a way Verlaine's "De la musique avant toute chose" and his "menthe" and "thym", while "ni o čem pogovorit'" becomes, as it were, a paraphrase of Verlaine's declaration. Mandel'-stam's words from his article "Zametki o Šen'e", "ironičeskaja *pesenka* Verlena" connected with "La chanson grise" in the same text directly comment on his lines: "Ja ne znaju s kakich por/Éta *pesenka* načalas'".[8]

La chanson grise is, in fact, mentioned in Mandel'štam's book *O poèzii*

(1928), but in the essay "Slovo i kul'tura", and not in "Zametki o Šen'e". This is the relévant text:

Sovremennaja poėzija, pri vsej svoej složnosti i vnutrennej ischiščrennosti, naivna:
  Écoutez la chanson grise. . .
Sintetičeskij poėt sovremennosti predstavljaetsja mne ne Vercharnom, a kakim-to Verlenom kul'tury.

It should be noted that the line quoted by Mandel'štam is a contamination of two different texts: (1) No. XVI from "Sagesse", the first and last lines – "*Écoutez la chanson* bien douce"/"*Écoutez la chanson* bien sage"; (2) the end of the second stanza from "Art poétique" – "Rien plus cher que *la chanson grise*/Où l'Indécis au Précis se joint". The last two lines could serve, I belive, as a precise characterization of Mandel'štam's own naïve "pesenka".

While accepting Levinton's and Timenčik's suggestions, we should attempt to trace the sources of Verlaine's imagery in the more distant past. In the first place, the *"grata thyma"* from the famous Horatian ode *Carminum liber* IV:2 come to mind:

> . . .*Ego apis Matinae*
> More modoque
> *Grata* carpentis *thyma* per laborem
> Plurimum circa nemus uvidique
> Tiburis ripas operosa parvus
> Carmina fingo.

Possibly, Mandel'štam knew also the following free translation of these lines by Fet:

> . . .s matinskoj
> Schoden pčeloju,
> P'juščej na tmine otradnuju vlagu,
> V rošče Tibura ja, vnemlja žurčan'ju
> Rečki, s usiliem pesni slagaju,
> Mal po prizvan'ju.

It is worth mentioning that Fet translated Latin *thymum* as *tmin,* although he knew, no doubt, that the Latin equivalent of Russian *tmin* was *cuminum.*

As early as 1963 Nils Nilsson pointed out the Horatian bee and the bee of Ronsard ("Je resemble à l'Abeille") as possible predecessors of Mandelštamian bees – blind rhapsodists.[9] In his later book on Mandel'štam,[10] he also quoted the following lines by André Chénier (which are very similar to those of Horace):

Ainsi, bruyante abeille, au retour du matin
Je vais changer en miel *les délices du thym*.

In these lines we are primarily interested in *"les délices du thym"* which is the exact translation of the Horatian *"grata thyma"*. Besides the Horatian ode, Verlaine obviously knew the poem by Chénier; it is a well-known fact that he repeats the rhyme of Chénier: *matin/thym*. Mandel'štam also must have known the Horatian ode which was normally included in Latin textbooks and anthologies. It is very likely that he was familiar with Chénier's verses as well, since he was deeply impressed by his poetry.

Mandel'štam's *tmin* is not the only reminiscence from Horace in his "Hayloft" poems: the second "Hayloft" contains a direct reference to another celebrated Horatian ode, "Exegi monumentum" (*Carminum liber* III:30). Mandel'štam's "ėolijskij čudesnyj stroj" is in fact Horace's "Aeolium carmen".

August 1983

NOTES

1. *Pamjat'*, no. 4, Moscow 1979 – Paris 1981. The authorship of this article is no longer a secret. It appeared in Serbocratian translation in a literary journal published in Zagreb *Književna smotra* (year XVII, no. 57–58, 1985), signed by Elena and Evgenij Pasternak.
2. "Zametki", pp. 289 and 290.
3. *Essays on Mandel'štam*, Harvard University Press (Cambridge, Massachusetts and London, England, 1976), 23; *Knjiga o Mandeljštamu*, Prosveta (Beograd, 1982), 54; "On the Poetics of Boris Pasternak", *Russian Literature* X–IV (1981), 350.
4. Strangely enough Pasternak here uses the verb *pylit'* as a transitive verb with a direct object in the accusative case: "Mlečnyj Put' pylit (= zasorjaet pyl'ju) glaza."
5. *Essays on Mandel'štam*, 34–38; *Knjiga o Mandeljštamu*, 69–76.
6. "Kniga K. F. Taranovskogo o poėzii O. Ė. Mandel'štama", *Russian Literature* VI 2 (1978), 196–211.
7. *Ibid.*, p. 208, note 18.
8. *Ibid.*, p. 201.
9. "Osip Mandel'štam and His Poetry", *Scando-Slavica* IX, 48. The primary source of Mandel'štam's bees-poets was, however, Plato's dialogue "Ion". Cf. *Essays on Mandel'štam*, 86–87; *Knjiga o Mandeljštamu*, 180.
10. *Osip Mandel'štam: Five Poems*, Almqvist and Wiksell International (Stockholm, 1974), 75 & 78.

Jan van der Eng

Types of Inner Tales in *Red Cavalry*

I.

Babel's cycle *Red Cavalry*[1] shows a modernist, mosaic-like thematic pattern. This applies to the stories taken separately as well as to their arrangement in the cycle. As a rule the motifs and the stories are not connected according to the principles of a causal-temporal and concomitant psychological organization. Though most tales convey the suggestion of a linear sequential order in the subsequent observations of the narrator, they are usually not formed into a whole with interdependent parts. In Stepanov's, much quoted, words: "The plot in Babel's stories develops not according to the sequential outline of events but according to the associations 'hidden' in the story itself" (Stepanov. 33; quoted by Mendelson: 37).

This associational pattern is even more striking in the cycle: more 'hidden' in some respects, more 'foregrounded' in others. It is more hidden as the sequential order of the narrator's observations tends to get lost in the arrangement of the separate tales, these being as varied as the fragments composing them; it is more foregrounded as the main themes become ever more discernible through the kaleidoscopic sequence of the tales and their thematic mosaics. These main themes are: the horribly violated and ultimately almost annihilated Jewish way of life, its human and moral ethos, superior to the revolutionary ethos of destruction and construction, the more and more degraded and in the end nearly lost campaign against Poland, the artistic alternative as a means of escape. In the following paragraphs I will examine only one aspect of Babel's modernism: the several types of inner stories, their relevance for the narrative form in which they are embedded as well as their function for the cycle as the encompassing whole. But first I will discuss some characteristics of the inner tale and distinguish this narrative form from other modes of breaking the story into virtually independent fragments, sidelines, etc.

II.

As an inner story I regard the tale which interrupts another narrative. The latter serves as a frame introducing the inner story and sometimes comments upon it in a straightforward or oblique manner. In its most reduced form it merely provides the reason for telling the inner story. Mostly, however, the narrative frame has many events and situations that are unrelated to the

128

inner story. The inner story always differs from the narrative frame in that it has characters of its own, its own temporal scheme and sequence of events.

It should be noticed that numerous stories of the cycle do not include an inner tale but are nevertheless split up into a series of distinctive, more or less elaborated and often quite different episodes. We can think of the story *The Death of Dolgušov*: it has sections on the disgraced commander, seeking death; on the troopers' desperate endeavour to go and fight; on the machine-gun-cart hanging about between two walls of fire and – most of all – on the situation indicated by the title. None of these, however, are marked by an independent temporal system: they are integrated into the chronological order of the narrator's subsequent observations. Furthermore neither do any of these show completely different groups of characters: the narrator is always present as a witness, sometimes he is involved as the antagonist. Sometimes other characters play a role in successive situations of great variety, linked together only by a strong suggestion of doom and impending disaster.

In one case – in the story *Squadron Commander Trunov* – the concoction of events and situations shows a tendency towards the shaping of a plot. This, however, is done unobtrusively so as to keep the impression of a mosaic-like construction. The story is split up into five more or less independent narrative fragments: the funeral of commander Trunov, the heat of a religious contention between several Jewish parties, the appearance and behaviour of a strange Galician, the narrator's quarrel with Trunov over the two Polish prisoners, killed by the latter, Trunov's unequal combat with Faunt Le Roy's bombing-planes. As may be inferred from this summing-up, Trunov is assigned a major role in three of these episodes, the narrator acting as his main antagonist in one of them. These episodes are causally and temporally interrelated: some motifs of Trunov's heroic fight against the bombers have crept into the part about his burial; the end of the episode about the narrator's quarrel with Trunov comes with the sudden appearance of the bombers. In between, however, two unfinished and totally unrelated episodes break the causal-temporal connection. This is all the more diverting as one of them consists of a series of suspensive remarks about a Galician as lanky and cadaverous as Don Quichote. There are some more intriguing allusions to what might become an inner tale. Thus it is said that the Galician "was arrayed as though for his funeral ... upon his huge body was set the nimble, tiny, pierced head of a serpent ... his gibbetlike frame cleaving the burning brilliance of the skies." But then the expectations roused by these images are cut short: the narrator meets a Cossack who severely reproaches him for his quarrel with Trunov. Thereupon follows the episode about the registration of the Polish prisoners and the killing of two of them. The preceding suspensive images now turn out to have only an associational purport for the theme of the story and the cycle as a whole. Within the story they can be connected with the three narrative sections on Trunov: the last hours of his life mark the approaching debacle of the Polish campaign which runs evermore conspicuously as a black thread through the second part of the cycle. In this perspective the images of the funeral, the serpent and the gibbet, look like ominous signs of doom, they foreshadow disastrous events: in this capacity they are related to Trunov's fate and to the ultimate outcome of the campaign.

It may be clear that the inner story is not the only Babelian device of arranging seemingly disconnected events and situations (Cf. Terras: 150–151). It is, however, one of the most captivating and refined aspects of Babel's art.

III,1.

The first instance of an inner tale occurs in the opening story: *Crossing the River Zbruč*. The distinctive mark of this type of inner tale is that it strikes the keynote of the theme, to which only indirect or passing references were made in the preceding part of the text. In this capacity the inner story tends to rule over the narrative frame, over the complex of diverse fragments centered in the narrator's observations. To put it more precisely: the pregnant Jewess's report prevails over the foregoing eight paragraphs of the text; her explanations in the last paragraph but one and her emotional outcry in the "coda" assign a definitely sinister significance to the suspensive signs of impending evil in the preceding sections. She tells how her father died at the hands of the Poles. Her story has a catalytic power provoking the true measure of horror hidden in the contrastive images of the landscape, in the opposition of rustic and colorful metaphors to figures of bloodshed and to blackening details of the world at nightfall. Comparable effects are also brought about in other phenomena of the narrative frame, in the narrator's representation of the sound and the fury at the crossing of the river Zbruč, of the dreadful silence in the house where he is billeted, etc. The woman's story conveys in Frank's words "a moment of revelation", induces the reader to what he calls "reflexive reference" that is to the suspension of the immediate referential functions of the text "until the entire pattern of internal references can be apprehended as a unity" (13). This so-called "spatial form", which is so characteristic of modernist writing, is most powerfully called forth by the short inner tale at the end of *Crossing the River Zbruč*. Thus I could say with Nilsson that the minor parts, played by the Polish Jews in the second half of Babel's story, "in the final scene nearly become leading roles" (70).

This tendency to rule over the narrative frame manifests itself most clearly in several effects of correction and rejection of the narrator's point of view. What the latter arrogantly blames as a filthy way of living is in fact the damage done to the house of the Jewish family. Just as he misunderstood the vestiges of oppression and desecration, he misinterpreted the behaviour of the inhabitants: this is obvious in his metaphorical description of their cleaning activity ("They skipped about noiselessly, monkey-fashion, like Japs in a circus act"). Regressively, however, their doings become symptomatic of panic-stricken conduct. It may even be argued that the sudden changes in the imagery of Volyn's landscape regressively acquires its true emotional significance, set against the murder of the old father.

The purport of the inner story in relation to the narrative frame lies in its significance for the narrator's gradual insight into the world of war, for his initiation into a reality of destruction and bloodshed, for his descent into hell, as one commentator put it (Falen: 137–8; Cf. also Nilsson: 65). Thus the lyric mood and its appropriate metaphors, the provocative war imagery, the haughtiness of the victor, is put to silence. The last words are with the pregnant woman. Her emotions, her sense of human worth and life's value, her despair, prevail. The narrator's understanding is implied.

The function of the opening story for the cycle as a whole is connected mainly with the initiation theme and hence with the facts of the inner story. According to Patricia Carden "the narrator of *Red Cavalry* will never come to understand more than he understands at the end of the first story" (50). It is indeed from the start that the narrator touches upon one of the most repugnant atrocities and it is from the start that a true sense of human value is set off against the violation of it. As Falen has said "an epiphanic revelation has emerged" (140). But further aspects of this human value and of its intricate connection with brutalized Hasidism and with the religious inspiration of the Jewish community in general, will still be unfolded. And also the paradoxically competing forces of this Jewish way of life on the one hand and of the revolution on the other, will be still further elaborated in startling images, emotional outbursts and laconic registrations: the tragic downfall of both runs through several stories and reaches its climax in the last tale of the cycle (in the first four editions: cf. Luplow: 116). Moreover, no mention has yet been made of the artistic alternative as an escape from the world of terror and stagnation to the realm of creation and renewal, a guarantee of human and spiritual values: the artist, not only in service of his craft, but an explorer of deep emotions, of unprecedented wit and beauty is set against the miseries of an irremediably deficient life.

III,2.

An intriguing story is *The Cemetery at Kozin*. It seems to be no more than the summing up of some characteristic details of a Jewish graveyard. The static character of this description is underscored by a series of nominative sentences. It is only the end of the second paragraph that is marked by a sentence with a simple predicate expressed by a verb in the indicative mood. This sentence contains the text of an inscription on one of the memorial stones. In fact it marks the transition to a sort of inner tale: a family chronicle in statu nascendi, which covers almost half of the short text (less than one page). This inner story is set against the introductory narrative frame: the individual and particular vs. the collective and general. In relation to the narrative frame it does not have a function of correction and rejection but of completion and emotional intensification: the deceased are specified by name and the dramatic culmination of their lives is reported in one sentence, hewn out in the granite. Thus the inner story imparts emotional vigour to the high-reliefs of anonymous rabbis, to religious symbols and emblems. Most remarkable is its closing statement: a rethorical exclamation, a never answered question launched to God: "O death, o covetous one, o greedy thief, why couldst thou not have spared us, just for once?" It echoes the outcry of the pregnant woman at the end of the first story, it has its roots in a universal experience shared by all men and it is a problem of the deepest concern in all forms of religious and philosophical thought. Therefore I regard it as main element of the narrator's point of view: in this respect the choice of his Jewish mouthpieces seems significant. Through them the narrator is connected with what affects him most and what is emphatically propounded in the cycle. The reverberatory quality of this inner tale is also connected with the inscription: "Wolff, son of Elijah, prince robbed from the Torah in his nineteenth spring." It may be remembered that the story, *The Rabbi's Son*, describes how Elijah Bratslavsky (Il'ja Braclavskij) died: "He – that last of the princes", as the narrator says. The narrator's reaction to this young man's death is marked by the awareness of the debacle of the campaign and the desintegration of Hasidism. It is this desintegration in particular that causes the effusive utterances at the beginning and the end of the story, the sweet memories of the Sabbath eves, the Talmud and the Torah rolls of childhood, "the tempest of my imagination with this age-old body of mine", as the narrator puts it in his last paragraph. His reaction recalls the effusion of emotions at the end of *The Cemetery at Kozin*, also at the beginning of *Gedali* and *The Rabbi*.

III,3.
A kind of apocryphal tale is inserted into the narrative *Pan Apolek*. In its relation to the narrative frame this inner story is neither a corrective nor a completing factor. The thematic core of the apocryphal story told by Apolek reflects the thematic essence of the narrative frame, devoted to the story proper of the painter's life. The purport of this common theme may be indicated as follows: Apolek's gospel of artistic freedom against ideological oppression; his libertine innocence against narrow-minded norms, etc. The content of Apolek's story is announced by him as Jesus's marriage to Deborah, "a Jerusalem maid of obscure birth". The narrator thereupon renders Apolek's provocative play with evangelical themes and turns of

expression: with Jesus's compassion on Deborah, who was repudiated by her betrothed; with His willingness to join her though she lay in loathsome dirt after she had vomited out all she had eaten; with His aloofness in opposition to Deborah's noisy triumph of a woman proud of her fall; with His suffering and sorrow indicated by the fact that "a deathly perspiration had broken out on His body"; with His unnoticed withdrawal from the banqueting hall and His retirement "to the wilderness eastward of Judaea."

The crux of this uncanonical tale seems to be a challenge of the sexual taboo in catholicism on the one hand, a somewhat irreverent approach of the saintly disregard of filth, on the other.

More important even may be its proof of Apolek's insight into the human heart, into the narrator's artistic fancies in particular. This faculty of wit and wisdom is related to all that is told in the narrative frame about Apolek's Bohemian way of life and alluring artistry, about the sympathy he meets in the people, about the war he wages against the church, and above all about the vow the narrator makes: to follow Apolek's example. At this point the story links up with one of the main themes of the cycle: the artist's way of life as an alternative to war and revolution. The theme is further elaborated in such stories as *The Church at Novograd, In St. Valentine's Church.* It has received a searching comment in a chapter of Patricia Carden's book: "Art Renders Justice." She observes that "artistic freedom as an outpouring of the spirit is a moral act" (148). And indeed "moral sensibility" may be connected with Apolek's intriguing and enigmatic painting, e.g. "The Death of John the Baptist" and with the narrator's awareness of the painter's message: in the shape of John the Baptist he recognizes the faithless and pitiless monk, pan Romual'd; the painting of Mary Magdalene appears to be a portrait of a loose Jewish girl named El'ka, the painting of St. Paul a portrait of a lame convert, Janek by name, etc. The narrator's delight in Apolek's fancies should not make us forgetful, however, of the mild irony in his view of Apolek's art, nor of adjusting the necessary shading to the solemn vow in the beginning of the story. This vow is above all concerned with Apolek's witty and facetious art of living, of which his paintings are the telling expression.

III,4.
The significance of art as a means of escape from the world of war determines the connection between the narrative frame and the inner tale in the story *Italian Sunshine.* Two ways of escape are at variance with each other: escape into the artistic world of imagination, escape into the allegedly real world of Italian sunshine.

The inner tale is presented in the form of a letter. It is written in a sophisticated idiolect not free from stylistic pretensions, though interspersed with party jargon and vulgar turns. It is addressed to a certain Viktorija, who appears to be the fiancée of its sender Sidorov. He mockingly launches a bitter complaint about his lot: he is bored in the army as he cannot ride (because of his wound), bored in a Moscow which is organized according to plan, witness the bureaucracy, display of pomposity, etc. Sidorov's point is his appeal for help to have him sent to Italy, land of sunshine and bananas ... "just to get well again ..."

The narrative frame provides the letter and its writer with several metaphorical qualifications of a rather ambiguous significance: they may pass a partly favourable, partly unfavourable, judgment upon the narrator's imagination, but also upon Sidorov's project. Thus it is said that the latter wrote at the light of a humpbacked candle, "ill-omened beacon of dreamers"; his letter "tore into shreds the pink wadding" of the narrator's imagination and dragged him "into the corridors of Sidorov's ... commonsense madness." The "pink wadding imagination" of the narrator is rather negatively set against Sidorov's fancy, but soon it becomes clear that there is nothing of Sidorov's madness in the narrator's imaginary world, nothing of the latter's lack of sound judgment. He finds relief from the hardship of circumstance in a jocular play with imagination. His view of the scorched, moonlit town evokes reminiscences of well-known theatrical scenes. He then ironically extends the vehicle (the theatrical scenes) of his figure of analogy so as to disturb the relation to the tenor (the wretched buildings of the town): "The damp mold of the ruins flowered like the marble of opera seats. And I waited, disturbed in spirit, for Romeo to appear from the clouds, a satin-clad Romeo singing of love, while a dismal electrician in the wings keeps a finger on the moon-extinguisher." Thereupon the narrator's strong sense of beauty again for a moment delivers him from the hardness of fate. He feasts his eyes upon the moonlit sky and gives expression to a sensation of overflowing life; his hyperbole sets forth a striking contrast with the phenomena of death and destruction: "Blue roads flowed past me like streams of milk spurting from many breasts." At the end of the narrative frame the exuberancy of the moon-night is emphasized again: "and only the window, overflowing with moonlight, shone forth like a deliverance." It is set as a moment of relief against the evil omen of Sidorov's brooding face above the yellow flame of the candle. By this opposition the narrative frame both heightens the impression of frustration in Sidorov's yearning after the Italian sunshine, and displays the narrator's intensely felt artistic delight in the power of his playful imagination in the as yet untouched beauty of the night.

In other stories of the cycle, too, the narrative frame has a corrective bearing on the inner tale told by a secondary character. Thus the last paragraph of the story A letter exposes the brutal and stupid outward appearance of the Kurdjukov family: father and sons. This closing statement of the narrator serves as an indirect commentary on the complete lack of emotional concern in Kurdjukov's letter to his mother, though he informs her of the atrocious killing of one of her sons by his father and of his father's death at the hands of his brother Simon. The final paragraph furthers, moreover, the narrator's implied moral position, which is far less ambiguous than might appear from the stories worded by a character and not encompassed by a narrative frame. These stories could ascribe a semblant justification to awesome atrocities as seems the case in *The Life and Adventures of Pavličenko, Matvej Rodionyč*. In relation to these stories the cycle as a whole functions as a narrative frame. The cyclic structure is conditioned by specific thematic essentials that occur in several variants. One of these essentials is the human factor as reflected in religion, beauty, compassionate behaviour and the concomitant abhorrence of violence.

III,5.

A somewhat more complicated connection between narrative frame and inner tale is shown by the story *The Road to Brody*. Its narrative frame conveys details of the ride to the town mentioned in the title. Traveling along Volhynie the narrator comments on the idyllic landscape and bitterly deplores the extermination of the bees. Thereupon the narrative flows into two successive inner tales: first a tale about the bee and its good qualities, then one about a light bay stallion. The latter tale is presented as a song, struck up by Afon'ka Bida.

The relation of the first tale to the narrative frame seems obvious: it stresses the atrocities of the red soldiers, victimizing even the innocents, those whom they pretend to release from oppression. This is, of course, a theme which runs through several other stories of the cycle as well, e.g. *The Remount Officer, Berestečko,* etc. But there is an aspect of this theme, which is explicitly put forth only in the story under consideration, or, to be more precise, which comes to the fore in an observation made by the same Afon'ka Bida, just before he starts his song. This observation then is again part of the narrative frame which is resumed after the pointed conclusion of the inner tale: the point of the latter is the bee's refusal to follow the example of all kind of midges and to strike at Jesus hanging upon His cross: "Can't", says the bee ... "He's a carpenter like us." In his comment Afon'ka Bida not only justifies the victimization of the innocents, but also requires their understanding: ... the bee's got to stick it now; it's for them too that we're messing about here." Needless to say that this point of view is not shared by the narrator: even within the scope of the story under discussion it is emphatically dismissed by him in the introductory narrative frame: he laments the extermination of the bees in the first two paragraphs, in the third he concludes: "The chronicle of our workaday offenses oppressed me without respite, like an ailing heart."

The second inner tale, contained in Afon'ka Bida's song, seems thematically rather removed from both the narrative frame and the other inner tale.

It may, however, be connected with the ride on horseback to Brody, and in particular with the narrow escape at a jolting gallop when the enemy suddenly opens fire. But its main function is to propound a thematic element which appears to be the core of some other stories, too: the Cossack's infinite attachment to his horse, the very staff of his itinerant way of life. This theme is the heart of stories like *Afon'ka Bida, The Story of a Horse,* etc. In these tales it is rendered dramatic by the death or the loss of the four-footed friend. Such a most embarrassing event in a Cossack's life also signifies fateful developments of the campaign: reckless sallies of personal revenge, loss of confidence in the revolution, awareness of the inevitably approaching catastrophe. In his utterly pessimistic letter to Chlebnikov Savickij suggests (*The Story of a Horse, Continued*) that one of the calamitous aspects of the campaign is the fact that "the white stallion is no longer beneath me. So that in accordance with war's change of fortune do not expect to see your beloved Divisional Commander Savitsky, Comrade Khlebnikov, but we shall meet again, to put it bluntly, in the Kingdom of Heaven ..."

Thus the thematic side-line about the significance of the Cossack's horse, links up with a main theme of the cycle.

IV.

To conclude I will summarize the main aspects of the inner story in Babel's *Red Cavalry*. Several types can be distinguished, dependent on their relation to the narrative frame and the cycle. The first of them occurs in the story *Crossing the River Zbruč*. This type fundamentally changes the significance of the narrative frame: the spokesman is a character. Her point of view collides with that of the narrator, propounded in the narrative frame. The narrator's view is overruled as an evident misinterpretation of facts. Another factor in this prevalence is the emotional intensity of expression. Most decisive is, of course, the universal purport of the character's effusions. This universality strongly furthers the important thematic function of this type of inner tale in the cycle. But determinative of this function are, above all, the variations of this universal element in other stories of the cycle, its association with instances of comparable emotional intensity and perception of the human predicament.

The second type can be found in the story *The Cemetery at Kozin*. It has all the characteristics of the first type, except one: it does not change the thematic essence of the narrative frame but completes it with illustrative details and thus provides it with an intensely emotional and reflexive shading.

The third type (the tale about the bee in *The Road to Brody*) surprisingly deepens the insight into the thematic core of the narrative frame. This narrative frame shows a twofold mental attitude: the narrator's view is connected with an important issue of the inner tale and the cycle as a whole (this view implies self-blame); the character's approach is linked up with a thematic side-line of an intriguing contrastive quality (this approach implies self-justification).

The fourth type, too, is part of the story *The Road to Brody*: Afon'ka Bida's song. The thematic shift produced by this inner tale is so diverting that the relation to the narrative frame is almost non-existent; moreover, its thematic function for the cycle is at first undeterminable. It is only gradually that variations in several stories will present the deviating theme to the reader's mind as a character's view of an intensely emotional strength. It will acquire more general thematic importance by associative links with other stories, which add new aspects and shadings and bring about effects that express also the narrator's position (Afon'ka Bida's song in its relation to several "horse-stories").

The fifth type is exemplified by the apocryphal tale in *Pan Apolek*. This inner story functions as a sort of parable: it symbolizes the human and artistic qualities of the painter, who is the author of the tale and the central character of the extensive narrative frame. As such the inner tale is connected with the thematic essence of the narrative frame and it is linked up with a main theme of the cycle.

In the sixth type the relation of the inner story to the narrative frame and to the cycle as a whole, is clearly that of a subordinate part to a dominant part. This type of inner story is frequently put into the mouth of a character who distinguishes himself by the idiosyncracies of his idiolect, made up of vulgar turns of expression, ideological sterotypes, and so on (so-called 'skaz'). The view propounded by this character is questioned and corrected in an indirect way by the values expressed in the narrator's narrative frame (*A Letter*). When this frame is lacking the cycle acts as a corrective medium (It has this function in *The Life and Adventures of Pavličenko, Matvej Rodionyč*).

The relation of dominance and subordination between narrative frame and inner tale becomes more complicated when both are played off against each other as comparable themes. An example of this type of inner tale (put in the mouth of a character using 'skaz') is to be found in the story *Italian Sunshine*. At first sight neither of the themes is represented as the more important: the narrator uses ambiguous expressions that are no more depreciative or appreciative of the theme in the narrative frame than of that in the inner tale. On second thoughts, however, the narrative frame exerts its corrective power, loses its ambiguities and gradually imposes itself upon the reader's mind as the more important part. The significance of this part becomes still more apparent because of its links with the contents of foregoing and following stories in the cycle. Hence the theme of the narrative frame fits in with a major thematic line.

NOTE

1. Quotations from: Isaac Babel, The Collected Stories. Edited and translated by Walter Morison, with an introduction by Lionel Trilling, New York and Scarborough, Ont., 1974.

References

Carden, Patricia, 1972. *The Art of Isaac Babel* (Ithaca and London).

Falen, James E, 1974. *Isaac Babel: Russian Master of the Short Story* (Knoxville).

Frank, Joseph, 1963. "Spatial Form in Modern Literature", in: *The Widening Gyre* (New Brunswick, New Jersey), 3–62.

Luplow, Carol, 1982. *Isaac Babel's Red Cavalry* (Ann Arbor, Michigan).

Mendelson, Danuta, 1982. *Metaphor in Babel's Short Stories* (Ann Arbor, Michigan).

Nilsson, Nils Åke, 1977. "Isaak Babel's Perechod čerez Zbruč", in: *Scando-Slavica,* t. 23, 63–71.

Stepanov, Nik., 1928. "Novella Babelja", in: *I. E. Babel': Stat'i i materialy* (Leningrad), 13–41.

Terras, Victor, 1966. "Line and Color: The Structure of I. Babel's Short Stories in *Red Cavalry",* in: *Studies in Short Fiction,* III, 141–156.

Henrik Birnbaum

Text, Context, Subtext:
Notes on Anna Achmatova's "A Poem without a Hero"

Glanz und ruhm rausch und qual traum und tod.
Stefan George

Rabotaet podtekst ... Ničto ne skazano v lob. Složnye i glubokie vešči izloženy ne na desjatkach stranic, kak oni pri- vyčny, a v dvuch strokach, no dlja vsech ponjatnych.
Anna Achmatova (in a comment on "A Poem Without a Hero")

In the poststructuralist age of hermeneutics and deconstruction students of literature have increasingly turned away from seeking to lay bare the structure inherent in a work of verbal art or to reveal the principles organizing its orchestration, imagery, and composition. Yet the new approach inspired, in particular, by Jacques Derrida and some of his more or less orthodox followers, notably in America, has been applied primarily to narrative discourse, much less to verse. Naturally, it is not possible, in the limited space of a few remarks offered here as a tribute to one of the truly empathic interpreters of modern Russian literature and a friend of nearly four decades, to enter into a detailed discussion of the merits and shortcomings of this fashionable, flexible, yet frequently challenged method which is bent on viewing a literary text more in terms of the human experience reflected in it and of its intentional or inadvertent impact than conceiving of it as a self-contained, carefully structured artistic whole. While not merely a return from the strictly text-immanent to a biographically and sociologically oriented type of literary scholarship, the new approach certainly includes elements of both, focusing as it does on the relationship between the author and his work as well as on that of the work and its reception. Clearly, Derrida's acknowledged indebtedness to Kant notwithstanding, the way to read, interpret and evaluate creative writing advocated by the French thinker does not bring to mind, in the first place, the Kantian concept of the aesthetic as capsulized in the oft-cited reference to the evocation of *interesseloses Wohlgefallen*. Though something presumably is lost when we no longer care to find or even doubt the existence of an intrinsic structure once thought crucial

139

to the process of converting chaos into cosmos, disorder into order, and entropy into form, expressed in the dense texture of poetically shaped language, there is also something to be said for searching, in a novel and probing way, for the reality and the existential predicament behind the artistic achievement mirroring yet transforming them, and for grasping the message not only as it is projected onto the syntagmatic axis of the unfolding text from the paradigmatic axis of the accessible code (to paraphrase Jakobson), but also as this message can be read, subliminally, between the lines, as it were. Put differently, only when, in addition to perceiving the structural elements of a text as combined and recombined by the poet, we also know and understand the wider context in which the text is embedded, or at least some of it, will we, as readers, be able to catch a glimpse of the subtext frequently artfully encoded beneath the readily apparent surface of the literary work. And only when we find ourselves in a position to carry out this two- or even multidimensional interpretive operation, thus involving much more than just straight reading, will we – by beginning to take in also the hidden message and deeper meaning – more fully enjoy the pleasure that the poetic text either was initially meant to convey or turned out to impart to the reader as a result of the latter's co-creative effort and ability. Or, if outright aesthetic enjoyment is perhaps not always the proper word to describe the effect achieved, such a more comprehensive understanding of a text would still prompt an emotional and/or intellectual response on the part of the reader that a different, more narrowly focused, albeit attentive ("close"), reading could simply not produce.

The œuvre of Anna Achmatova, rightly considered a reticent poet, provides a telling example of the potentials of the approach to literature just sketched. This is particularly true of her longest and most difficult piece, "A Poem Without a Hero," which she herself in part two of the poem (stanza XVI) characterized as a box with a triple bottom ("U škatulki ž trojnoe dno"); cf. Kunitz & Hayward 1973, 169; van der Eng-Liedmeier & Verheul 1973, 101; Haight 1976, 148–9, with fn. Note also the repeated reference to mirrors and the – distorted – images they reflect as well as the poet's admitting (in part two, stanza XVII) to having used secret ink and writing in mirror handwriting ("No soznajus', čto primenila / Simpatičeskie černila . . . / I zerkal'nym pis'mom pišu") – this "admission" not only having political implications but also countering criticism for liberal borrowing from other writers. Written over a period of twenty-two years (1940–62) and summing up much of her own life's experience in an almost Proustian manner (cf. Kunitz & Hayward 1973, 169), this crowning achievement of her poetic creativity is by the same token a hymn to and a mythopoetic transfiguration of Achmatova's familiar ambience – her beloved city with its immediate environs. In this context it is worth noting, however, that the title of her work is probably not meant to allude to the nameless urban masses, or even to some segment of Petersburg society in which the poet had once moved about in her youth. Rather, it is to be understood as referring in a more personal fashion to herself only and to her own life's difficult and painful shifts of bliss and despair. In claiming her poem to be without a hero, she therefore possibly echoes Mandel'štam who in what may be regarded as his Petersburg tale – *Egipetskaja marka* – had written: "Stranno podumat', čto naša zizn' – èto povest' bez fabuly i geroja, iz pustoty i stekla ..."; see also van der Eng-Liedmeier & Verheul 1973, 109, n. 51. But see now also the Postscript at the end of this essay. Constructed explicitly as a triptych – an asymmetric triptych, to be sure, considering the uneven length of the three parts – with its digressing mid portion, "Intermezzo/Tails," reflecting over the task of the poet, the text of Achmatova's "Poem" in its first, most elaborate part, "The Year Nineteen–Thirteen/A Petersburg Tale," contains reminiscences, or rather carnivalesque flashes of memories, of a long gone past in pre-Revolutionary Petersburg centered around a tragic real event, a suicide. In tune with the tale's general atmosphere, it is swarming with mummed shadows and receding mirages. As for the Russian word for 'tails,' *reška,* used as the heading of part two, it not only means the reverse side of a coin or medal but also suggests self-defeat and failure. It is along these lines also that the poet's declaration (again, in stanza XVI of part two) are to be understood when she says that she agrees to failure and does not hide her embarrassment ("Ja soglasna na neudaču / I smuščen'e svoe ne prjaču ..."); on the ambiguity of *reška*, see, e.g., van der Eng-Liedmeier & Verheul 1973, 96, with n. 37; Achmatova 1976, 517 (in the notes by Žirmunskij). By contrast to the playful, though phantom-filled and dreamlike sequences in the first part of the "Poem", with some unsettling hints about the imminent turning point in Russia's fate (and by implication that of the poet) enhanced by strong associations to the Don Juan motif of guilt and disaster, with its specific Russian echoes (in Puškin and Blok), its last section, titled "Epilogue," foreshadows the poet's mere spiritual presence in a postwar Leningrad, slowly rising from its sufferings, set in an uncertain future sometime after 1942 (when this part was first written in Tashkent); cf. also the foreboding appearance of the "guest from the future" already in part one. On Achmatova and Puškin, cf. esp. Žirmunskij 1973, 75–84; Timenčik 1968 and 1974: Haight 1976, *passim*. Achmatova was tied to Puškin by a peculiar affinity (particularly apparent in some of her earlier pieces, esp. in the collection *Belaja staja* of 1917/18) as well as by an almost metaphoric/ metonymic relationship marked by similar themes and their analoguous artistic treatment, in addition to sharing some physical settings important to their poetic careers: Odessa, Carskoe Selo, Petersburg. Achmatova's own Puškin studies (1977) bear further testimony to this life-long influence. Concerning Achmatova and Blok, see Žirmunskij 1970 and 1973, 85–110; Maver Lo Gatto 1970/72; Haight 1976, 68–9, 155–8, and *passim*. For an in-depth analysis, cf., moreover, Toporov 1981 (where, 157–77, also the Russian poet's allusions to and echoes of Hoffmann, crucial to part one of the "Poem," are discussed).

Composed in Achmatova's characteristic anapestic-iambic meter, or regularized *dol'nik,* in irregular strophic form in part one, regular, six-line stanzas (except where, following Puškin's occasional manner, left blank) in part two, and without any strophic division in part three (cf. van der Eng-Liedmeier & Verheul 1973, 65, with the reference to Žirmunskij's coinage *achmatovskaja strofa*), and interspersed with prose, the unique genre of *Poèma bez geroja* could perhaps be termed a novel-poem (*Romangedicht*) of sorts, though in the last analysis no traditional label will quite fit it; for discussion, see Birnbaum 1984. In any event, the "Poem" lends itself eminently for the approach attempting to establish if not the full, irretrievable subtext – contrary to her own claim made in the comment quoted as an epigraph to these notes – partly rendered opaque and cryptic by the poet herself, then at least some of the underlying elements of reality and reference which, with some assurance, can be recovered and interpreted. Thus a more complete understanding of the text can be gained, mindful though we must be of Achmatova's penchant for, and (in the days of Stalin's repression) perceived necessity of, elusiveness and vagueness as part of her poetic technique as well as her concern for the fate and safety of those dear to her.

In her long evolution as a poet, Achmatova, although in essence remaining true to the credo of her Acmeist youth throughout her career – with the exception of a few well-known and properly understood lapses – can therefore be said to have moved along a path from the articulate and transparent (if occasionally deliberately only half-spoken) toward the concealed and obscure. This trend she shared, to some extent, with her fellow Acmeist Mandel'štam, while, for example, Pasternak's development as a poet rather followed the opposite course, notwithstanding some profound parallels between "A Poem Without a Hero" and Pasternak's crowning life synthesis, *Doktor Živago;* for details, see Birnbaum 1984. Achmatova's "Poem" is no doubt the best illustration of this particular trait of the creativity of her mature years; cf. Lotman *et al.* 1975, 11–12; Birnbaum 1980, 31 and 54, n. 19. On the general drift of Achmatova's poetic evolution, see also Driver 1975. For some discussion of the chief tenets of Acmeism, see, e.g., Driver 1968 and Mickiewicz 1975. By the same token, the claim made by some critics that the "Poem" in fact marks a return, or even regression, to unadulterated Symbolism appears quite uncalled for despite of its frequent, but very specific and different recourse to symbolic language and imagery; cf. Kunitz & Hayward 1973, 170.

The text of "A Poem Without a Hero" is known in several versions exhibiting substantial differences. These differences are both of a quantitative and qualitative nature, with the chronologically latest variants, as could

142

be expected, reaching maximum expansion. Yet in some instances certain phrases and even whole passages forming part of an earlier redaction have subsequently been deleted. As is well known, Achmatova began writing her "Poem" in earnest in late 1940 when, as she reports in the prefatory note (*Vmesto predislovija*), "Pervyj raz ona prišla ko mne v Fontannyj Dom v noč' na 27 dekabrja 1940 goda, prislav kak vestnika ešče osen'ju odin nebol'šoj otryvok." Dated 8 April 1943 in Tashkent, the note then states that that night she wrote two sections of part one – "1913" and the first dedication, in memory of Vs(evolod) K(njazev), the young poet, appearing in more than one guise in "A Petersburg Tale," with whom the poet had been in love but who had killed himself because of his own unrequited love for the sophisticated and beautiful Ol'ga Afanas'evna Glebova-Sudejkina. The latter, to whom Achmatova had previously inscribed a few of her poems was the object of the "Poem's" second dedication, dated 25 May 1945 and occasioned by the news of her death in Paris. In a sense, Ol'ga ("Putanica-Psicheja") is the poet's double in part one, now merging with her, now viewed (and acting) separately, with an identity of her own. The third and last dedication – a poetic device in its own right – Achmatova did not write until 5 January 1956.

Until recently, the version published by A. Haight in 1967 was generally considered the definitive one. However, see also Achmatova 1968, 95–133, with the additions and deletions indicated in the same volume, 603–6. Also, the version published in Achmatova 1976, 352–80, edited by Žirmunskij, adding (on the last two pages) some stanzas which were eventually omitted from the text of the "Poem", ought to be consulted. For more details and discussion regarding earlier and later variants, the reader is referred to the account given in the Appendix in Haight 1976, 208–9, indicating, among other things, corrections not considered by the editors of the standard edition.

There can be little doubt, then, that all these emendations and variant readings, studied carefully, have substantially contributed to clarify certain obscure passages in the "Poem", although the basic structure of the first redaction of 1940–42, composed as if in three movements of a symphony, did not essentially change in subsequent versions; cf. van der Eng-Liedmeier & Verheul 1973, 64–5, with n. 5 (and the reference to Dobin); see also *ibid*. 134, in the poet's own reflections. Note in this connection merely the "Poem's" first version and Verheul's keen observations, pointing out, in particular, the substantial rewording in part three after the break with V. G. Garšin, the poet's last life companion, to whom *Reška* was originally dedicated. The epigraph "My future is in my past," attributed to Mary Stuart, is thus a later addition expressing the poet's renunciation of the world. See further van der Eng-Liedmeier & Verheul 1973, 115–41. Thus it can be said that the existence of several versions, with additions and deletions, provides an invaluable clue to the interpretation of "A Poem Without a Hero," whose comprehension and hence full appreciation is, in any event, impeded by the many mere hints and oblique references both to the poet's own contemporaries and to events in which they were involved, and by a number of allusions (not readily understood by the uninitiated) to Western literature and art.

In addition to work already cited (including Žirmunskij 1973, esp. 143–77, and Achmatova 1976, 512–23, containing Žirmunskij's notes), Čukovskij 1964, Dobin 1968 (esp. 190–245), and Pavlovskij 1982 (esp. 128–61), are major sources for the elucidation and decipherment of Achmatova's "A Poem Without a Hero," and notably its context in reality and creative imagination – the backdrop against which the coming into being of the memories, dreams and visions surfacing in it must be viewed. Only then will also the "Poem's" powerful subtext, the message of love and death (cf. Birnbaum 1982, esp. 11), time and eternity (cf. Verheul 1971, esp. 180–220), take on a life of its own and stay with us – its readers.

Postscript: This essay had already been submitted when the excellent study by S. Leiter, *Akhmatova's Petersburg* (1983) came to my attention. Chapter five, "Poem Without a Hero" (143–190), in particular, complements and supersedes much of what could only be briefly sketched in this contribution. Note, incidentally, that the author uses precisely the Mandel'štam quotation referred to also by me as an epigraph for her treatment of Akhmatova's crowning piece; see further for a general assessment also Ketchian 1984.

References

Achmatova, A., 1968 *Sočinenija*. Tom vtoroj, G. P. Struve and B. A. Filippov, eds., Munich and Washington.

–, 1976, *Stichotvorenija i poėmy*, A. A. Surkov and V. M. Žirmunskij, eds., Leningrad.

Birnbaum, H., 1980 "On the Poetry of Prose: Land- and Cityscape 'Defamiliarized' in *Doctor Zhivago*," in: *Fiction and Drama in Eastern and Southeastern Europe: Evolution and Experiment in the Postwar Period*, H. Birnbaum and T. Eekman, eds., Columbus, Ohio, 27–60.

–, 1982 "Face to Face with Death: On a Recurrent Theme in the Poetry of Anna Achmatova," *Scando-Slavica* 28, 5–17.

– 1984 "Gedichtroman und Romangedicht im russischen Postsymbolismus (Zu einigen tiefgründigen Übereinstimmungen und oberflächlichen Unterschieden zwischen *Doktor Schiwago* und dem *Poem ohne Helden*)," in: *Text, Symbol, Weltmodell. Johannes Holthusen zum 60. Geburtstag*, J. R. Döring-Smirnov, *et al.*, eds., Munich, 19–36.

Čukovskij, K., 1964 "Čitaja Achmatovu," *Moskva* 1964/5, 200–3.

Dobin, E., 1968 *Poėzija Anny Achmatovoj*, Leningrad.

Driver, S., 1968 "Acmeism," *Slavic and East European Journal* 12, 141–56.

–, 1975 "Directions in Axmatova's Poetry Since the Early Period," *Russian Language Journal*, Supplementary Issue (Spring 1975), 84–91.

Haight, A. (ed.), 1967 "Anna Akhmatova's *Poema bez geroya*," *The Slavonic and East European Review* 45: no. 105, 474–96.

–, 1976 *Anna Akhmatova: A Poetic Pilgrimage*, New York and London.

Ketchian, S., 1984 (Review of) Leiter 1983, *Slavic and East European Journal* 28, 406–7.

Kunitz, S. & Hayward, M. (eds.), 1973 *Poems of Akhmatova / Anna Achmatova, Izbrannye Stichi. Selected, Translated* and *Introduced,* Boston and Toronto.

Leiter, S., 1983 *Akhmatova's Petersburg,* Philadelphia.

Lotman, Ju. M., B. A. Uspenskij, V. V. Ivanov, V. N. Toporov, A. M. Pjatigorskij, 1975 *Theses on the Semiotic Study of Culture (as Applied to Slavic Texts),* Lisse.

Maver Lo Gatto, A., 1970/72 "Sfumature e contrasti nella poesia di Anna Achmatova (Anna Achmatova e Aleksandr Blok)," *Ricerche Slavistiche* 17/19, 305–405.

Mickiewicz, D., 1975 "The Problem of Defining Acmeism," *Russian Language Journal.* Supplementary Issue (Spring 1975), 1–20.

Pavlovskij, A. I., 1982 *Anna Achmatova. Očerk tvorčestva* (2nd ed.), Leningrad.

Timenčik, R., 1968 "Achmatova i Puškin (Razbor stichotvorenija 'Smuglyj otrok brodil po allejam'),", in; *Uč. zap. Latv. gos. un-ta im. P. Stuchki* 106 *(Puškinskij sbornik),* Riga, 124–31.

–, 1974 "Achmatova i Puškin. Zametki k teme," in: *Uč. zap. Latv. gos. un-ta im. P. Stuchki* 215, Riga, 32–55.

Toporov, V. N., 1981 *Achmatova i Blok (k probleme postroenija poétičeskogo dialoga: "blokovskij" tekst Achmatovoj),* Berkeley.

van der Eng-Liedmeier, J. & Verheul, K., 1973 *Tale without a Hero and Twenty-Two Poems by Anna Axmatova: Essays. With unpublished poems by Anna Axmatova,* The Hague and Paris.

Verheul, K., 1971 *The Theme of Time in the Poetry of Anna Axmatova,* The Hague and Paris.

Žirmunskij. V. M., 1970 "Anna Achmatova i Aleksandr Blok," *Russkaja literatura* 3, 57–82.

–, 1973 *Tvorčestvo Anny Achmatovoj,* Leningrad.

Erik Egeberg

The Pilgrim, the Prophet and the Poet: Iosif Brodskij's "Piligrimy"

ПИЛИГРИМЫ

Мимо ристалищ, капищ,
мимо храмов и баров,
мимо шикарных кладбищ,
мимо больших базаров,
мира и горя мимо,
мимо Мекки и Рима,
синим солнцем палимы
идут по земле
пилигримы.

Увечны они, горбаты.
Голодны, полуодеты.
Глаза их полны заката.
Сердца их полны рассвета.
За ними поют пустыни,
вспыхивают зарницы,
звезды дрожат над ними,
и хрипло кричат им птицы,
что мир останется прежним.

Да. Останется прежним.
Ослепительно снежным.
И сомнительно нежным.
Мир останется лживым.
Мир останется вечным.
Может быть, постижимым,
но всё-таки бесконечным.

И значит, не будет толка
от веры в себя да в Бога.
И значит, остались только
Иллюзия и Дорога.
И быть над землей закатам.
И быть над землей рассветам.

Удобрить ее солдатам.
Одобрить ее поэтам.

Iosif Brodskij's *Piligrimy* (Pilgrims), published in the author's first collection of verse *(Stichotvorenija i poėmy,* 1965) may seem a plain and simple poem: the subject is indicated in the title, the pilgrims also appear in the text, and we are told what they do and how they look. True, their appearance may seem strange, and a closer investigation of the pilgrims' conduct will be necessary in order to elucidate the message of the poem. And if we want to reveal the deeper layers of meaning we shall have to examine the elements that may seem accidental as well.

An analysis of a lyrical poem may be conducted in different ways. However, a poem is a work of art with extension in time (corresponding to the space of the printed text), i.e., with an inherent axis from beginning till end. Therefore, in my opinion, the most significant of the various schemes which may be applied, is that which emerges when we follow the succession of verses, constantly evaluating every new verse as a combination of positive and negative responses to the expectations generated by the preceding lines.

Starting to read a sentence one picks out the most important parts of it – first the predicate, then the subject. But the first sentence of *Piligrimy* does not bring these parts in the opening lines, on the contrary, what the reader finds is a long sequence of parallel adverbial sentence elements, all with an initial *mimo* 'past'. This word not only fits into the syntactic structure, but it also hints at the reader's way past these elements towards the heart of the sentence.

A common denomination for all the things the pilgrims pass in the first four verses (and which the reader also has to pass on his search for the subject) is 'public places'. These may be divided into two groups – secular and sacred ones. To the first category belong *ristališča* 'stadiums', *bary* 'bars', and *bazary* 'markets', to the second *kapišča* 'heathen sanctuaries', *chramy* '(heathen or Christian) temples' and *kladbišča* 'graveyards'. These items are arranged according to a special pattern: The two first verses contain each one item of either category, while the following two verses have only one noun – either a secular (v. 4) or a sacred one. The six nouns, though being of opposite categories, are mutually connected by phonetic or morphologic devices (the suffix *-išče, bazarov* being phonetically an "expansion" of *barov, barov* and *chramov* containing identical (*a, o, r, v*) or similar (*b, m*) sounds), whereby the borderline between the two semantic groups of words is blurred. This again leads to a compromise of the values usually associated with the sacred items because the secular ones are connected with such activities as public amusement and commerce. This effect is additionally enhanced by the two adjectives, introduced in v. 3 and 4, both of which (*šikarnyj* 'ostentatious' and *bol'šoj* 'big') stress the external side of the objects.

Every poem can be viewed as an interplay of repetition and variation: repetition intensifies the effect but must be counteracted by variation lest the effect be spoiled by monotony. The author also has a limited number of devices by which he can develop the theme signalized in the first verse. In this poem we have already noticed an arrangement of the verses in pairs, leading us to expect a change also in the fifth verse. Our expectations are not disappointed, here the preposition *mimo* disappears from the front position of the line, but only after the reader has been deceived by the first syllable of the word *mira*. However, *mimo* reappears at the end of the same verse, and when this same word opens the following (6th) line, the reader is confirmed in his belief in the stability of the system.

To this point the things which the pilgrims have been passing by have been denominations for places. Now we can observe a shift: *mimo* has been connected with the abstracts *mir* 'peace' and *gore* 'sorrow', and in the following verse with two proper nouns: Mecca and Rome. These cities are not only the main cities of the world's two predominant religions, but also centres of world empires; thus the ambiguity secular : sacred is preserved. The chiastic arrangement of these verses, centred on the double *mimo*, also underlines the correlation between the opening and the closing word, *mira* and *Rima,* the last one being a (partial) phonetic reversal of the first, whereby also the second important meaning of the word *mir* is activated – 'world'.

This correlation may seem a sufficient explanation of the order of the two religious centres, which contradicts the chronological sequence. But this pecularity can equally be viewed as an indication of the direction of the pilgrims' wandering – from sunrise towards sunset.

Now at last the period approaches its end, that is the elements required for making this long chain of adverbials a full sentence. Already the new dominant consonant of the following verse – *s* – signalizes the advent of a new phase, and its concluding word, *palimy* 'burnt', anticipates the presence of the grammatical subject. This verse, however, also confirms the impression of a very long wandering, evoked by all the *mimo*'s: blue is a very uncommon epithet of the sun, but it actually is the colour it assumes when looked at for more than a short moment, and *palimy* hints at a long time of exposure to the sun's rays.

Together, the two last verses of this section have the same rhythmic structure as the preceding verses. But by splitting this structural unit in two the author emphasizes the main element of the sentence, the subject *piligrimy*. The importance of this word is furthermore stressed by its phonetic composition, which makes it appear as a total of the repeated sounds of the preceding lines.

When the subject, hinted at in the title, at last occurs, it is usually focused throughout the rest of the poem. In *Piligrimy* it is different. True, the pilgrims are still the subject of the following sentence, which introduces the second section of the poem. But the word *piligrimy* itself is not repeated; it is replaced by the pronoun *oni* 'they', and the place of this word is far from a prominent one – *oni* is almost hidden between its predicates. And after this the pilgrims do not occur as the subject of any sentence of the poem. Nevertheless, the second part of the poem must be defined as the section in which we find a description of the pilgrims. As in the foregoing lines the description is segmented in pairs of verses. The four predicates of the pilgrims (represented by *oni*) all stress their low status in this world and their detachment from it: crippled, humpbacked, hungry and half-clothed. At the same time these adjectives imply that the pilgrims have continued their wandering for a long, long time.

Verses 2 and 3 of this section form a syntactic parallelism, the main word of which is the repeated *polny* 'full'. Subjects are the pilgrim's eyes and hearts, the words governed by *polny* 'sunrise' and 'sunset'. This segment thus affirms the seclusion of the pilgrims from the world: the pictures in their eyes and their hearts (associated with their senses and their memory) do not reflect the earth, but what is above it. These phenomena are continuously changing, but their change follows a pattern endlessly repeating itself.

In the following verses the subjects are neither the pilgrims nor parts of their bodies, but things surrounding them and signalizing to them, their message remaining hidden until the reader reaches the end of the section, where he sees: "The world remains as before." This subordinate clause is dependent upon the only clause with an animate subject (*pticy* 'birds'), but it can be read as subordinate to all the preceding clauses (from v. 5 of this section on) as well.

One should take notice of the transformation of the pronoun *oni* in this section, which deals especially with the pilgrims. In the first pair of verses it appears in the nominative, but only once. In the next two verses it is in the genitive, and in the following four verses in other oblique cases (*za nimi – nad nimi – im*). By this arrangement of the material and the shift in the use of cases the author creates the impression that the pilgrims are now passing the point where the reader is standing.

The last subordinate clause does not fit into the predominant pattern of verse pairs. This odd verse, however, calls for a continuation, a response, and the author uses it as a starting point for the third section of his poem.

This section does not deal with the pilgrims, but with the world, the subject of the last clause of the foregoing section. The whole third section can be considered as an expansion of this clause, which is repeated at its beginning with the only alteration that the conjunction and the subject itself are replaced by the affirmative *Da* 'Yes'. This immutability of the world, already hinted at but only now explicitly pronounced, is, however, not a state of security and stability. In this part, where the ambiguity of the introductory section reappears, the content can be summarized in the words forming its centre: *Mir ostanetsja lživym* 'The world remains false'. The suggestive play of repeated sounds, so striking in the first verses, also reappears, the dominant sounds now being sibilants and affricates.

The following, fourth, section has all the characteristics of a conclusion. It opens with the words *I značit* 'Well then', repeated at the beginning of the 3rd verse. A system of anaphoric *I* 'And', so common in the conclusion of poems, creates an impression of unhindered movement: The solution is at hand.

The fourth section consists of three verse pairs, the two first of which have the formal shape of deductions. In v. 1 and 2 the meaning of a belief in oneself and in God is denied, from which follows – in the two next verses – that the only remaining things are the Illusion and the Road. The section ends with two parallel sentences emphasizing the immutability underlying the changes of the world. They do not possess the logical, argumentative structure of the foregoing ones. Their more descriptive nature creates a mood that may be perceived as an emotional concentrate of the whole poem, a "poetic" picture illustrating the phrase: "The world remains as before."

However, the poem does not end with these two smooth verses, describing the beautiful sky. They are followed by another pair of verses, rhyming with the preceding ones. By presenting these two concluding verses as a section of their own the poet stresses the opposition to the foregoing pair. Brodskij once more ends a poem with a crude contrast.

The two last verses not only rhyme with the preceding ones, but also repeat their particular syntactic pattern, stressing the impersonal aspect of natural phenomena occuring irrespectively of the two (logical) subjects (which here are in the dative), both animate and masculine. Against this common background the differences stand out very distinctly. First, the concluding section brings the reader back to earth, from *nad nej* 'over her' to *ee* 'her'. Second, they for the last time stress the prevalent ambiguity of the poem. And third, they do this in a way that underlines the contrast between the two components of the ambiguity and thereby point at the falseness of the world. The constellation of *udobrit'* 'to fertilize' and *odobrit'* 'to approve' questions the purport of *dobryj* 'good'.

We may ask if this is a poem about the world, and not primarily about the pilgrims. In the latter half of the poem the words *mir* and *zemlja* 'earth' are repeated several times, while the pilgrims seem to have passed by and out of sight. But the attentive reader will notice that items associated with the pilgrims reoccur in the conclusion about the world.

And in fact the pilgrims have not disappeared from the poem, even though the reader may have observed them passing by. But to discern their role one has to establish the place of Brodskij's poem in a particular literary tradition. This tradition is not primarily that of "pilgrim poems", even if we can observe certain important points of resemblance to other poems about wanderers, in the first place with Nekrasov's *Razmyšlenija u paradnogo pod"ezda* (Meditations at a main entrance), which seem to have been Brodskij's direct point of departure. In the central part of this rather long poem we find the description of the *stranniki* who are rebuffed at the grandee's front door and continue their wandering with the words: "May God judge him." But also Lermontov's *Tuči* (Clouds) may be mentioned; in this poem we recognize the separation of the pilgrims from the people and from the world, their perpetual movement and their connection with the sky. Nevertheless, there are other poems which have a still stronger affinity to Brodskij's poems about the pilgrims: the Russian poems about the prophet, of which Puškin's and Lermontov's are by far the best known. These poems (and the poems *Prorok* 'The Prophet' by Nekrasov and Rozengejm as well), even though internally closely connected with the social realities of 19th-century Russia, are stripped of all accessories of a special time and place.

Puškin and Lermontov both show us their prophet as a wanderer, but their wanderers represent two different stages in the career of the man of God. In Puškin's poem the prophet receives the Lord's order to go and bring His word to the peoples of the world. In Lermontov's poem the prophet has already tried to fulfil this task, but he has been rejected by his audience and has left society. The fellowship of other men, however, of which he has thus been deprived, is replaced and more than made up for by communion with nature. If we regard Brodskij's poem as a third phase in the prophet's development, we can describe this phase as a state where the prophet / pilgrim has lost even this sense of communion with nature (and of nature's communion with God).

The poem opens by stressing the lack of contact between the pilgrims and objects synecdochically chosen to represent civilization. But in the following section of the poem we discover that the pilgrims are also wandering through nature, apparently without paying any attention to its earthly objects: their eyes and hearts are filled with sunrises and sunsets, representations of pure time, seen as endless monotony.

The prophet's mission was to change the world. As a consequence of the world's unchangeability the belief that God wants to change the world through His servant and messenger has vanished. What is then left? The pilgrims have no goal for their wandering, their hearts and eyes only reflect the alternation of night and day. It may seem that the result is emptiness.

Here the initial four verses of the fourth section are especially important because they explicitly express the lack of meaning. But these verses need a closer examination. The two last elements of the second verse are *v sebja* 'in oneself' and *v Boga* 'in God', and they correspond with the two nouns *Illjuzija* "Illusion' and *Doroga* 'Road' in the fourth line. The correspondence between God and Road is moreover emphasized by a marked phonetic repetition: *da v Bóga* vs. *Doróga* (pronounced with an *a* in the unstressed first syllable). These verses may be interpreted in the following way: A reasonable belief in oneself is replaced by (or has turned out to be) an illusion (or even "the Illusion"), while belief in God is replaced by the road. This shift from God to the road corresponds with the substitution of the prophet by the pilgrim.

But what then is *the Road,* this notion that has replaced the notion of God? The author gives us no explanation, and each different purport of this word gives the whole poem a new significance, a new "colour". It must be emphasized that there are several possible interpretations of the word.

One interpretation stands out among the others because it is in accord with the religious setting of the entire poem. The notion 'road' or 'way' is very frequently used in the Bible, often with the meaning 'way of life'. When Christ says: "I am the way," his words fit into an ample Jewish context.

Doroga in this poem can be interpreted as Christ, but it can also be given a broader significance: a new representation of God, not recognized by everyone, as the pilgrims' way is the opposite of the traditional religious movement eastwards. However, if we take the whole utterance in John 14, 6 into consideration, the image of Christ emerges still clearer: "I am the way, the truth and the life." In the light of this passage the pilgrims' devotion to their wandering becomes understandable not only on the ground of negative arguments.

Nevertheless, an even more convincing interpretation presents itself if we go beyond the borders of traditional European culture, and such a perspective is in fact hinted at in the poem itself, where the pilgrims seem to originate from a place east of both Rome and Mecca, and where the arrangement of secular and sacred places at the beginning suggest a wandering through the centuries from before the emergence of Christianity. Thus, we turn to the third great world religion, Buddhism, the impact of which was felt in our culture just at the time when Brodskij's poem was written.

In Buddhism both *illusion* and *road / way* are well-known concepts. The various branches of this religion may differ in their views on which phenomena actually are to be classified as illusions, but they all agree that *man's self* is illusory. When one has seen this, one longs for a liberation from the world's painful and monotonous round of meaningless events, and one of the four holy verities, preached by Shakyamuni, the Buddha, maintains that there is a way, leading from suffering to Nirvana. This Nirvana is a state beyond the Illusion and therefore very well may correspond to the already noticed impression of emptiness.

Piligrimy is a pessimistic poem, even if we accept that the old belief in God may be replaced by a new appearance of the Highest Being or of an hitherto unknown way to salvation. The split between God and the world is wider, there is no hope for a redemption of the world any more.

But what about the two concluding verses? Here a new person turns up: the poet. The old poems about the prophet were – implicitly – poems about the poet too, and his appearance in Brodskij's poem may be perceived as an echo of Puškin's and Lermontov's verses. But in *Piligrimy* the role of the man of God and that of the poet have been completely dissociated: the former has no connection with the earth any more and the latter is entangled in its compromises. That may be the most tragic aspect of the poem – from a poet's point of view.

(An earlier version of this paper was presented to an audience at Stockholm University in May, 1986, and the author thanks all those who then – and on other occasions – have contributed with comments.)

Fiona Björling

Morality as History: An Analysis of Jurij Trifonov's Novel *Starik*

Notwithstanding a set of devices which are reminiscent of modernist and post-modernist fiction, Jurij Trifonov is a writer who must be understood within the context of the Russian realist and socialist-realist traditions of fictional narrative. I refer specifically to the following devices which have all in turn been considered typical features of modern (i.e. modernist and/or postmodernist) as opposed to realist fiction:

1. Multiperspective or polyphony (cf Doležel 112–114).
2. Achronology of fictional time (cf Doležel 121; Lodge 46, 155, 231–235; Frank).
3. Ambiguity as regards the status of literature to life, fact to fiction (cf Lodge 239 ff; Hollowell passim, especially chapter I).

In a previous article devoted to an analysis of *Dom na naberežnoj* (DNN) I considered these devices under the designation of 'narrative confusion' (Björling). From *Drugaja žizn'* (DŽ) to DNN and *Starik* can be noted an increasing development of the principle of multiperspective. Not only does the author intermingle the characters' point of view with that of the narrator through extensive use of free indirect speech, but he further renders the narrative position in itself unstable and ambiguous. In DNN no less than three distinctive narrative situations can be distinguished; of these the first person narrative sections are not integrated with the other two situations and the question as to their authorship is not resolved from within the text. This situation renders the interpretive position of the implied author elusive which in turn poses a problem for reader interpretation.

The mysterious first person narrator in DNN I understand to comprise Trifonov's genuine autobiographical voice: this is introduced not as literary device, but by way of a statement from the historical writer (as opposed to the implied author, cf Chatman 147–151) as to his own limitations when mediating reality. The shift between literature (fiction) and life (autobiography) is not intended as a comment on the mutual status of the one regarding the other as is the case in post-modernist fiction (Lodge and Hollowell op. cit.). Its purpose is rather to lay side by side two strikingly different witnesses – the fictional Glebov's and the writer Trifonov's personal reminiscences. By introducing himself rather than another fictional character, Trifonov breaks

154

out of the security of the fictional word and projects the problem of truthful witness to the past into his own life and by analogy into the lives of his readers.

Both the theme and the method which are developed in Trifonov's mature works have to do with the reconstruction of the past. Only by honestly facing and taking into account our past acts can we be moral beings in the present. The situation in Eastern Europe however encourages an attitude of blindness as to what happened yesterday. Insistence on the need for a historical rooting – for individual and nation alike – is emerging as a pressing theme in Eastern European literature today.[1] The characters in Trifonov's stories *Obmen, Predvaritel'nye itogi* (PI), *Dolgoe proščanie* (DP), DŽ and DNN are all engaged in reconstructing their past lives by way of dealing with a personal crisis in the present. None of them fully succeed in the attempt. Their failure reflects at the private, individual level the political tendency to erase the past systematically.

As a writer Trifonov has shown persistent interest in history. He has not written traditional historical novels (with the exception of *Neterpen'e*) but rather examined the recent past with a view to understanding the present which it has helped to form. A fascination with documents and archive material is revealed in the book which Trifonov wrote about his father, *Otblesk kostra*. This same research provides much of the raw material for *Starik*. Furthermore several of Trifonov's fictional characters are professional and amateur historians, to wit Griša in DP and Sereža in DŽ. This interest in a confrontation with the past will help us to define Trifonov's understanding of the role of the writer. Implicit in Trifonov's work is an approximation of the role of the writer to that of historian. What is even more telling is that the dividing line between professional and amateur historian, between public and private reconstruction of the past, is drawn so finely, that in the last resort each and every individual citizen is placed in the role of historian. Thus writer, historian and individual citizen all share a common task. Far from raising the wirter onto a pedestal whence he may proclaim omniscient truths, Trifonov brings him down to the level of each and every individual. Within the tradition of Soviet Russian literature this stand is original and innovatory.

The novel *Starik* marks a new development in Trifonov's 'historical' interest. The main character Pavel Evgrafovič (PE) has taken upon himself the role of semi-professional historian and set himself the task of establishing the fact as to whether the Cossack revolutionary Mironov, here thinly disguised under the fictitious name of Migulin, was or was not faithful to the revolution. To this end he has conducted extensive correspondence, interviews and archival research. Ostensibly a public historical issue has superceded the personal interest of the earlier stories. But it soon emerges that PE's interest in

Migulin is chanelled through a highly personal involvement in Migulin's fate; not only was PE secretary and a witness at Migulin's trial, but he was obsessed with Migulin's person owing to his romantic attachment to Asja, for a short time Migulin's wife. Thus the public and the personal historical issues are intimately intertwined. The public issue is given status in the novel through the introduction of documentary material which clearly stems from Trifonov's own research into the life of his father (*Otblesk kostra*). In this book Trifonov considers directly the case of Mironov (pp. 143–157); further he elaborates his interest in the past in general. Discussing *èta dalekaja, vzbudoražennaja, komu-to uže neponjatnaja sejčas žizn'*, Trifonov continues:

> *Začem že ja voroščǔ ee stranicy? Oni volnujut menja. I ne tol'ko potomu, čto oni ob otce i o ljudjach, kotorych ja znal, no i potomu, čto oni o vremeni, kogda vse načinalos'. Kogda načinalis' my.* (125–126)[2]

Like Trifonov's other Moscow stories (*Obmen*, PI, DŽ and DNN), *Starik* has a hierarchial structure as regards both story and discourse levels. As story it revolves around a situation in the early seventies (1972) which situation in turn revolves around the events of the civil war, 1917–1921.[3] The 1972 situation does not merely act as a frame for the civil war events but interacts with the same through the personal involvement of the protagonist PE in both situations. PE's retreat into the past is in part brought on by increasing debility due to old age as well as by his failure to communicate with his squabbling family and neighbours. At the same time the petty immorality – and basic unhappiness – of the inhabitants of the dača settlement at Sokolinyj bor in 1972 is set in relief against 'the time when it all began', that is the revolution and civil war. Similarly the title of the novel *Starik* refers ostensibly to the old man in 1972, PE; at the same time it involuntarily rubs off on the second level of the story to refer to Migulin himself. PE refers to Migulin as an old man on more than one occasion; Migulin was more than twice the age of Asja and PE himself never quite mature enough for her. In this way the two levels of the story are consistently brought to bear on one another.

The 1972 situation revolves around PE's preoccupation with his research on the one hand, and around an intrigue concerning a vacant dača on the other. The fictional interest may be termed 'psychological-realistic' and is strongly reminiscent of the earlier Moscow stories. PE's interest in Migulin is also 'psychological': he wants to know why Migulin desobeyed Red Army orders and left for the front and whether Migulin was wrongly or rightly condemned as a traitor. The story of Migulin bears the seeds of a truly epic novel, but this epic potential is fragmented into a thousand tiny pieces which never come together in coherent narrative. The novel comprises but a modest

234 small pages and it introduces more than 150 characters by name. It covers in panoramic if fragmentary description the situation of the revolution in Petersburg through the civil war as experienced in the Don region. Although fragmentary the description of the 1972 heatwave summer in and around Moscow is extensive. It entails PE's family life; the string-pulling in connection with the vacant dača; the story of Kandaurov's plans for an extended visit to Mexico, his desertion of his mistress, medical check-up and discovery of a fatal illness; the story of Sanja Izvarin's childhood ostracism in the dača community of Sokolinyj bor during the fateful purges of the late 1930s; PE's references to Petersburg in 1914 and his childhood attachment to Asja; PE'S allusions to his wife, Galja; PE's cryptic allusions to his own 'doubtful' behaviour in 1925 when he helped to vote Prichod'ko out of the party (103) and again later in the 1930s (37); finally the material introduced directly by Asja in her letters, and the documents quoted from the civil war and Migulin's trial. To sum up: an enormous amount of material is presented and touched upon but it is never organised into coherent narrative. The effect is to suggest the vast range of the upheavals which occurred in Russia during and after the revolution as well as the consequences in the 1930s and the resulting situation today (i.e. 1970s). The chaotic and fragmentary nature of the presentation as regards orientation of person, time and place gives expression to the fact that this remains raw material, a material which no human mind can as yet comprehend in its entirety – whether that human mind belong in the fictional world (PE) or in the real world of the Soviet writer and historian (Jurij Trifonov).

Turning from story to discourse, we find a situation no less complicated than that in DNN. In *Starik* five basic narrative situations are to be distinguished and these are complicated in turn by the extended inserts of Asja's quoted letters on the one hand, and the historical documents on the other.[4] The five narrative situations are distinguished as follows:

1. N1: The 'primary' narrator is of a traditionally omniscient type and he introduces PE in the third person describing the situation in 1972: PE's research project, the atmosphere in the dača settlement and the effect of the heatwave. Omniscient narration occurs only sporadically and is never sustained. The omniscient narrator describes PE from without bringing to the reader's attention the symptoms of old age which PE does not admit to himself:

Nakaljajas' obidoj i vdrug zabyv pro pis'mo ot Asi, Pavel Evgrafovič spustilsja vetchoj lesenkoj vniz, namerevajas' vzjat' na kuchne sudki, čtoby idti v sanatorij. (9)

Descriptions of the heat narrated by N1 occasionally manifest a rhetorical style generally absent from *Starik* as well as from Trifonov's works in general. In the following description the heat is described as an apocalyptic force:

Čugun davil, lesa goreli, Moskva gibla v uduš'e, zadychalas' ot sizoj, pepel'noj, buroj, krasnovatoj, černoj – v raznye časy dnja raznogo cveta – mgly, zapolnjavšej ulicy i doma medlenno tekučim, steljaščimsja, kak tuman ili kak jadovityj gaz, oblakom, zapach gari pronikal vsjudu, spastis' bylo nel'zja, obmeleli ozera, reka obnažila kamni, edva sočilas' voda iz kranov, pticy ne peli; žizn' podošla k koncu na ėtoj planete, ubivaemoj solncem. (150–151)

2. N2: Interwoven with the omniscient narration describing PE and his situation from without is the narrative situation which rests on extended use of free indirect speech and describes, in third person, PE's thoughts and emotions from within. This is a narrative situation much used by Trifonov and familiar from his earlier stories such as DŽ and DNN. It ensures that the reader identify with the point of view of the character described and is used by Trifonov to reveal both sympathetic and unsympathetic characters. N1 and N2 modulate from one to another as follows:

Nikogo i ničego ne zamečal Pavel Evgrafovič, dumal o pis'me, i čto-to vdrug nedodumannoe, nedočitannoe do konca neprijatno stalo sverbit'. Čepucha kakaja-to. Čuš' ničtožnaja, frazočka: "Ne ponimaju, počemu napisal imenno ty". Otčego že ne ponimaet? Glupo ne ponimat'. Da i vse pis'mo kakoe-to, prosti gospodi, nemnogo, čto-li, starušeč'e, glupovatoe. (15)

I suggest that the transition between N1 and N2 occurs towards the end of the first sentence so that the verb *sverbit'* is understood to be coloured by PE's own internal thoughts. Both N1 and N2 are orientated towards description of the 1972 situation in Sokolinyj bor; but while N1 focuses on the heatwave and PE's old-age, N2 describes from within PE's annoyance and impatience, particularly with his family and their problems.

3. N3: After ten pages of text the narrative situation switches to first person narration with a marked preference for the present tense. This narrative shift is marked by a typological spacing, used throughout the text to designate segmentation (i.e. there are no chapter divisions). It is PE himself who conducts the first person narration and he uses it to describe the past – specifically the years 1917–1921. Referring to his narration time (1972) PE describes only his inner life, that is the family situation at the dača is barely alluded to in the first person sections:

158

Dni moi vse bolee perelivajutsja v pamjat' ... (15)

On the following page, after another typological spacing, the narration plunges abruptly into the distant past with a stark sense of dramatic present.

Ona ešče dyšit. No mne kažetsja, umerla. (16)

The present tense dominating, first person narration extends for over half the book (128/239pp). It mediates the years of PE's acquaintance with Asja and the Migulin episode in staccato, achronological fragments. In this way narration descends onto another level regarding discourse as well as story. What is story time for N1 and N2 (i.e. 1972) is discourse time for N3. So that notwithstanding the integration of the two levels through the character of PE with his emotional rooting in both, the two levels nevertheless remain distinct. The narrative situations which distinguish them lend to each a distinctive tone and significance.[5]

4. N4: The remaining two narrative situations adopt the heavy use of free indirect speech which defined N2, but this time their character of orientation is another. N4 is orientated towards presenting Kandaurov, a character only indirectly connected with PE. Since the use of free indirect speech is so entirely focused on one specific character, I consider the two sections concerned with Kandaurov to constitute an independent narrative situation, notwithstanding the fact that the technique used is similar to N2. A typical Soviet character, Kandaurov has succeeded in doing well for himself. In his egocentricity he is both callous and immature. Like Glebov in DNN he is a character who one as reader would certainly condemn as immoral were it not for the fact that the extended use of free indirect speech forces a certain amount of identification between reader and character. Kandaurov is presented from within just as is PE and subsequently the obviously sympathetic character Sanja Izvarin (cf N5). It is by lining up different characters with equally persuasive point of view technique that Trifonov breaks down the usual moralising tabulation of good and bad, typical for tendency literature, not least of the socialist realist variety. Thus a narrative situation, just as much as story matter, is used by Trifonov to convey an important part of the novel's theme, namely the fact that all individuals are to a certain extent trapped within their own egocentric circles.

5. N5: The final narrative situation occurs on only one occasion and introduces a character who plays little part in the web of the novel's characters and intrigues. The childhood memories of Sanja Izvarin relating to Sokolinyj bor in the late 1930s are related in the third person in the familiar style of free indirect speech. Sanja is introduced on the pretext of his being a lawful claimant in 1972 to the vacant dača, having lived there as a child. But Sanja's memories of the dača settlement are painful and he declines to put in a claim. Thereby his role in the story is complete. From the point of view of both story and discourse, this section (124–139) is reminiscent of the first

person sections in DNN: not only does it mediate the painful childhood experience of social ostracism and split families at the time of the purges, but it does so with a sense of nostalgia and even lyricism which is lacking in the narrative situation focused on for example Glebov and Kandaurov. The following is a description of Majja:

> Isčezlo lico, zabyt golos, no požiznenno veet kakim-to dunoveniem tepla ot imeni: Majja. Možet li byt' ljubov' v travjanom, motyl'kovom vozraste? U Sani byla. On byl vljublen v volosy. Kogda videl sredi zeleni mel'kanie sijajuščej zolotoj golovy, čuvstvoval ispug i radost', i budto sily pokidali ego: chotelos' upast' i ležat' nepodvižno, kak žuk, pritvorjavšijsja mertvym. (135)

Although not presented in the first person as in DNN, I suggest that the Sanja section is autobiographical. Like the autobiographical sections in DNN it is not integrated into the fictional web of the novel, but stands apart, a comment with a status of its own. From the thematic point of view, that is from the point of view of the historical reconstruction, the interlude with Sanja is significant: on the level of public reconstruction it interpolates between the two story levels – the beginning of the Soviet state (1917–1921) and the present situation (1972) – the black period of the 1930s, a period which grew out of the original revolutionary situation, and which likewise led to present Soviet society. On the level of personal reconstruction, Sanja's memories give new glimpses into the past lives of the 1972 characters, in particular of PE and his family (133–134).[6]

These five narrative situations are tabulated in the figure below.[7] Together they constitute three different kinds of narration:
1. N1 narrates epically from without presenting as fictional fact the situation in 1972 which centers around PE.
2. N2, N4 and N5 effect psychological-realistic description directed towards Soviet society in 1972, presenting from within the thoughts and emotions of three very different characters; PE, Kandaurov and Sanja Izvarin.
3. N3 is used almost exclusively to relate the distant past and presents PE's personal, first person witness.

All the archive material is presented within N3 sections, that is to say that it is mediated and chosen by PE himself. Asja's letters on the other hand are introduced within N1 and N2 sections; their effect is to challenge PE's personal witness (N3), for the material they present gives a view of the distant past which is not congruent with his version.

An interesting structure now emerges which includes both story and discourse levels and which effects the theme of the novel. Each of the main characters plays in turn two roles: on the one hand he is the object of another's discourse, he is presented as someone's story; and on the other he

160

NARRATIVE SITUATION	N 1	N 2	N 3	N 4	N 5
PERSON	3	3	1	3	3
TEMPUS	past	past	present + past	past	past
FREE INDIRECT STYLE	–	+	–	+	+
CHARACTER'S POINT OF VIEW	–	PE	PE	Kandaurov	Sanja Izvarin
STORY CONTENT	PE as old man, PE's research, heatwave	family, neighbours, dača acquisition	revolution, civil war, Asja, Migulin	dača acquisition, trip to Mexico/ mistress, check-up sickness	childhood memories, dača community, purges, social ostracism
PLACE	Sokolinyj bor	Sokolinyj bor	Petersburg/ Don	Sokolinyj bor/ Moscow	Moscow/ Sokolinyj bor
STORY TIME	1972	1972	1917/ 1921	1972	1972/ 1930s
DISCOURSE TIME	0	0	1972	0	0
QUOTATIONS	+ Asja's letters	+ Asja's letters	+ historical documents	–	–
NUMBER OCCASIONS	passim	8	6	2	1
NUMBER PAGES	passim	66	128	21	16

generates his own discourse, introducing another character on the story level:

	DISCOURSE		STORY
N1	Omniscient narrator	presents	PE and other characters
N3	PE	”	Asja (and Migulin)
Letters	Asja	”	Migulin
Documents	Migulin	”	Civil war

For while PE believes himself to be engaged in research on Migulin's role in the civil war, his interest in fact goes via his personal interest in Asja and again through his guilty conscience for having himself betrayed Migulin at the latter's trial. This 'betrayal' is hinted at on several occasions throughout the novel but is finally spelled out by the research student who, after PE's death, arrives at the dača settlement to partake of his material:

> *"Istina v tom, čto dobrejšij Pavel Evgrafovič v dvadcat' pervom na vopros sledovatelja, dopuskaet li on vozmožnost' učastija Migulina v kontrrevolju-cionnom vosstanii, otvetil iskrenne: "Dopuskaju", no, konečno, zabyl ob ètom, ničego udivitel'nogo, togda tak dumali vse ili počti vse, byvajut vremena, kogda istina i vera splavljajutsja nerastoržimo, slitkom, trudno razobrat'sja, gde čto, no my razberemsja".* (240)

The tragedy lies in the fact that PE himself has bewailed the selectivity of human memory on more than one occasion. Above all Asja's inability to see in Migulin any other than the man she loved irks and provokes PE:

> *No počemu ty ne upominaeš', Asja, čto na tom mitinge, kotoryj ty tak podrobno opisyvaeš', on nazyval Kazačij otdel "sobač'im otdelom" i "čer-veobraznym otrostkom slepoj kiški". Èto ego podlinnye slova!* (190)
> *(Vidiš', Asen'ka, èti fakty počemu-to tebe ne zapomnilis'. Da, naša čelove-českaja pamjat' – ešče bolee čudo potomu, čto umeet porazitel'nym obra-zom odno otseivat', a drugoe sochranjat'!)* (191)

On another occasion PE refers to the conflicting witnesses of a group of old men who had met Migulin:

> *Stariki ni čerta ne pomnjat, putajut, vrut, im verit' nel'zja. Neužto i ja? I mne? Ved' otlično pomnju, . . .* (55–56)

In the light of these remarks, the research student's casual dismissal of all PE's laborious truth-searching as being founded on a fatal lapsus of his own is indeed condemning. Whether or not Trifonov is to be considered a truly pessimistic writer depends on whether we interpret the research student's confidant *"no my razberemsja"* as a real guarantee that one day the truth will out, or whether we understand it as an irony on the part of the author who merely implies that a new round of biassed truth-searching has begun.[8]

Multiperspective exposes the selectivity of every individual point of view. The novel's narrative structure, just as much as its story content, has an important part in realising the historical theme. The Reconstruction of History is not only PE's self-avowed mission, but also that of his creator, the writer Jurij Trifonov. In fact every character in the novel is shown in the act of creating his own story, accounting for his own past. In the last resort,

Trifonov's works are not concerned with the establishing of true and false facts, but rather with the way in which human beings go about reconstructing history, the way they relate to the facts of their own lives and the life of the society in which they live.

By way of concluding my analysis I shall return to the initial statements of this article to consider Trifonov's writings in the light of modernism and post-modernism on the one hand, and socialist realism on the other. Thereafter I shall compare the impact of Trifonov's writings to the impact of Čechov's writing at the beginning of the century. Finally I shall consider peculiarities in the position of reader which Trifonov's writing compel.

1. In Trifonov's works objective truth proves elusive and one man's truth gives way to another's with chinese-box effect. On the surface this syndrome might be compared with the modernist and post-modernist eschewing of a final truth position; accordingly the writer begins from a zero position and creates his own truth. This position has led to a situation where, from the point of view of the realistic tradition, art and life stand in a new relationship the one to the other. Art creates reality, it does not merely mediate or reflect the same. In contemporary Russian literature, Andrej Bitov's *Puškinskij dom* provides a superb example of fiction which is obsessed with the status of its own fictionality. In this book the author and writer Bitov intrudes regularly to elaborate on how he might have written his book otherwise: he thereby stresses the arbitrariness of the author's will. The fact of the writer's intrusion may be compared with Trifonov's autobiographical appearances but the motivation and effect is of another order altogether.

At the end of *Puškinskij dom* the hero Leva Odoevcev dies but is subsequently resurrected, not as literary hero, but as real person. As the hero escapes his existence in the past and invades the author's present time, so too he usurps reality itself and threatens the author's position:

"Posle vstuplenija geroja v nastojaščee vremja, sovpadajuščee s avtorskim, možno liš' vjalo sledovat' za geroem, tupo sogljadatajstvovat' (čto, kstati, i osuščestvljat'-to praktičeski nevozmožno) i opisyvat' posledovatel'nost' ego dviženij, kotorye neizvestno kuda vedut, krome kak v sledujuščee mgnovenie nastojaščego – opisyvat' so skorost'ju samoj žizni. Èto bylo by ešče kak-to vozmožno, esli by avtor sam byl geroem svoego proizvedenija i vel svoego roda dnevnik. No avtor želaet žit' svoej žizn'ju, i emu ne očen' lovko stol' nazojlivo presledovat' geroja. I potom, èto beskonečnoe oži-danie, poka geroj proživet stol'ko, čto, obrativšis' v prošloe, otrezok ètot možno budet izložit' so skorost'ju svjaznogo povestvovanija..." (372. The above is taken from an italicised section designated: (KURSIV MOJ – A.B.); see also the section ACHILLES I ČEREPACHA (Otnošenija geroja i avtora), 397–408).

Trifonov's literary works betray nothing of the literary self-consciousness to be found in *Puškinskij dom* or indeed those other postmodernist works which, in trying to erase the distinction between life and literature, in fact provoke the same, as for example the non-fiction novel in post-war USA (Hollowell and Lodge passim; Björling n. 23, 30). Trifonov's erasion of the borderline between life and literature is of a traditional, artless kind and stems from the basic premise of nineteenth century realism that the business of literature is to teach us something about life. Trifonov is a writer in the spirit of Belinskij.

2. Within the context of socialist realism, such a standpoint is in fact innovatory. In the Soviet Union realist literature is distinguished by its tendentious function and the idea that literature mediate reality and thereby enlighten, in the spirit of Belinskij, has been undermined. Socialist realist literature substitutes the IDEAL for the REAL, presents what OUGHT TO BE as though it were what IS. Readers of Soviet and anti-Soviet literature alike have come to expect that a work of literature – even if it relies on a reading between the lines – will reveal, on the level of the implied author, a clear set of moral values by which the characters and events of the work are to be judged, a scale of desirability, of good and bad.

As I have attempted to show, Trifonov does not offer a clear scale of moral values so that it is difficult for his readers to play the normal game of condemning and condoning. For if Trifonov the author does not condone a character like Kandaurov, then neither does he condemn him. On the one hand he reveals Kandaurov from within, and on the other he shows the old man PE, despite his basic will to be honest, to be guilty of emotions and behaviour which are similar in kind to those of Kandaurov.[9] This attitude of social tolerance seems to irk Soviet and anti-Soviet readers alike. The following judgements are typical for Soviet critics:

> *"Ju. Trifonov predel'no točen v vypolnenii svoich zadač, kogda izobražaet vnutrennij mir geroev, kogda vgljadyvaetsja v sokrovennye, tajnye dviženija duši. I on byvaet ne vsegda točen, a podčas i protivorečiv, kogda zatragivaet takie aspekty čelovečeskich otnošenij, takie kollizii, kotorye po samomu svoemu charakteru trebujut uglublennosti v obščestvenno značimuju problematiku."* (Sinel'nikov 61)

> *"No golos avtora ne osmelilsja, esli možno tak vyrazit'sja, otkryto vystupit' rjadom s golosom Glebova v kul'minacionnych scenach. On predpočel ustranit'sja voobšče. I éto prinizilo obščij smysl povesti."* (Kožinov 46)

Shneidman gives a convenient orientation in Soviet responses towards Trifonov's work. Shneidman makes two other interesting points: firstly he quotes Trifonov as claiming "that his art is in the tradition of nineteenth-century classical literature" (343); and secondly he refers to the fact that Trifonov "resents the fact that most western critics overemphasize the social aspects of his work at the expense of the literary qualities of his art." (347. Cf Håstad 35 who quotes Trifonov's attitude to the censor.)

3. Trifonov's position with regard to the Soviet literary situation may be compared with Čechov's situation at the turn of the century. Both Čechov and Trifonov refrain from drawing tendentious conclusions from the realistic material which they present (Shneidman 343). But there lies a significant difference in the fact that Čechov, at the turn of the century, could still take a clearly positivistic standpoint and assume the possibility of describing reality objectively. Trifonov, after seventy years of post-Einstein civilization, and fifty years of Soviet power, faces the dilema that objective truth eludes human understanding. This, according to my interpretation is precisely what his fiction is concerned with. And yet Trifonov is at heart still a positivist; he reiterates time and again the necessity of persuing the search for truth: *Značit, vot radi čego nužno starat'sja, vot čto vykapyvat' iz zemli – pravdu, vo vsech ee vidach (Prodolžitel'nye uroki, 508); . . . osnovnaja ideja – napisat' pravdu, kakoj by žestokoj i strannoj ona ni byla. A pravda ved' prigoditsja – kogda-nibud' . . . (Otblesk kostra 55); Ob''jasnil kak mog: tem, čto istinoj ne delilsja. Choronil dlja sebja. A istina, kak mne kažetsja, dorogoj kandidat medicinskich nauk, ved' tol'ko togda dragocennost', kogda dlja vsech . . .* (PE, *Starik* 231). In a head-on truth confrontation with some old men, witnesses of the incidents surrounding Migulin, PE says: *A ja, govorju, udivljajus' tomu, čto est' ljudi, kotorym soveršenno ne interesna istorija svoego naroda.* (47) The will and the passion for truth, for history, are prevalent, but inability to ride above personal bias and suppression of the truth proves to be a fatal stumbling block. I believe this goes for the characters in Trifonov's works, for Trifonov himself as writer (Björling 25), and, by implication, for each and every human being. There is only one possible vehicle for truth, and that is a human mind: truth does not reside in archives and documents, but in the human mind which composes, the human mind which interprets, those documents. The question of objective reality and its availability accordingly has a different significance for the two writers, Čechov and Trifonov, notwithstanding their common lack of tendentiousness.

4. On the one hand I have attempted to analyse the peculiar narrative technique which is adopted in *Starik,* and on the other I have pointed to the novel's theme as having to do with the need for human beings, in private as well as in society, to reconstruct their past truthfully. In conjunction these two aspects have an interesting effect on the position of the reader, in *Starik* as well as in Trifonov's mature work on the whole.

In the constellation: *historical writer – implied author – narrator – characters – narratee – implied reader – historical reader*, the position of implied author and accordingly its counterpart implied reader are deliberately played down (Björling). This is measured by the difficulty for the historical reader of identifying an adequate implied reader position, in other words of discerning the authorial message, the moral of the story. In realist literature, and even more so in socialist realist literature, the implied author plays a game of collusion with the implied reader: he sets up, so to speak, a set of moral assumptions which he expects his reader to abide by. Thereafter the implied author and the implied reader walk hand in hand in shared approval and disapproval of the characters and events portrayed.

In Trifonov's work, lack of narrative collusion is not the mark of postmodernist fiction, but rather the opposite. Far from insisting on the fictionality of the worlds portrayed in his stories, Trifonov renders their fictionality immaterial. For the undermining of the implied author position has the effect of easing up the distinction between the fictional world and the real world. In literature with a clearly defined authorial position, the reader is able to take shelter, conveniently knowing himself to be in collusion with the implied author and therefore automatically on the "right" side. The participation of the reader is in such cases relatively passive; as a historical person he sits apart from the fictional world and he is not called upon to share the moral responsibility for the conclusions presented to him. But in Trifonov's mature works, the distinction between fictional world and real world is not so clearly defined: the distance to the events portrayed which is automatically achieved through the presence of a strong implied author position, is reduced in these works. The reader stands as it were face to face with characters and events unmediated. Hereby moral onus is transferred onto the reader: he has actively to engage in sorting out the good and the bad of the story, to choose sides, to draw moral conclusions. At the same time the lack of distance between the historical reader and the fictional world portrayed undermines the hierarchy of the fictional communication. Historical writer and historical reader are drawn into the web of the text and inculpated by it. The problem effected through the characters (how to overcome personal bias and reconstruct true history) rubs off on writer and reader alike. Trifonov through his autobiographical inserts, above all in DNN, "admits" his own personal bias. Similarly the reader must ask himself whether or not he too is guilty of betraying the truth of the past in one way or another.[10]

Implicit in Trifonov's work is the idea of the writer as bearing the responsibility of a historian, one whose business it is to transcend his personal bias of the moment in order to guarantee his country a truthful picture of its past. At the same time Trifonov shows that even serious investigators of the past (the anonymous first person narrator in DNN, PE in *Starik*) suffer from human prejudices which obstruct a truly objective vision. Further: the narrative technique used in these stories has the effect of widening the circle of those who play a historical role, to include the reader.

166

Each and every human being bears the responsibility of being truthful to his past, both as private individual and as member of a society. Trifonov's message can therefore be interpreted as a call to the individual – not least in Soviet society – to share the business of being the conscience of the nation. It is not only those in power who are responsible, and not only the writers, but each and every citizen.

NOTES

1. Compare for example Milan Kundera's *Žert* and *Kniha smíchu a zapomnění;* in the latter the fatal disposition to erase the past is indicated in the title and interwoven as the most persistent theme of the work. It is interesting to note a superficial similarity between Trifonov's *Dom na naberežnoj* and Kundera's *Žert.* The intrigues of the two novels both revolve around the reconstruction of an act of political consequence commited by the hero in his youth. In both cases memory – the hero's as well as the other characters' involved – turns out to be an unreliable witness to the truth. Furthermore the novels share two significant features of narrative technique: on the one hand multiperspective, and on the other achronology and complexity of fictional time. In his analysis of *Žert*, Doležel shows precisely these two narrative features to be the means by which the novel emancipates itself from the realist tradition and establishes itself firstly as a modern novel and secondly as an ideological novel (cf. pre-realist traditions), a novel that is which bypasses the "preference for homogeneous narrative ... established in the realist schools of fiction." (113) Doležel analyses "the basic feature of fictional time in the *The Joke* /which/ is quite typical for modern fiction: the proper chronology of events is done away with and replaced by achronological confrontations and clashes of narrated events occurring on different time-planes, in different time-periods." (121) I note that this description would apply aptly to DNN. The intermingling of fiction and autobiography which is a prominent feature of DNN finds its parallel in Kundera's *Kniha smíchu i zapomnění.* Yet despite common themes and common devices of narrrative technique Trifonov's and Kundera's writings must be placed at opposite ends of the pole realist/ non-realist fiction.

2. *Otblesk kostra* contains several comments relating to history, time and the human accounting of the same. These comments illumine and confirm these matters as a constant theme in Trifonov's work. Concerning reports from the February revolution Trifonov writes: *Čem bolee prochodilo vremeni, tem rassuditel'nee stanovilis' ocenki.* (57) An aphorism *(lučšij chudožnik – vremja)* is given a twist in the comment which admits that while time has rendered more beautiful both Tacitus' and Puškin's words, it has also been ready to transform into art that which was not art originally. (58)

3. In DNN the narrative revolves around a situation in the summer of 1972, a situation which in turn refers back to two crucial periods in the lives of the heroes, namely 1938 and 1947. It is interesting to note that both DNN and *Starik* have the first story level set in the heatwave of 1972, when the woods around Moscow were ravaged by forest fires. Natural catastrophe signals the fact that something is wrong in the lives of the characters. Their attempts to delve into the past are accompanied by a manifestation in nature.

4. Since I myself have not had access to the relevant archives, I do not here take issue with the authenticity of the documents quoted in the text. I presume that Trifonov's research into the life of his father (*Otblesk kostra*) provides the groundwork from which the documents, perhaps paraphrased, are taken. In any case real historical figures are introduced into the fictional web of the story, see for example the reference to a meeting between Migulin and Lenin (Vladimir Il'ič) and the conversation which took place between them. (173)

5. Cf a Czech novel mentioned by Doležel: "In the novel *Follow the Green Light (Jdi za zeleným světlem,* 1956) by Edvard Valenta, linear structure is associated with a specific

organization of the fictional time: the 'contemporary' action is narrated in the *Er*-form, whereas the 'prehistory' is rendered in the *Ich*-form." (114)

6. To a certain extent of course both N4 and N5 are interspersed with the more neutral comments of N1. An interesting distinction can be noted here: In the two sections orientated towards Kandaurov the use of free indirect speech is heavy and it is hard to find any passage where the neutrality and distance of N1 is indisputable. In the description of the love scene the use of free indirect speech is subdued, e.g.: *Ona povernulas' i smotrela na nego s neprosochšimi slezami na glazach, no s poistine učeničeskim ljubopytstvom. A on smotrel na nee s toskoj* ... (121) But the perspective could even here be attributed to Kandaurov himself, albeit moved to sincerity in the act of leaving his mistress. In the section orientated towards Sanja Izvarin, on the other hand, the use of free indirect speech is milder. This has to do with Izvarin's specific status as a character in the novel. His story is self-contained and apart: firstly he does not put in his lawful claim for the vacant dača, and secondly his memories refer back to the late 1930s, which period is otherwise not illuminated in the novel. The relatively mild use of free indirect speech, notwithstanding the fact that the passage is entirely orientated toward Izvarin's point of view, indicates a corresponding lack of distance between the various posts in the narrative hierarchy (author/narrator/character). In the last resort I believe it indicates an identity between Izvarin and the voice behind all the narrators, namely the writer Trifonov. See for example the description of the history of the dača settlement at Sokolinyj bor. (132–133)

7. My figures are based on a segmentation of the text into 18 narrative sections, which for the most part are indicated typographically by a double spacing. From 177 onwards, however, the alternation of narrative sections becomes less well-defined: more abrupt on the one hand, and without typographical indication on the other. Thus an N2 section begins on 215 and modulates gradually into a page-long section under N3. This in turn is broken off on 221 (*otvet iz VCIKa* ...) and narration continues under N2 (*Pavel Evgrafovič dlja čego-to vzjal so stola papku* ...). On 222 first person narration (N3) suddenly intrudes mid-paragraph (*Pomnju davjaščee ožidanie ... Jansonu dvadcat' vosem'* ...). On the thematic level these narrative switches indicate that PE is no longer able to keep the present and the past distinct; sitting on the veranda talking to Polina about his work on Migulin, PE slips inadvertently back into the past situation. Significantly the final N3 section (227–239) describes PE's visit to Asja, i.e. its story is set in 1972; PE has finally lost his sense of orientation in time. (Note: the N2 section, 222–227, includes a short orientation towards PE's son, Ruslan. The final section, 239–240 describes briefly the situation after PE's death.)

8. In *Otblesk kostra* Trifonov considers his grandmother's (T.A. Slovatinskaja's) memoirs. He is disturbed that these memoirs, written in 1957 and referring to the 1930s, bear no witness to the grief and tragedy to her own family caused by Stalin:
Čto ž èto: neponimanie istorii, slepaja vera ili poluvekovaja privyčka k konspiracii, zastavljav-šaja konspirirovat' samuju strašnuju bol'? Trifonov mentions his own doubts about including these memoirs and his final decision to do so – *potomu čto osnovnaja ideja – napisat' pravdu, kakoj by žestokoj i strannoj ona ni byla. A pravda ved' prigoditsja – kogda-nibud'* ... (55)

9. In his article "*Vybirat', rešat'sja, žertvovat'* ", Trifonov replies to the critical allegations that his stories contain so few positive heroes. Discussing *Obmen* he explains that he is not interested in primitively categorising characters as 'negative' and 'positive', since this cannot be done in real life. Trifonov wishes to create literary characters who are representative of real people. Thus he does not condemn Lena as a person, but only those traits of hers which he abhors and which are common to many real people. These remarks find an echo in *Starik* when PE says: *Vot ètogo ne ponimaju: černye da belye, mrakobesy da angely. I nikogo poseredke. A poseredke-to vse. I ot mraka, i ot besov, i ot angelov v každom* ... (47–48)

10. Cf note 9. In "*Vybirat', rešat'sja, žertvovat'* " Trifonov testifies to his desire directly to involve the reader in the problems with which his stories are concerned. It is only by

presenting characters who are true to life (= *pravdivye*, cf the article *"Vozvraščenie k 'Prosus' "*) that the writer can hope to affect the reader: *I zadača, možet byt', v tom i sostoit, čtoby pomogat' – slabymi silami literatury – odnomu svojstvu preodolevat' drugoe, čeloveku menjat'sja k lučšemu.* (544–545) The article ends with a touching story concerning the son of a friend of Trifonov's, who at first was unable to go through with the family plan of joining households with his grandmother: *"Ja pročital povest' "Obmen" i ne mogu s"ezžat'sja s babuškoj. Nu ne mogu"*, and Trifonov continues: *Delo v tom, čtob čitatel' zadumalsja – chotja by na minutu. Èto grandiozno mnogo.* (545)

BIBLIOGRAPHY

Bitov, Andrej, *Puškinskij dom*, Ann Arbor, Michigan 1978.

Björling, Fiona, "Jurij Trifonov's *Dom na naberežnoj:* Fiction or Autobiography?", *Biografi og Værk = Svantevit* IX-I, Aarhus 1983, pp 9–30.

Chatman, Seymour, *Story and Discourse. Narrative Structure in Fiction and Film*, Ithaca etc. 1978.

Doležel, Lubomír, " 'Narrative symposium' in Milan Kundera's *The Joke"*, *Narrative Modes in Czech Literature*, Toronto 1973, pp. 112–125.

Frank, Joseph, "Spatial Form in Modern Literature", *The Widening Gyre*, New Brunswick 1963.

Hollowell, John, *Fact and Fiction. The New Journalism and the Nonfiction Novel*, Chapel Hill 1977.

Håstad, Disa, *Samtal med Sovjetiska Författare*, Stockholm 1979.

Kožinov, V. V., *"Problema avtora i put' pisatelja"*, *Kontekst* 1977, pp 23–47.

Kundera, Milan, *Žert*, Prague 1967.

Kundera, Milan, *Kniha smíchu a zapomnění*, Toronto 1981.

Lodge, David, *The Modes of Modern Writing*, London 1977.

Sinel'nikov, M., *"Ispytanie povsednevnost'ju: nekotorye itogi"*, *Voprosy literatury* 1972/2, pp 46–62.

Shneidman, N. N., "Jurij Trifonov and the Ethics of Contemporary Soviet City life", *Canadian Slavonic Papers*, 19, 1977, pp. 335–351.

Trifonov, Jurij, *Otblesk kostra*, Moscow 1966.

Trifonov, Jurij, *Povesti*, Moscow 1978 (*Dom na naberežnoj*).

Trifonov, Jurij, *Izbrannye proizvedenija*, TI-TII, Moscow 1978 (TI, *Neterpenie*; TII, *Obmen; Predvaritel'nye itogi; Dolgoe proščanie; Drugaja žizn'; Prodolžitel'nye uroki; Vybirat', rešat'sja, žertvovat'; Vozvraščenie k* "Prosus").

Trifonov, Jurij, *Starik*, Moscow 1979.

169

Lars Kleberg (Stockholm)

Poland Reconsidered: Fredrik Böök's Polish Travelogues

One of the first and certainly the most influential Swedish writer to visit Poland in the beginning of our century was Fredrik Böök. Professor of History of Literature at the University of Lund between 1920 and 1924, member of the Swedish Academy since 1922 and leading literary columnist in *Svenska Dagbladet,* Fredrik Böök was a critic of outstanding influence for almost a half-century.[1] Between the wars, whenever Böök's essays appeared in the daily newspaper of the conservative Swedish cultural elite, they had a significant influence on the circulation.[2] The judgement of Böök was decisive for the career of Swedish and foreign writers alike. "He was", as one Swedish observer says, "the leading authority of the educated bourgeois Sweden who with a mere wink of his hand could decide over the life or death of a book on the book store counters".[3] Böök's importance for the 1924 Nobel prize being awarded to Władysław Reymont and not to Stefan Żeromski (as was expected by many observers) is well-known.[4]

Fredrik Böök's powerful intervention against Żeromski and in favour of Reymont is just one example of his paramount influence in Swedish literary affairs at the time. The underlying motivation for the intervention was certainly not a matter of literary taste only. Böök was a passionate Germanophile all his life, and his negative appraisal of Żeromski's *Wiatr od morza (Wind from the Sea)* was conditioned by his German-oriented mode of reception. In fact, it seems that Böök never read Żeromski's novel but only the German reactions to it.[5]

Fredrik Böök visited Poland for the first time in spring 1916, i.e. during the first part of World War I when Warsaw found itself under German rule. The writer was impressed by the "triumphs of the German administration" after the Russians had retired. The future of Poland and Polish culture, Böök concluded in his book of travel sketches published in fall 1916, could only be guaranteed by Germany as a defense against Russian domination.[6] The defeat of Germany and the resurrection of independent Poland in 1918 obviously forced Böök to reconsider this conception.

When Fredrik Böök made an extensive tour through Europe in 1922, reflected in the collection of travel sketches *Journey to Constantinople through Central Europe in Spring 1922,* his explicit purpose was to make a

170

diagnosis of Europe after the fall of the German and Austro-Hungarian empires.[7] The book is an excellent example of the right wing critic's journalism. Böök's Odyssey went through Denmark, Germany, Austria, Czechoslovakia, Poland, Hungary, Rumania, Turkey and Serbia. Every time he encounters a new (non-German) country, the writer has an opportunity to reflect on the pleasure of being a Swedish conservative of rural origin. The feeling of South Swedish superiority only fades when Böök encounters officers in uniform: whatever country they represent, his admiration is almost lyrical.

Confronted with the various new states built on the ruins of the former empires, Böök remains faithful to his utopia of a united Central Europe under German or at least German-speaking leadership. German culture, according to Böök, is the backbone of Europe and the only defense against Russian barbarianism, now in addition communist, as well as against Roman decadence. Needless to say, Jews are constantly suspected to be agents of either or both evil forces. There is only one positive effect to be seen from the German-Austrian defeat in World War I, according to Böök 1922:

By destroying the dynasties of Hohenzollern and Habsburg this peace treaty /i.e. Versailles – L.K./ has cleared away the two main obstacles for the German expansion in Central Europe, for the cultural and political hegemony which seems inevitable when one considers the position of the almost hundred millions /i.e. German-speaking people – L.K./ in the heart of Europe. As long as the Hohenzollerns governed, the /.../ idea of the unification of Central Europe was impossible, because it would have been interpreted and perceived as a manifestation of feudal dynastic politics. As long as Habsburg held together the bundle of small nationalities, the idea was utopian. Now the ground is cleared, and fifty or hundred years from now the Germans will perhaps no longer carry the stigma of the Versailles peace.[8]

As one perceptive reader of Böök's travelogue quietly noted in the margin of my copy of the book, "one had only to wait for another sixteen years", that is until Munich 1938. The quotation from Böök is illuminating, not only because it demonstrates his Germanophile attitude, but also because it has a clearly Hegelian ring, based on the concept of the evolution of the *Weltgeist*.

Böök's travel sketches are, in view of the ideological subtext, astonishingly concrete, vivid and witty. Böök was undoubtedly one of the best reporters we have had in this country. The seventy pages devoted to Poland and Polish matters in *Journey to Constantinople*, covering visits to Poznań, Gdańsk (which Böök of course prefers to call Danzig) and Kraków, undoubtedly give a dynamic picture of social life and ideological tensions in Poland shortly after independence. The political situation in the republic is certainly better analyzed by the well-known Slavist translator and critic Alfred Jensen, whose travel sketches appeared under the title *On the Ruins of the Romanovs and the Habsburgs* one year earlier, in 1921.[9] But Fredrik Böök was by far the better writer of the two. A comparison with Georg Brandes, Böök's implied opponent and superior in almost all respects, is in fact not out of place. While Brandes in his famous book *Polish Impressions* of 1888[10] stayed in Russian-governed Warsaw, our local anti-Brandes now avoids the capital and stops in Poznań and Kraków, which had been until recently ruled by Germany and Austria, respectively. While Brandes wrote extensively on Polish Romantic literature, Böök's literary points of reference are now the realists Żeromski and Reymont. Brandes kept strictly to the literary and intellectual salons; Böök eagerly turns to the rural landscape and to the historical monuments which evoke the memory of earlier Polish-Swedish contacts.

In the Poznań area, Böök obviously finds himself especially at ease. He correctly identifies Poland as an agricultural country and Polish culture as one based on the contradiction between aristocracy and gentry on the one hand and peasantry on the other. His two visits to the surroundings of Poznań are in this respect especially interesting. The first visit is a pilgrimage to Jankowice, the former estate of count Lars von Engeström, the famous Swedish minister who married Rozalia Chłapowska and died at Jankowice in 1826.[11] Böök finds Jankowice almost void of concrete traces of the Swedish and Polish patriot but full of memories. The present mistress willingly tells the story of the magnificent park and the well of Dorothea, named after von Engeström's youngest daughter. We do not learn, however, who the present – 1922 – owners of Jankowice are. The Swedish guest then pays a visit to the nearby village of Ceradz, where he finds – as one can still do today – the family chapel of the von Engeström family. Böök notes that he found that the chapel could not be opened, because the Catholic priest had just ran away with the local midwife and the presbytery was closed in expectation of an investigation commission. So Fredrik Böök could only inspect the mausoleum through a little window from which, nevertheless, the tombs and the bust of Lars von Engeström could be seen. In the chapel are also buried the son, Gustaw Stanisław, who died as a Russian officer, a career strongly disapproved of by the family, the grandson Wawrzyniec and the grandgrandson Edmund, both important propagators of Swedish and Scandinavian culture in Poland. The surprising anecdote about the adventurous parish priest can be confirmed: visiting the church of Ceradz Kościelny in 1985, I myself read on the table of notable dates in the history of the parish, that in 1922 a new priest had to be appointed after a vaguely described incident in the parish.

The other estate Böök visits is definitely more impressive than the anonymously ruled Jankowice. The estate of Winnagóra flourishes – and "not

172

only", Böök says, "because it is situated in the former German province of Posen, the healthiest, best cultivated and most prospering third of the new state".[12] Winnagóra was given to the legendary general Dombrowski by Napoleon. At the time of Böök's visit it is both a private museum of patriotic relics – "a Polish national pantheon" – and an expansive agricultural enterprise where the farmhands live "better than most other Polish peasants" although strict patriarchal relations are still in force.[13]

Böök's sketches from the Poznań area are full of freshness and poignant observations from the point of view of a conservative son of Skåne. Taken only as such, however, they would not deserve more attention than any other travelogue by the conservative or anti-Russian Swedish writers who made pilgrimages to Poland, the unstable "safeguard of the Western world" between the wars (Essén, Serner, Rogberg et. al.).[14] In 1940, however, professor Böök published one of his recurrent ventures into belles lettres, a collection of short stories entitled *The Dancing Girl of Aleppo,* where the thematic material of 1922 is skillfully transformed into a fictional narrative, much more ambiguous than the political statements of the author.[15]

The four novellas contained in *The Dancing Girl of Aleppo* are all based on the contrast and confrontation of Swedish and foreign, or other variations on the opposition between *ours* and *theirs*, *we* and *they*. The thematic material is taken from Böök's travels or from his encounters with East Europeans in Sweden; the basic structure of the novellas is the *embedded narrative.* The dancing girl of the title story is not the daughter of the Syrian city but a mysterious Russian emigré girl, who dances the *kolomyjka* in a Aleppo night club. She tries to persuade a Swedish businessman to take her with him up to the North and the birch trees to which she longs to return, but the bewildered Swede escapes. The second story, entitled "A Russian Decameron", relates the author's encounter with a young Baltic nobleman who tells strange episodes from his life in Russia. The Baltic storyteller returns in the fourth and final novella, "The Brothers of Riga". The third part of the book, which is the one that interests us here, is entitled "Hamlet in Poland".

"Hamlet in Poland" is a fictitious diary of a Swedish engineer of simple manners and common sense, who carries some autobiographical traits. The engineer comes to Poznań in 1923 in order to sell sugar-mill installations to Count Czapski, the owner of the prospering estate Lipowagora (sic). The diary-writing engineer tells us about his encounters with the Polish businessmen in Poznań, who try to bribe him (unsuccessfully, of course) but also with the distinguished Czapski family. The efficiency and faultlessness of count Ignacy are, however, counter-balanced by the ardent Catholic countess, and by the melancholic son, count Wladislaw (sic). Through an article in the Swedish press (we easily recognize Böök's own travel sketches of 1922), the engineer has learned about the Jankowice estate and the von Engeström family story. He asks the Czapskis to help him pay a visit to the neighbour. This idea, although eagerly supported by young count Wladislaw, meets with obstacles. Jankowice is simply a place one does not frequent.

The countess Twardowska, whose late husband had inherited Jankowice from the last of the von Engeströms, has recently commited a horrible mésalliance and consequently been excluded from good company.

This last moment is indeed in accordance with historic realities, although they were *not* revealed by Böök in his 1922 travelogue. Countess Zofia Zamoyska, married to a Mr Kielecki, owner of Jankowice, had in fact remarried after her husband's death and become the spouse of her own chief steward, a certain Mr Dziewulski. In his novella, however, Böök changed some of these facts, about which he must have been informed when visiting Poznań and Jankowice, in order to construct a *fictional microcosm* representing post-World War I Poland as he saw it.

Thus, the widowed countess of Jankowice in "Hamlet in Poland" has married her own chief steward. But his name is not Dziewulski but Josef Mandelstam: he is thus not only a servant but also a Jew. This double mésalliance of course excluded the countess of Jankowice, née Zamoyska, from society. The Swedish engineer's insisting on going to Jankowice, however, pleases the young count Wladislaw enormously. As a matter of fact, his late mother (the present mistress of Lipowagora is his step-mother) was the sister of of the now excommunicated countess of Jankowice and Wladislaw suffers from the lack of contact with his beloved aunt. Through the initiative of the foreign guest, he is now able to visit her at Jankowice. The person who is most pleased with the visit, which is prolonged to a series of visits to other estates as well, is of course Josef Mandelstam, for whom all doors of the Polish gentry are closed. Mandelstam not only uses the Swedish guest as a vehicle for intrusion in the Polish homes. He also breaks into the sealed presbytery, from whom the amorous priest has fled with his mistress, the midwife, and finds the key to the von Engeström chapel. Thus, the Swedish engineer manages to see the inside of the chapel (i.e. more than Böök himself did) before leaving Poznań and Poland with a signed contract for the sugar-mill installation in his pocket.

But why "Hamlet in Poland"? Just as the other novellas, the fictitious diary contains an embedded narrative, and this is the story of the enigmatic young count. Having made friends with the foreigner, Wladislaw Czapski tells the sad story of his aunt, now married to her Jewish chief steward, and also reveals his own story. Educated in the German army he has served his own country in the war against Russia in 1920. He is pro-German and a patriot at the same time. But he is also closely related, he tells the Swedish quest, to the disdained Jewish people. Wladislaw, who neither wants to be a country squire nor an officer, has studied jurisprudence with Isak Feldman, *Privatdozent,* who has become his mentor and only friend. Now the old count has demanded that Wladislaw break his relations with Feldman, since they would obviously hamper the diplomatic career which his father has prepared for him. Feldman, who has lived in a little house on Lipowagora for years, is to be sent away. How shall I, says Wladislaw with tears in his eyes, be able to behave like a scoundrel towards my friend, like a scoundrel no better than that Josef Mandelstam who has married my aunt in order to get hold of her heritage?

Isak Feldman is however not only Wladislaw's only friend. He is also a historian, whose views on the fate of Europe make up a kind of doubly embedded narrative, retold by Wladislaw in his monologue and reported in the fictitious diary. Space does not allow us here to discuss in detail the geopolitical and historiosophical concept of Wladislaw's friend, which he, Wladislaw – the Polish Hamlet – also has made his own. The essence of this concept is a resigned acceptance of the cruel laws of history. Poland is situated, by fate, between Germany and Russia; neither is better than the other. In his final conversation with the Swedish engineer, Wladislaw exclaims:

> It is not wisdom, it is not reason, it is not good faith that forges the fate of the nations, that creates the history of the world. No. It is hate and violence, it is extacies and intoxications, it is heroism and unreason, in the nations and in the individuals. /. . ./ The men of fate are marching, Isak Feldman used to say, the wars and the revolutions have cleaned the way for them – the play can begin, the real, great drama. It is called world history. Clio is a whore.[16]

Isak Feldman's desillusioned conception of history, which by its mere weight seems to be close to the author's voice, is not immediately compatible with the Germanophile Hegelian idealism of Fredrik Böök who visited Poland in 1922. And yet the Jewish *Privatdozent,* through his student count Wladislaw, is a strong voice in the composition of the narrative. As we know from other sources, professor Böök's views had changed during the 1930's in a pessimistic materialistic direction, what did not, however, stop him from eagerly supporting Hitler's Germany.[17] But a literary text does not equal the political opinions of its author. "Hamlet in Poland", then, is a *transformation* of the thematic material from the travel sketch of 1922, according to the rules of ambiguity of *narrative prose.* The dynamic, playful oppositions between the good estate and the bad estate, the lonely foreigner and the enigmatic Polish Hamlet, between the villainous Jew and the wise Jew, between the Swedish observer and the Jewish observer etc. become the basic tenets of the story.

However, the changes from 1922 to 1940 are not only intratextual, not only a matter of "belletrization of facts". Fredrik Böök's own worldview had also, in the meantime, become more desillusioned, not to say cynical, in its acceptance of *Das Wirkliche,* of the march of the *Weltgeist.* And last but not least – the entire historical context was radically different in 1940. This is also reflected in the text of the novella. The fictitious diary of the Swedish engineer in Poznań is dated 1923. But it ends with a postscriptum, carrying the date of December 24, 1939. The engineer, now in Stockholm of course, has met a Swedish colleague, who has managed to escape from the burning Warsaw.

From him he learns about the fate of count Wladislaw. He was killed in action at the beginning of the war at Bromberg (Bydgoszcz), that is, while fighting the Germans. About the fate of his mentor and friend Isak Feldman we can only guess, because Feldman, expelled from Lipowagora, emigrated to Moscow already during the engineer's visit to Poland in 1923. Thus, Fredrik Böök's Polish Hamlet, and probably his Jewish mentor as well, are both destroyed by the ruthless march of History, as is Poland itself.

To sum up: in my opinion, Fredrik Böök's Polish travelogues, taken together make up a quite unusual manifestation of a controversial writer's work and of Swedish reaction to Polish reality between the wars.

NOTES

1. Tomas Forser's dissertation, *Bööks 30-tal. En studie i ideologi,* Stockholm 1976, is an excellent study which, however, focusses mainly on the contradictory ideological evolution of the critic and his relation to Hegelianism, Marxism, and Nazism.
2. Ivar Andersson, *Svenska Dagbladets historia,* 1, Stockholm 1960, p. 204.
3. Erik Hj. Linder, quoted in *Svenskt litteraturlexikon,* Lund 1964, p. 74.
4. Zenon Ciesielski, *Zbliżenia skandynawsko-polskie,* Gdańsk 1972, p. 157–160; Nils Åke Nilsson, "Sienkiewicz and Reymont in Sweden", in *Swedish-Polish Literary Contacts,* ed. Nils Åke Nilsson, Stockholm 1979, p. 107–114.
5. Nilsson, op. cit., p. 113.
6. *Resa till Tyskland och Polen 1916,* Stockholm 1916.
7. *Resa till Konstantinopel genom Mellan-Europa våren 1922,* Stockholm 1922.
8. ibid., p. 350.
9. Alfred Jensen, *På Romanovs och Habsburgs ruiner. Kulturpolitiska nutidsstudier,* Stockholm 1921.
10. Georg Brandes, *Indtryk fra Polen,* København 1888.
11. On the Engeström family, cf. Ciesielski, op. cit., p. 9–18.
12. Böök, op. cit. p. 179.
13. Ibid., p. 184.
14. Cf. Kazimierz Ślaski, *Tysiaclecie polsko-skandynawskich stosunków kulturalnych,* Wrocław etc. 1977, whose enumeration, however, for some reason or other, leaves out Böök.
15. *Danskerskan i Aleppo,* Stockholm 1940.
16. Ibid., p. 157–158.
17. Forser, op. cit., p. 139 ff.

Thomas G. Winner

Text and Context in the Aesthetic Theories of Jan Mukařovský

Questions focal today in literary scholarship that were already being explored in the 1930s by the Prague Linguistic Circle include the issues of aesthetic axiology, and the dynamic character of aesthetic structures in cultural context which lead directly to the notion of intertextuality, although the term was not used by the Prague Linguistic Circle. Among the notable searchers in these areas was Jan Mukařovský (1891–1974). Unfortunately, the theoretical and applied studies of the Prague group, most of which were written in Czech, were not translated until the 1970s, with some notable exceptions,[1] and so remained largely unknown to scholars outside of Czechoslovakia. This isolation of the Prague scholars during their years of greatest florescence is astonishing, since the blossoming Czech artistic avantgarde movement of the 1920s and 1930s proceeded in close contact with groups abroad, especially France, Germany, and Russia. For example, there were close connections between the Czech and French surrealist movements, and between the German Bauhaus and the Czech modern architectural tradition.

While the language barrier prevented the thought of the Prague scholars from penetrating significantly the intellectual life outside of Czechoslovakia, this obstacle did not exist in the opposite direction, and the Prague scholars were well versed in such traditions as Husserlian Phenomenology, Russian Formalism, as well as the artistic avantgarde of all of Europe. But the work of the Prague scholars, especially of those members of the circle who were Czech,[2] was also part of the Czech scientific past, especially of Herbartian aesthetics and the Czech Formist movement, whose most important representative, Otakar Zich (1887–1933), was Mukařovský's teacher and his predecessor in the chair of aesthetics at the Charles University in Prague (cf. Winner 1986).

Mukařovský's most important contribution in the thirties was his elaboration of a theory of the sign character of art and its individual textual realizations; but he did not come to this immediately. Mukařovský's teacher, Otakar Zich, had been especially interested in formal aspects of art such as its phonic structures, leading his pupil Mukařovský to investigate concepts of the Russian Formalists. While Mukařovský accepted the Russian Formalist

177

view of the immanent character of the work of verbal art early in his career, he soon revised this view, finding the Formalists' indifference to context inadequate.

Mukařovský soon became vitally interested in problems of mutual relations between different artistic texts, going so far as to consider interrelations across modalities, such as links between verbal and visual texts. He also raised the issue of the interrelation between artistic and non-artistic texts. Finally, he considered the manyfold interconnections of all texts in culture. Culture became for him a complex of interrelated structures, a position in which he laid the basis for the later development of a semiotics of culture (cf. I. Portis Winner 1982) especially among the Moscow-Tartu school in the Soviet Union.

Mukařovský's theoretical departures were based on various questions and assumptions concerning the key concept of the aesthetic function, the aesthetic norm, and aesthetic value (cf. Mukařovský 1936). In the area of pragmatics, where Mukařovský departed most dramatically from the Russian Formalists, questions turned to the relation between the artistic text, its creator and its audience, since Mukařovský held that all artistic modalities share a history of uninterrupted dialogues between the author of a work and all those who, through the generations, are the receivers of the work. Here was raised for the first time the issue of artistic reception, foreshadowing theories of the Konstanz school today.

In the following pages we shall consider in more detail certain of the focal issues in Mukařovský's work.

1. *The question of immanence of the artistic work*

The concept of the immanence of the artistic text was focal in the work of the Russian Formalists, and was most consistently advanced by Viktor Šklovskij (cf. Šklovskij 1925:5–6). It was later independently held by the Anglo-American New Critics who were apparently not acquainted with Šklovskij's work. The validity of the position of immanence was first questioned in Jakobson's and Tynjanov's 1928 manifesto about the relation between literature and language (Jakobson and Tynjanov 1928), which denied the existence of closed systems as well as the separation of diachrony and synchrony on which the view of the closed system rested. At this time, Mukařovský was still under the spell of the Formalist position. Thus in his preface to his study of the Czech Romantic writer Karel Hyněk Mácha, he described the work of verbal art as

a phenomenon *sui generis* which is freed from all relation with other series of phenomena ... For example, the relation of the work of art to its creator, or its relation to external reality ... (Mukařovský 1928:9).

By 1934 Mukařovský had revised his position. Thus in his preface to the Czech translation of Šklovskij's *Theory of Prose* (1934b), he rejected the idea of the work of art as isolated from other literary and extraliterary series. In another essay of the same year he suggested that while art and society each had their own laws of development, their interrelations were dialectic, hence dynamic and changeable (1934c:168).

2. *Literature and natural language*

Mukařovský always saw the literary text as complexly related to the system of the natural language in which it is written, and this system, in turn, as closely linked to the system of cultural values of a given time of writing as well as to values of the past. He regarded social language levels in a literary text as not reduceable to social structure. Rather, he conceived them as shaped by transformations, oppositions and mediation. In an essay of 1940, Mukařovský gives an example in discussing Jakobson's treatment of the relation between language and the verbal arts (Jakobson 1926:52–3). The example is A. V. Jung's translation into Czech of Puškin's line *Burja mgloju nebo kroet* as *Bouře mlhou nebe krýje,* which Jakobson had criticized, although the translation follows the original exactly in meter, rhythm, word stress and word boundaries, as well as semantically. Mukařovský asked why it was that the Czech version does not capture the flavor of the Russian original, and finds the answer in the rhythm of the line. Since Russian is characterized by free word stress, the coincidence of word boundary and the regular first syllable stress in Puškin's line is extremely rare, and thus sounds fresh and unusual. On the other hand, in Czech, where the coincidence of word stress and word boundary is normative and thus unmarked, such a coincidence does not convey the freshness and newness it has in Russian; rather it is redundant. Thus the context of the natural language, its rules and relations, play a part in the creation of a poetic line and affect its poetic value (1940).

3. *Function, norm, and value*

Among Mukařovský's best known contributions to poetics are his notions of function, norm and value and their complex relations. He first touched on this question in an essay in 1929 (1929), and returned to it frequently. His important 1936 monograph, *Aesthetic Function, Norm, and Value as Social Facts* (1936) is devoted to these issues, departing from the perspectives of the 1929 *Theses* of the Prague Linguistic Circle. Important stances of the *Theses* had been that language is a polyfunctional system in which different functions are related in changeable hierarchies, one function always being in a dominant position in relation to the other functions active in a given message. The aesthetic function, seen as autotelic and thus directed towards the expression as such, is only one of several functions. When it is discerned as dominant in a text, that text is perceived as aesthetic. An artistic work where the aesthetic function is dominant from the point of view of the author, can, due to contextual pragmatic circumstances, be decoded by a receiver in such a way that another function may be propelled into the dominant position. Thus, under certain circumstances, a novel may be read as an historic document in which the referential and not the aesthetic function is dominant. And, vice versa, a communication encoded as dominantly referential can be received as an aesthetic text. Thus the boundary between the aesthetic and the non-aesthetic is not firm but it is relative, unsteady, and dependent on temporal, spatial, and general cultural contexts.

Value is the measure of the success of a work in fulfilling its dominant function. But how this may be translated into practice or tested is never made clear. In addition, value is based on teleological considerations: a communication is evaluated in a certain way because author and/or receiver(s) imbue it with a certain orientation, in other words, see it as governed by a certain function. In considering the relation between value, the aesthetic function and the intention of the receiver, Mukařovský presents an example where different interpretations of the sentence "Evening is setting in" are compared (1938:157–58). If we regard this sentence as a referential communication, then we consider its truth value. It could be a grammatical example without relation to the immediate material situation. If, however, we see it as a poetic quotation, we attend to the message first and only secondarily to other values, including those attendant to the context, even if such a context must be imagined where we do not know the text from which the line is cited.

Turning now to the question of the aesthetic norm with which the aesthetic function is always in dynamic relations, Mukařovský considered the dynamics of the aesthetic function. Since the creative artist can always choose between normativity and anti-normativity, in the most extreme cases we can envisage a totally normative, thus redundant, text, or a totally anti-normative creation which is thus not decodable. However, aesthetic value always depends on some degree of artistic norm violation, since such violations increase tensions between what is expected and what happens, and between norms and anti-norms, and thus increase the artistic information of a text. Mukařovský compares the aesthetic norms for art to grammatical norms in non-aesthetic verbal texts in natural language. The difference is that the aesthetic norm is not binding as are grammatical norms. While no norms are seen as having the force of a law (since norms are essentially only conventions), aesthetic norms are more changeable than other types of norms. Norms are grounded on cultural perspectives, on such fundamental perceptions as space and time. This is later dealt with by semiotics of culture as

180

developed by the Moscow-Tartu school, but not by Mukařovský who simply described norms as unstable regulative energy principles (1937).

4. *The semiotic perspective*

The most significant contribution of Mukařovský in poetics and general aesthetics was the elaboration of a semiotic perspective. Mukařovský and Roman Jakobson were looking for a non-reductive, interrelated and dynamic view of all texts both in the verbal arts and in non-artistic verbal constructs. While Saussure's semiotic concepts were fundamental here, the Saussurean concept of the static synchronic slice was not accepted. (Peirce was not known at all in Prague during the 1930s.) However, Saussure's notion of the inseparability of the expressive and semantic strata of the sign, which he described as being related like the two sides of a sheet of paper, seemed to Mukařovský and his group to be the first scientific basis for a serious critique of the Formalist's concept of the primacy of form over meaning. Saussure's concept of the arbitrary relation of the sign to its object was not completely accepted by the Prague group, although a theoretical taxonomy of signs had to await Jakobson's introduction of Peircean classifications in the 1960s, and his later elaborations upon these such as the concept of introversive semiosis and that of the artifice. But this was too late in Mukařovský's life, and he never concerned himself with these new views. Mukařovský and Jakobson saw the artistic sign as polysemic, attracting the attention of the receiver to its own structuration and thereby conveying diffuse meanings. Mukařovský delved into the complex questions of the meaning of artistic texts. Meaning involved the multifarious relations of the work of art to its producer and its recipients; the intricate mutual relations between art, culture, and society; interrelations of different artistic modalities and genres; and the problem of the evolution of artistic series. All these issues, which are aspects of meaning and are still vital today, were raised in Mukařovský's influential lecture presented to the 1934 International Philosophical Congress in Prague (1934a). The essay contained the following main points: 1. Every psychological act which exceeds the boundaries of individual consciousness becomes by this a communication and hence a sign, defined as a perceptible reality, which is connected to a reality which exists outside its boundaries and to which it points and which it evokes. 2. A work of art is thus a sign, since it mediates between members of a collective. 3. The work of art, as an autonomous sign, can not be identified with the point of view of the author or with its psychological effect on the receiver in the sense of traditional psychological aesthetics. 4. The work of art as a communicative semiotic phenomenon can not be reduced to its material shape, to its *Dinglichkeit.* This is so because this *Dinglichkeit,* which corresponds to Saussure's *signifiant,* is also part and parcel of the meaning of the sign which exists in the collective consciousness. By implication, this view contradicts Saussure's split between *signifiant* and *signifié* because, although Saussure held that they could not be separated, he also saw them as independent entities which could not exchange their qualities. 5. The semantic aspect of a work of verbal art is inextricably bound to the linguistic system. But the work of art is not reduceable to the linguistic system with which it stands in an indefinite relationship.

Mukařovský foreshadowed many problems at the center of discussions in aesthetic semiotics today: Inevitably, in his interest in meaning, Mukařovský was led to the area of the pragmatics of art which had been bracketed by the Russian Formalists. As early as 1934, in his lecture to the Prague Linguistic Circle (1934d), Mukařovský spoke of the roles of author and receiver of the work of art as unstable and mutually interchangeable. For example, he wrote, the author of a text can temporarily place himself in the position of a receiver. Thus a painter may step back from his easel to study his painting from a distance, or a composer may play a few bars of his composition to reflect upon how it sounds. Thus the structure of a work arises through an interaction of the producer and the recipients of the evolving text. Mukařovský, long before Morris, saw the three domains, syntactics, semantics, and pragmatics as highly interpenetrative and as never isolated from each other.

5. *Culture*

To Mukařovský culture was a kind of hypostructure, a "structure of structures". He saw all structures in a culture as dynamically and hierarchically interrelated, and dominance in the hierarchy as constantly shifting. Mukařovský described the hypostructure of culture in the following way in his 1934 preface to the Czech translation of Šklovskij's *Theory of Prose:*

> The sphere of social phenomena to which literature belongs is composed of many series (structures), each of which has its autonomous development. These are, for example, science, politics, economics, social stratification, language, morality, religion, and so forth. Despite their autonomy, however, the individual series influence each other. If we take any of them as a starting point in order to study its functions, that is, its effects upon other series, it will appear that even these functions create a structure, that they are constantly regrouping and counterbalancing each other. Therefore none of them must be made dominant *a priori* over the others, for the most various shifts occur in their interrelations ... (1934b:349)

Later Mukařovský stressed particularly the dynamic relational shifts between the various structures composing culture, between texts within the same art, between different artistic modalities, and between art and non-art:

182

It becomes clear that if we want to understand the evolution of a certain branch of the arts, we must examine the art and its problematics in relation with the other arts ... Furthermore, art is one of the branches of culture, and culture, as a whole, in turn, forms a structure, the individual elements of which (for instance art, science, politics) are in mutual, complex, and historically changeable relations to each other. However, the structure of culture as a whole is again not an isolated phenomenon, for the basic source of its dynamics is the movement of society ... (1946–7:47–50).

Thus, as we suggested at the beginning of this paper, literary texts are not only part of their own evolving series in which texts stand in complex relations to texts, but also part of a larger artistic series including music or painting, for instance. Here was laid the basis for a new and broader kind of non-reductive comparative study in which the work of art is seen as autonomous, and yet intricately related to a complex context. In his statement about the dynamic hierarchical relations of the various series, Mukařovský anticipated the interesting contemporary discussions about the temporary dominance of one art over the other, such as for instance the dominant position of music in the late nineteenth century and that of the visual arts in the early years of the European avantgarde.

Mukařovský's theories were a beginning. Certainly they laid a theoretical basis for contemporary studies of intertextuality. They also brought to the fore the issue of the interrelation of different artistic modalities, as for example the primarily linear verbal arts and music as compared to the primarily non-linear arts (the visual arts), a focal interest to scholars in contemporary aesthetic semiotics. However, explorations are still in their infancy, and many areas suggested by Mukařovský are in need of greater scrutiny. For example, the problem of the relations of artistic to non-artistic series and the nature of the artistic function needs to be further refined.

In general, Mukařovský foresaw and suggested most of the fields of inquiry that occupy modern poetics, no longer satisfied with traditional comparative studies of "influences", reductionism, the inherently closed systems of literary hermeneutics, or pure formalism. Rather, the quest is for meaning and aesthetic value derived from a vast area of interrelation of structures as perceived by author and audience in a broadly conceived cultural context.

NOTES

A somewhat different version of this essay has just appeared in German: "Nachwort," Jan Mukařovský, *Schriften zur Ästhetik, Kunsttheorie und Poetik.* Herausgegeben und übersetzt von Holger Siegel. Tübingen (Günther Narr Verlag), 1986.
1. Much of the credit for the translations of Prague school works belongs to Ladislav Matejka, who gave the pioneering impetus to these translations in his *Michigan Slavic Contributions,*

Michigan Slavic Publications, and elsewhere, and to Peter Steiner and John Burbank, who issued a monumental two volume edition of translations of Mukařovský's work under the imprint of Yale University Press. Of course, a limited number of significant Prague publications were written in languages more accessible to Western scholars in the 1930s. Thus a limited number of Jakobson's essays were written in German, and Mukařovský wrote a few essays in French (cf. 1934a and 1938). And of course, Jakobson began writing in English after his arrival in the United States in the early 1940s.
2. As is known, several prominent members of the Prague Linguistic Circle were Russian, notably, Jakobson, Bogatyrev, and Trubetzkoy.

REFERENCES
Jakobson, Roman, 1926. *Základy českého verše*. Praha.
Jakobson, Roman (with Jurij Tynjanov), 1928. Problemy izučenija literatury i jazyka. *Novyj LEF*. Moscow.
Mukařovský, Jan, 1928. Machův Máj. Estetická studie. Praha. Cited from Mukařovský, 1948. Vol. III.
— 1929. O současné poetice. *Plán* 7:387–97.
— 1934a. "L'art comme fait sémiologique." Actes du VIIIe Congrès international de philosophie à Prague 2–7 septembre 1934. Republished in Czech as "Umění jako sémiotický fakt," in Mukařovský 1966.
— 1934b. K českému překladu Šklovského Teorie prózy. *Čin* (Praha). VI. Cited from Mukařovský, 1948, I:5–6.
— 1934c. Polákova Vznešenost přírody. Pokus o rozbor a vývojové zařadění básnické struktury. *Sborník filologický*. X. Praha.
— 1934d. Záměrnost a nezáměrnost v umění. Cited from Mukařovský 1966:89–108.
— 1936. Aesthetic Function, Norm, and Value as Social Facts. English translation by Mark Suino. Ann Arbor (= Michigan Slavic Publications). Originally published as *Estetická funkce, norma a hodnota jako sociální fakty*. Praha (Borový).
— 1937. Estetická norma. *Travaux du IXe Congrès International de Philosophie*. Paris. Cited from 1966.
— 1938. La dénomination poétique et la fonction esthétique de la langue. *Actes du IVe Congrès International des Linguistes*. Cited from 1948, I.
— 1940. O jazyce básnickém. *Slovo a slovesnost* VI:113–45. Cited from 1948, I:129-53.
— 1946–47. Problémy individua v umění. University lecture. Printed from manuscript in 1971:49–84.
— 1948. *Kapitoly z české poetiky*. Praha. Vols. I–III.
— 1966. *Studie z estetiky*. Praha. Odeon.
— 1971. *Cestami poetiky a estetiky*. Praha. Čsl. spisovatel.
Prague Linguistic Circle, 1929. Téze předložené prvému sjezdu slovanských filologů v Praze. Reprinted IN *Základy pražské jazykovědné školy*, edited by Josef Vachek. Praha (Academia).
Šklovskij, Viktor, 1925. *O teorii prozy*. Moscow.
Winner, Irene Portis, 1982. The State of the Art of Semiotics of Culture. Monographs of the Toronto Semiotic Circle. Toronto. Victoria University.
Winner, Thomas G., (1986). "Otakar Zich as a Precursor of Prague Literary Structuralism and Semiotics, With Special Reference to Dramaturgy." IN *Poetics Today*, and Karl Eimermacher, ed., *Die slawischen literarischen Theorien*. (Forthcoming.)

Aleksandar Flaker

Krleža's Culinary Flemishness

> "Thus, within the Flemishness, paintings of feasts, regardless of their introduction into the bourgeois everyday life [orig. *bytovizacija*] still retain, though to a lesser degree, their positive, popular-festive nature, which explains the power and attractiveness of these images in Flemish art." (M. Bachtin, Tvorčestvo Fransua Rablė i narodnaja kul'tura srednevekov'ja i renessansa, Moskva 1965, p. 328.)

In his comparison of Krleža's *Balade Petrice Kerempuha* (The Ballads of Petrica Kerempuh) to the poetry of Eduard Bagrickij, Russian poet from Odessa, Zdravko Malić calls one of the chapters of his study *I Consume, Therefore I Am,* and, consequently, dubs the "point of view from which the world starts to assume the shape of an object of culinary interest" *"pantagruelism"*, after Rabelais, of course, but without reference to Bachtin's chapter *Piršestvennye obrazy u Rablė* (The Feasting Scenes of Rabelais). "Pantagruelism" is seen as a "caricature of every spiritual interpretation of the world, its materialization in the most drastic form, and thus highly characteristic of the Ulenspigelian tradition"[1]. Malić gives numerous examples of the "pantagruelism" of *Balade* on the level of style: comparisons and metaphors in which the first member is a man and his action while the second is an "object of culinary interest", but – we might add – from socially varied menus.

As for "objects of culinary interest" in the *Ballads*, the most representative is certainly the *Keglovichiana*, in which we find an entire catalogue of edibles and scenes of feasting prepared in heaven for the late Count Keglovič. It is observed from the wings like a "heavenly paradise" by "Imbro Skunkač, chicken filcher and thief" (M. Krleža, *Balade Petrice Kerempuha*, Ljubljana 1936, p. 39) who, on earth, "pecked at corn with the turkeys and the chickens" (51), but who is then taken from the heavenly feast and thrown into hell. The point of view in this "Ballad" is that of the people, a Kerempuh-Ulenspigel point of view, and the *popular* source of the main motif is confirmed by a Russian, somewhat earlier example. In 1923, the Soviet "proletarian" and folk poet Demjan Bednyj, relegated today to the margins of literature, published his sacrilegious text *Kak 14 divizija v raj šla* (How the 14th Division Went to Paradise), in which the "Lord's virgin" Malanja must wait at the gates to heaven while the entire 14th division, after having stumbled on a mine field (in the World War), enters – with the generals and priests at its head, of course. The *cook*, in the very rear, takes pity on God-fearing Malanja. Bednyj's "folk buffonade" was performed on the Moscow music hall stage in 1932[2]. In both works, Krleža's as well as Bednyj's, those who ruled, and (in Krleža) gorged themselves on earth, are the ones who enter heaven, while simple people are outsiders there. In Krleža's work there is an emphasis on the "particular connection of food to death and hell"[3], significant also in the folk rituals of "karmine" (among the Catholics) and "daća" (among the Orthodox) – in South-Slavic areas post-funeral feasts equivalent to a wake – treated by Mickiewicz as well in the beginning of his dramatic text *Dziady* (Forefathers' Eve): a "feast with many dishes, beverages and fruit, to which the spirits of the deceased are invited"[4]. In the imagination of Mickiewicz's folk "fiddler" heaven is also filled with edibles ("doughnuts, pasta, milk and fruit and strawberries") which goes together with the basic refrain of this part of the text where the chorus points out that "he who has never tasted bitterness" on earth "will never taste sweetness in heaven"[5] (to be stressed here are the concepts of 'bitterness' and 'sweetness', belonging to the sense of taste!). In Krleža's text the reverse applies, for with a glance from "below", Krleža claims that whoever has tasted of pleasure on earth will taste of it in heaven as well; heaven becomes an extension of earthly space, undergoing a "drastic materialization".

Krleža's text (the *Balade* in general) is based on a duality in the folk picturesque, dedicated to feasts and food: the representatives of the ruling classes eat differently from ordinary people, who within the categories of their own diet dream more of food than eat: the rulers of life, in distinction from the oral tradition (Kraljević Marko in the poetry of the Serbian or Croatian language), "are not feasting in the name of the people, but at the expense of the people and to the people's detriment", but – with Bachtin – it is important to add that "the bread stolen from the people does not cease to be bread, wine is always good, even when the Pope is drinking it. *Wine and bread* have their logic, their *truth*, their *irresistible urge for an abundance that spilleth over ...*"[6]

It is important to stress, when discussing the "Flemishness" of Krleža's *Balade* and in particular Bruegel as their artistic model (or more correctly one of the artistic models), that the abundance and variety of edibles enumerated by Krleža is not paralleled in Bruegel's work. In the painting *The Fight Between Carnival and Lent* (1559), a picture Krleža had seen at the Viennese *Kunsthistorisches Museum*, the prince of the carnival rides on a barrel, his weapon is a skewer with a pig's head on it, and his shield – a ham impaled on the barrel; and in another painting from the Viennese museum, *Peasant Wedding* (1568) wine is poured in the foreground and dishes are carried, but the edibles on the table are hidden by human figures, Bruegel is indeed modest in his portrayal of feasts in comparison to Krleža. Only

Schlaraffenland (1567, *Alte Pinakothek*, Munich) has that "irresistible urge for abundance" that Bachtin speaks of, although its heaps of porridge, roasted suckling pig and fences made out of sausages are principally disputed as sinful. Sometimes Krleža is closer to Bosch than to Bruegel, as in the phantasmagorical folk grotesque *Scherzo* with its search for the "god of Bacchus" and a "Pauline friar with a tuft like 'mlinci' " (mlinci – a popular pasta dish), a friar who concludes that "of all literary chines, the most healthy are the sweet pheasant chines!" (26–28), in *Sanoborska* (Samobor Ballad) with its series of grotesque "images" in which pigs lay "eggs" and little "suckling pigs" crow (29), or in *Komendrijaši* (The Buffoons) with its popular-grotesque parallels drawn between people and edibles (a "baron" is compared to "štrukli" (cheese filled dumplings), "beans", "marinade", "goat", "ox", "tomato" and "lemon", 100).

However, Krleža's culinary Flemishness can be seen not only in *Balade*, where it is based on the cultural models of the 16th century, it also comes forth in the novels. Although we will be dealing here with examples from the last of his novels – *Zastave* (Banners), it should not be forgotten that the opening scene of the novel *Na rubu pameti* (On the Edge of Reason) is the chapter *Dinner Party in Domaćinski's Vineyard*, and that the act of the "domestic" capitalist who produces chamber pots for Persia, namely his murder of a peasant – an act that brings forth the indignation of the narrator and thus furthers the plot – is committed in the "defense of his own Riesling" (M. Krleža, *Povratak Filipa Latinovicza. Na rubu pameti*, Zagreb 1973, p. 207). The novel in which Krleža attempts to generalize the question of the mechanism of power in the states of Central Europe bears the characteristic title of *Banket u Blitvi* (Banquet in Blithuania), stressing in the title itself that it is a text in which there will be *conversations* between representatives of governments and those strata that attend "banquets". Although the "banquet" here is not a chronotope of the novel, it is important to note that the title indicates a "feast as the essential framework of wise words, speeches, merry truth" for "between words and feasts there is an underlying bond" rooted in the "antique symposion"[7]. The banquet is not, of course, a symposion, but a place where statesmen and politicians on the highest level meet with representatives of (official) culture and art, and such a gathering, with its inevitable disputes and mutual setting of accounts, is the fundamental principle of the novel's organization with its dialogue and soliloquy sections. In this connection one of the basic chronotopes of *The Brothers Karamazov* deserves mention, a tavern in which Ivan and Alyosha meet to converse on God "with fish soup, tea and jam", a situation Krleža clearly used as a model in the novel *In extremis*.[9] The "tavern", as Šklovskij established, is a locus of "geometric intersection of individual lines of the novel", it was "patented with purely literary goals" by Cervantes, and, early on, this "literary tavern"[10] became one of the frequent chronotopes of the

187

novel, as for instance in Stendhal's and Balzac's novels, where the characters meet in the parlor-salon; the importance of the salon is signalled by the fact that "there dialogues develop which acquire a special meaning in the novel, they disclose the characters, their 'ideas' and 'passions' "[11]. Krleža is relying on this tradition in the compositional pattern of *Zastave*, even if the novel is "dispersive" in many aspects, making plot and composition less important[12]. Organized formally and compositionally around the basic chronotope "path", as a projection of the metaphor "path of life" that "permits (the novel) to witness everyday life [*byt*] broadly"[13], *Zastave* underlines already in the headings of its chapters the meaning of the chronotope of "tavern", or, in Krleža's work, restaurant or "parlor"; in any case the *table*, around which the characters of the novel gather to lead dialogues, is where Krleža's Flemishness comes to the foreground. In the following chapter headings the "table" is emphasized: *Dinner in Honor of Mr. Stevan Mihailović Gruić* (M. Krleža, *Zastave* 1, Sarajevo 1979. This is the edition that I will refer to, with volume number, and where there are quotes, I will include page number), *Dinner at Old Kamráth's* (2), *A Silver Anniversary at the Jurjaveški Home* (4), *Dinner at the Grand Hotel* (5). Furthermore we encounter within the novel restaurants, inns, bodegas or (Hungarian) *csárdas* as *loci* facilitating dialogic interaction, lovers' trysts or as places of social characterization. Some of these *loci* can be identified. The Budapest "restaurant, reserved for the select of the presidential cream" is called "At King Matthias's" (see *Zastave* 1, Zagreb 1967, p. 168) in the first editions, but even under the name "Hungarian Crown" (Sarajevo edition 1, 144) it is recognizable as the *Mátyás Pince*; a comparison of newspapers with "Gerbaud's Profiterollen" (1, 193) invokes the famous Budapest Konditorei, and Kamilo meets with Kamráth at an "evening at Gundel's", a restaurant renowned even today in Budapest, where they "serve Balaton fish, bedewed with a yellow mist of butter from steaming, silver casseroles" (2, 293). There Kamilo looks at the "dark blue, tempestuous landscape on his platter: slender, chivalric towers, dark ominous Scottish fortresses on a misty shore" (2, 295), clearly an allusion to the famous Wedgewood china!

The vision of the first of the *loci* is marked iconic:

> Under age-old attics and with rustic, crudely hewn tables, with a floor of red, varnished brick, in the dim glow of orange lampshades, everything was patriarchal, everything was an imitation of a Renaissance tavern from the old days of Corvinus, with servants in tails, silver casseroles, crayfish, Balaton *fogas* in jelly, Martell, Courvoisier, "Szürkebarát" from Tokai, Transdanubian "Bikaver", rabbit, venison, game in general, pheasants, mayonnaise, English meat, grilled Danubian sturgeon, pineapple bowl, and of all these Kamilo chose the stuffed pepper (1, 144–145).

This is certainly not Grosz's satiric vision of a scene from the opulent Berlin restaurants of the 1920s, so esteemed by Krleža, but a catalogue of edibles, situated in the framework of an architectural "imitation" of the European Renaissance, and disputed within Kamilo's opposition to his "illustrious" father by his choice of a popular dish, and thus transferred into a culture to which the main character of the novel belongs, by genealogy alone. A similar catalogue of "rich" food will appear later in Kamilo's "half-dream" in which the *locus* of a meeting will become the "store window of a delicatessen bodega" on the corner of *Váci street* "with mixed pickles, Italian mortadella and salsas, with salmon and pickled herrings, with French cheeses and Cointreau", and then the *intérieur* with "pink pastries in marzipan, the pink glaze of punch and cream, with a large, massive cake in the middle of the dining room, as massive as a mill wheel" (2, 82–83), while in *Dinner at Old Kamráth's* the iconic model of these enumerations discloses the Budapest culinary opulence, with *game, fish* and *cheeses* in the focus of attention. In fact, we learn little of the menu of this "dinner" which actually serves only as a framework motivating the dialogue. All that we know is that "black coffee with Chartreuse was served" (2, 55) at the end, while at the beginning of the chapter, attention is focused on the iconography of the chronotope, i.e. on

> the still gloomy and funereal mood that reigned in the dark, heavy oak-panelled *Dutch* dining room, decorated with equally dark *still-lifes*, on which the *oily, pink fish* on *silver platters* stood out from *brown molasses*, and with slaughtered *corpses of furry rabbits*, on which *veinal blood* had clotted in the open wounds (my italics, A.F., 2, 42).

This classic Dutch *still-life*, familiar from the paintings of Snyder or Weenix, exhales death, as an accompaniment to food, and in this same vein of painting bloody corpses we furthermore find the "Quartered Ox" by Krleža's friend Petar Dobrović (1936, Dobrović Gallery, Belgrade) painted at the same Mlini, near Dubrovnik, where the *Portrait of Miroslav Krleža* (1938, same gallery) was made. "Dutch Settecento Stilleben" appears in an intérieur still later, but with the correction that these "still-lifes are not Dutch, but Dalmatian, probably by a provincial Venetian master – in the countryside, in our cities, there are many such things" (5, 148).

In the chapter *The Call of the Emperor's Trumpet* in which Kamilo becomes "an Austrian recruit" (2, 209) in the World War, a *locus* of farewell is the Hungarian *csárda* which appears as a popular inn on the outskirts of Budapest, on the Danube, with "sterlets on the grill and fisherman's soup, and fresh Sombor cheese, and wine thick and dark as ox blood" ("Bikaver" wine, in which the comparison with ox blood is included in the name). However, amid the "oily mass of fish meat" Kamilo recalls the "lordly" Budapest drinks of "cherries in rum of Mistress de Szemera, and cognac in a café, and Tokai and Kirsch and Armagnac" (2, 205). "In the maelstrom of images" which passes through his mind culinary motifs from other cultural regions appear, arosen by the memory of his already dead Serbian friend: faith in life, as faith in the "innocent joys of life, in Smederevo wine, grilled bulls' balls, good coffee, Turkish demi-tasse, Turkish coffee pot, decasyllable, gypsy violin" (2, 203) – and it should be pointed out that in this inner monologue the culinary motifs are placed in one and the same category as the decasyllable, the "heroic" verse meter of the oral epics mythologized in this culture.

In the chapter *Dinner in honor of Mr. Stevan Mihailović Gruić*, dedicated to the Serbian-Croatian dispute on the eve of the World War, the "dinner" in the Zagreb "salon" is only a framework for the conversation, but this framework explains why the "retired Serbian minister" (1, 337) is characterized with the aid of elements of popular culinary culture. Stevča returns from his military service "with a huge Užice smoked ham, two kilos of caviar from Kladovo, and a 5-liter jug of juniper brandy" (1, 342). He recalls in culinary concepts the Serbian army in the Balkan war: "heaps of amorphous masses of mutton wallow in the mud, skewers with pilfered rolls are turned here and there, juniper brandy is downed" (1, 344). Here contrast is also made to food from official banquets in the Kingdom of Serbia – "surprise with cognac and crêpes flambée", on the other hand, and popular dishes, "kaimak cheese from Užice or čevapčići" (352) on the other. The opposition between two cultural regions is designated sarcastically in culinary terms: "bloody liver" stands for the Serbian and "a silver casserole" (1, 363) for the Croatian side.

At the above-mentioned dinner with father and son in a Budapest restaurant, within the exposition of the novel, Emerički *senior*, representative of the traditional values, complains of the Croatian cuisine:

> We don't even know, brother, how to cook, no, not even how to cook, and all we can think about are some ideas, we've been ruined by Viennese cuisine, the devil knows why we've forgotten how to cook, a little of the old Croatian cuisine has held on in Varaždin, but that is disappearing by and by, I remember when I was there in secondary school, those turkeys, those sausages, those roast sirloins, buckwheat patties and mlinci pasta, those were dishes, and it is all disappearing, the good traditions are melting like snow, and that is our modern time (. . .).
> (1, 145)

In accordance with such a description, the chapters that bring the characters of the novel to the *table* in Croatian *loci* do not abound in information on "Croatian cuisine". The chapter *A Silver Anniversary at the Jurjaveški Home* is a real "banquet" chapter[14] which collects the social elite around the table, and where the exposition of the chapter is dedicated to the culinary content of the "jubilee" table – a description of a dinner that

> began with richly served caviar, on ice slabs, and progressed from turtle soup and chilled crayfish in their shells with mayonnaise to turkey with mlinci, only to continue with hunting-style venison and end with hot carnival doughnuts (. . .) (4, 8)

However, there is later mention of "a roast bearing the famous name of Archduchess Stephanie, served at Glavački's with a spicy mushroom sauce" (4, 10), "a burgundy of the Čazma prevost", comparable to (Hungarian) Tokai wine (4, 11), and at the end of the chapter, there appears even a "sizeable gilthead fish" and a "suckling pig", half of which is devoured by one of the guests "with head and brains" (4, 53); but this table is no longer presented as a *tableau*. The menu is composed of elements of representative European dining, but also of the "national" dishes of northern (turkey with mlinci) and maritime (gilthead fish) Croatia.

Dinner at the Grand Hotel, conveying the nervous mood of the three characters in an "agonizing, crepuscular and deadly game",[15] gathered around the table, introduces titbits from the hotel menu ("vol-au-vent of chicken livers with a mushroom sauce", "asparagus soup", "perch", "Odeschalchi's burgundy", 5, 81) in an argument with the waiter; "huge silver platters full of fish" (82) appear on the table once more, with associations to "various tasty specialties" of the domestic cuisine, but this is only a "dinner of friends, where all *pretend* to dine, though no one feels like eating" (84), and where the tension among the three persons grows when they are to select the "salon wine" (5, 89); coffee is finally served, and Kamilo Emerički, by now Mirković, remains with Ana Borongay, and a "bottle of Armagnac" (5, 97). It is worth remarking, however, how at the culmination of this tragic situation of the two loners, Ana, a poetess of Hungarian modernism, who has already embraced fashionable Cocteau and Picasso (5, 150), drinks a "mysterious mixture of pale green absinthe" only to turn, a moment later, to the "coloristic perfection of her already slightly *wilted self-portrait*" (5, 1-4-105, my italics, A. F.). These emphatically ironic details point to Picasso's painting *La buveuse d'absinthe* (1902, The Hermitage, Leningrad), all the more so since Ana, with the pathetic, tragic exclamation of "ah, my dear mask", intended for herself, turns to the waiter to continue the rounds of Armagnac.

And it is only at the end of the novel, in the chapter *Finale*, when Ana and Kamilo descend to the "abyss" of their love affair, in the brutal atmosphere of a tavern on the outskirts of the town, on the banks of the Sava (recall the csárda on the Danube!) where the waiter offers "gypsy-like concoctions", that a local, more plebeian menu appears – "Presswurst or fine, home-made head cheese with warm corn bread", and "for dinner: štrukli, blood sausage, devenica sausage, garlic sausage, pečenica sausage", and then "à la carte: crambambuli, Glühwein, pancakes with rum, barley, chicken soup, hot brandy, Eier-Cognac, Butellenwein, as you wish, and if you would have a French liqueur as well, then 'Heidsieck' and 'Veuve Cliquot' " (5, 168).

This is no longer the Dutch *Settecento-Stilleben*, nor is it Picasso's melancholic woman with absinthe and a siphon; this brothel-like atmosphere is thick with the "sweetly sickening smells" of spices, and dishes are not served in "silver casseroles", but instead "clay jugs" with "peasant grog" are put on the table (5, 17). This opposition of popular dishes to the predominantly high class "banquet" meals in *Zastave*, Krleža's last novel, is strictly functional and related to the pivotal events of the novel.

In *Zastave* the bearers of the textual structure are not ordinary people, and hence there is no "pantagruelism"; it has been replaced by a "Flemishness", shaped iconically only in the Budapest scenes. It appears, however, in the novel in which the grotesquely caricatured Grosz-like "noble" world is confronted with a peasant and a poacher, to whom "man is a gut with nine windows" (*Na rubu pameti*, 335), a peasant who farts in pantagruelian style, dreaming of a mother who baked štrukli (cheese pie) and cooked "tripe" that peasants "can't afford, God bless 'em" (335), or of "slabs of bacon" (343), and where someone steals the officers' chocolate rations, someone who is named after the most filling Zagorje dish – Valent Žganec (žganci – corn mush), a name that reminds us of the important place that food occupies in Krleža's texts, and of its very varied functions.

NOTES:

1. Z. Malić, *U krugu Balada Petrice Kerempuha. Krleža i Bagricki.* In: *Hrvatska književnost prema evropskim književnostima.* Zagreb 1970, pp. 562–563; English translation – *Within the Compass of 'The Ballads of Petrica Kerempuh'. Krleža and Bagritskii.* In: *Comparative Studies in Croatian Literature.* Zagreb 1980, p. 559.
2. Cf. afterword by Fritz Mierau in: D. Bedny, *Gedichte und Fabeln.* Leipzig 1974, p. 144.
3. M. Bachtin, *Tvorčestvo Fransua Rablé i narodnaja kul'tura srednevekov'ja i renessansa.* Moskva 1965, p. 327.
4. A. Mickiewicz, *Dzieła poetyckie.* Nowogródek (4th ed.) 1933, p. 128.
5. Ibid., p. 130.
6. M. Bachtin, op. cit. pp. 316–317.
7. Ibid., p. 308.
8. Vučković stresses the many "*banquet* situations" in Krleža, with examples from *Gospoda Glembajevi, Povratak Filipa Latinovicza,* the novels *Na rubu pameti* and *Banket u Blitvi,* the short story *Sprovod u Theresienburgu.* He attributes the frequency of such scenes to the "influence of Strindberg" and to the writer's personal experience as described in the text *Pijana novembarska noć 1918.* R. Vučković, *Krležini romani.* Radio-Sarajevo, XIII, 1985, 50, p. 323.
9. Cf. A. Flaker, *Književne poredbe.* Zagreb 1968, pp. 493–494.
10. V. Šklovskij, *O teorii proze.* Moskva 1929, pp. 108–112.
11. M. M. Bachtin, *Voprosy literatury i ėstetiki.* Moskva 1975, p. 395.
12. Cf. S. Lasić, *Struktura Krležinih "Zastava".* Zagreb 1974.
13. M. M. Bachtin, op.cit., p. 271.
14. R. Vučković, op.cit., p. 323.
15. R. Vučković, op.cit., p. 329.

A Selected Bibliography of Nils Åke Nilsson's Works

Compiled by Märta Bergstrand, Anna and Henryk Lenczyc

This bibliography focuses on Nils Åke Nilsson's scholarly writings. It does not include either his numerous articles in the daily newspaper EXPRESSEN 1946–1984, or his prefaces to Swedish translations of Russian and other Slavic writers; Nils Åke Nilsson's own translations (of Russian classical and modern prose and poetry as well as modern Polish and Slovene poetry) are not included either. A complete bibliography of Professor Nilsson's writings is to be published by the Department of Slavic and Baltic languages, Stockholm University.

Publications marked with an asterisk in Sections 1 and 3 are to be found with full data in Section 2.

1. Scholarly works

1946

1 000 vanliga ord. Rysk-svensk och svensk-rysk ordlista. Stockholm. 47 p.

1947

Sovjetrysk litteratur. *Europas litteraturhistoria 1918–1939.* Stockholm. pp. 429–506.

1948

Modern ryska. Stockholm. 54 p.
Sovjetrysk litteratur 1917–1939. Stockholm. 222 p.
Ryskspråkig litteratur efter 1900. *Vem skrev vad?* Stockholm. pp. 286–293.

1949

Die Apollonius-Erzählung in den slavischen Literaturen. Uppsala. 172 p. (Études de philologie slave. 3.)

1954

Gogol et Pétersbourg. Recherches sur les antécédents des contes pétersbourgeois. Stockholm. 71 s. (Études de philologie slave. 4.)
Das erwachene Petersburg. Eine Bemerkung zu "Eugen Onegin", erster Gesang, Strophe 35. *Scando-Slavica* 1. pp. 98–102,
Öst–Väst. Två världar. Amerikas Förenta staters och Sovjetunionens utveckling och ställning i vår tid. Vol.2. Sovjetunionen. (With Hagbard Jonassen & Juri Semjonow). Stockholm. 186 p.

1955

Zur Entstehungsgeschichte des Gogolschen "Mantels". *Scando-Slavica* 2. pp. 116–133.

1957

Mops-gaubica – rybar'-den'. Un type d'expression métaphorique dans la poésie moderne russe. *Scando-Slavica* 3. pp. 74–91.

1958

Ibsen in Russland. Stockholm. 253 p. (Études de philologie slave. 7.)
Strindberg, Gorky and Blok. *Scando-Slavica* 4. pp. 23–42.

1959

1 000 vanliga ord. Rysk-svensk och svensk-rysk ordlista. 2. tryckningen. Stockholm. 47 s.
Life as ecstasy and sacrifice. Two poems by Boris Pasternak. *Scando-Slavica* 5. pp. 180–198.

1960

Eight letters from Valerij Brjusov to Alfred Jensen. *Studia Slavica Gunnaro Gunnarsson sexagenario dedicata.* pp. 70–81.
Soviet student slang. *Scando-Slavica* 6. pp. 113–123.

1961

Intonation and rhythm in Čechov's plays. *Anton Čechov 1860–1960.* ed. T. Eekman. Leiden. pp. 168–180.

1962

Cataloguing in Puškin's epic poetry. *Studi in onore di Ettore Lo Gatto e Giovanni Maver.* Firenze. pp. 499–506.
Some notes on Slovene rhythm. *International journal of Slavic linguistics and poetics* 5. pp. 126–135.

1963

Osip Mandel'štam and his poetry. *Scando-Slavica* 9. pp. 37–52.

1964

Russian heraldic virši from the 17th century. A manuscript in the Diocesan and county library at Västerås, Sweden. Stockholm. 93 p.
The parabola of poetry. Some remarks on Andrej Voznesenskij. *Scando-Slavica* 10. pp. 49–64.

1965

1 000 vanliga ord. Rysk-svensk och svensk-rysk ordlista. 3. tryckningen. Stockholm. 47 p.
Through the wrong end of binoculars. An introduction to Jurij Oleša. *Scando-Slavica* 11. pp. 40–68.
"Usad'ba noč'ju, čingischan' ". Verbs derived from personal names as a means of expression in literary Russian. *Lingua viget commentationes slavicae in honorem V. Kiparsky.* Helsinki. pp. 97–101. (On the title-page 1964.)

1966

The dead bees. Notes on a poem by Nikolaj Gumilev. *Orbis Scriptus. Dmitrij Tschizewskij zum 70. Geburtstag.* München. pp. 573–580.
"Mužajtes', muži!" On the history of a poetism. *Scando-Slavica* 12. pp. 5–12.

Osip Mandel'štam's "Insomnia" poem. *International journal of Slavic linguistics and poetics* 10. pp. 148–154.

1967

1000 vanliga ord. Rysk-svensk och svensk-rysk ordlista. 3. tryckningen. Stockholm. 47 p.

Intonation and rhythm in Chekhov's plays. *Chekhov. A collection of critical essays.* Englewood Cliffs. pp. 161–174.

Ship metaphors in Mandel'štam's poetry. *To honor Roman Jakobson.* The Hague. Vol. 2. pp. 1436–1444.

The use of preterite + bylo in Turgenev. *Scando-Slavica* 13. pp. 39–57.

1968

Studies in Čechov's narrative technique. The Steppe and the Bishop. Stockholm. 109 p. (Stockholm Slavic studies. 2.)

Blok's "Vowel Fugue". A suggestion for a different interpretation. *International journal of Slavic linguistics and poetics* 11. pp. 150–158.

Bridge and Birič. *Annuaire de l'institut de philologie et d'histoire orientales et slaves.* Bruxelles. 18. No. 1. p. 307.

Chekhov and the European drama of his time. *Moderna språk* 62:1. pp. 67–72.

Leksika i stilistika pisem Čechova. *Scando-Slavica* 14. pp. 33–58.

Recepcja dzieł Sienkiewicza w Szwecji. *Henryk Sienkiewicz. Twórczość i recepcja światowa.* Kraków. pp. 423–434.

"Reduta Ordona". Kilka uwag o stylu batalistycznym. *Pamiętnik Literacki.* 59. No. 4. pp. 157–163.

1969

A hall of mirrors. Nabokov and Olesha. *Scando-Slavica* 15. pp. 5–12.

Ryska översättningar av modern svensk litteratur. *Moderna språk* 63:4. pp. 366–371.

Style and translation. *Moderna språk* 63:1. pp. 49–60.

1970

The Russian imaginists. Stockholm. 117 p. (Stockholm Slavic studies. 5.)

Dostoevskij and the language of suspense. *Scando-Slavica* 16. pp. 35–44.

Vasilisk Gnedov's One-Letter poems. *Gorski Vijenac.* A garland of essays offered to professor Elizabeth Mary Hill, ed. by R. Auty, L.R. Lewitter & A.P. Vlasto. Cambridge. pp. 220–223.

1971

Intonacja i rytm w sztukach Czechowa. *Czechow w oczach krytyki światowej.* Warszawa. pp. 393–414.

Osip Mandel'štam's poem "The Admiralty". *Scando-Slavica* 17. pp. 21–26.

1972

Mandel'štam and the Nurmis skates. *Scando-Slavica* 18. pp. 91–95.

1973

Rysk litteratur från Tjechov till Solsjenitsyn. Stockholm 148 p.

Mandel'štam and the revolution. *Scando-Slavica* 19. pp. 7–16.

Osip Mandel'štam and his poetry. *Major Soviet writers.* Essays in criticism. ed. by E.J. Brown. London. pp. 164–177.

"Proslavim, brat'ja" and "Na kamennyx otrogax". Remarks on two poems by Osip Mandel'štam. *Slavic Poetics*. Essays in honor of Kiril Taranovsky. The Hague. pp. 295–297.

Rhyming as a stylistic device in "Crime and Punishment". *Russian Literature* 4. pp. 65–71.

Den ryska litteraturen. *Litteraturens världshistoria*. Vol. 10: Sekelskiftet. Första världskriget. Stockholm. pp. 422–465. Danish translation: *Verdens Litteratur Historie*. København. Bd. 10. pp. 443–488.

Through the wrong end of binoculars. An introduction to Jurij Oleša. *Major Soviet writers*. Essays in criticism. ed. by E. J. Brown. London. pp. 254–279.

1974

Osip Mandel'štam. Five poems. Stockholm. 87 p. (Stockholm studies in Russian literature. 1.)

Mandel'štam's poem "Voz'mi na radost' ". *Russian Literature* 7/8 pp. 165–179.

Nya tendenser inom rysk litteraturforskning. *Humanist. forskning* 3:1. pp. 32–35.

De slaviska litteraturerna. *Litteraturens Världshistoria*. Vol. 11: Mellankrigstiden. Andra världskriget. Stockholm. pp. 412–447., Vol. 12: Efterkrigstiden. pp. 176–188. Danish translation *Verdens Litteratur Historie*. København. Vol. 11. pp. 447–482., Vol. 12. pp. 201–214.

1975

Adam Mickiewicz. "Stepy Akermańskie". *Meddelanden från Institutionen för slaviska och baltiska språk*. No. 12. pp. 12–18.

Gogol's The Overcoat and the topography of Petersburg. *Scando-Slavica* 21. pp. 5–18.

Soviet literature in the Paris literary magazine "transition". *Vladimir Majakovskij. Memoirs and essays*. pp. 179–183.*

1976

An exhaustive picture of spring. A poem by Majakovskij. *Scando-Slavica* 22. pp. 25–34.

"With oars at rest" and the poetic tradition. *Boris Pasternak. Essays*. pp. 180–202.*

1977

Isaak Babel's "Perechod čerez Zbruč". *Scando-Slavica* 23. pp. 63–71.

Jugoslavistiska u Švedskoj. *Naučni sastanak slavista u Vukove dane*. 3. pp. 169–173.

"Peredo mnoj" and "Pered toboj". Two formulas in the love lyric of Puškin and Fet. *Korrespondenzen. Festschrift für Dietrich Gerhardt* ... Giessen. pp. 289–297.

1978

Futurizam i primitivizam. *Književna reč* 25.5 pp. 10–14.

Jugoslavisk avantgardekonferens. *Meddelanden från Institutionen för slaviska och baltiska språk* No. 17. pp. 42–46.

Kručenych's poem "Dyr bul ščyl". *Scando-Slavica* 24. pp. 139–148.

Lermontov's poem "Parus". *Studia linguistica Alexandro Vasilii filio Issatschenko a collegis amicisque oblata*. Lisse. pp. 297–302.

Life as ecstacy and sacrifice: Two poems by Boris Pasternak. *Pasternak. A collection of critical essays*. ed. by V. Ehrlich. New York. pp. 51–67.

1979

Baratynskij's elegiac code. *Russian romanticism.* pp. 144–167.*

"The Bishop" – its theme. *A. Chekhov: Short stories.* ed. by R.E. Matlaw. New York. pp. 357–368.

"In vain" – "Perhaps". The Russian romantic poets and fate. *Scando-Slavica* 25. pp. 71–82.

Mandel'štam and the revolution. *Art, society, revolution.* pp. 165–178.*

Sienkiewicz and Reymont in Sweden. *Swedish-Polish literary contacts.* pp. 107–114.*

Spring 1918. The arts and the commissars. *Art, society, revolution.* pp. 9–53.*

Stichotvorenija Pasternaka "Složa vesla" i literaturnaja tradicija. *Boris Pasternak 1890–1960. Colloque de Cerisy-la-Salle.* Paris. pp. 273–280.

Swedish-Polish literary contacts over the centuries. *Swedish-Polish literary contacts.* pp. 1–3.*

1980

Avant-garde poetry and the cinema. *Voz'mi na radost':* To honour Jeanne van der Eng-Liedmeier. Amsterdam. pp. 135–138.

Futurism, primitivism and the Russian Avant-garde. *Russian Literature* 8. pp. 469–482.

The use of the predicative adjective in Russian. *Scando-Slavica* 26. pp. 149–160.

1981

The challenge from the periphery. *Scando-Slavica* 27. pp. 93–103.

Futurizm i primitivizm. *Umjetnost riječi.* 25. pp. 77–80.

The roaring parnassus: Art and revolution in Russia. *Les années folles. Les mouvements avant-gardistes européens. The roaring twenties. The avant-garde movements in Europe.* ed. Zbigniew Folejewski. Ottawa. pp. 39–49.

The sound poem: Russian Zaum' and German Dada. *Russian Literature* 10. pp. 307–317.

"To Cassandra". A poem by Osip Mandel'štam from December 1917. *Poetica Slavica. Studies in honor of Zbigniew Folejewski.* Ed. J. Douglas Clayton & Gunter Schaarschnidt. Ottawa. pp. 105–113.

Two Chekhovs: Mayakovsky and Chekhov's "Futurism". *Chekhov's great plays.* ed. Jean-Pierre Barricelli. New York. pp. 251–261.

1982

Babel – Guy de Maupassant. *Die russische Novelle.* ed. Bodo Zelinsky. Düsseldorf. pp. 182–190.

Evropski kontekst romana "Na rubu pameti". *Oko* (Zagreb) No. 7. pp. 23.

Futuryzm i prymitywizm. *Acta universitatis Lodziensis. Folia scientiarum artium et librorum.* Łódź. No. 3. pp. 37–51.

Isaak Babel's story "Guy de Maupassant". *Studies in 20th century Russian prose.* pp. 213–227.*

On the origins of Gogol's Overcoat. *Gogol's Overcoat.* An anthology of critical essays. ed. by Elizabeth Trahan. Ann Arbor. pp. 61–72.

Romanen i Ryssland-Sovjetunionen. *Romanen under nittonhundratalet.* pp. 115–127.*

Tolstoj – Čechov – Babel'. "Shortness" and "syntax" in the Russian short story. *Scando-Slavica* 28. pp. 91–107.

Tuwim's Sokrates tańczący. *International journal of Slavic linguistics and poetics* 25/26. pp. 307–312.

Virginia Woolf och den ryska litteraturen. *Litterär översättning.* Bidrag till forskarse-minariet översättning av litterära texter den 17–18 december 1981 Nedre Manilla på Djurgården. pp. 199–212.

1983

Att översätta rysk avant-garde-poesi. Några försök med Velimir Chlebnikovs Skratt-besvärjelse. *Från språk till språk.* Sjutton uppsatser om litterär översättning utgiven av G. Engwall och R. af Geijerstam. Lund. pp. 7–18.

Krleža's novel "Na rubu pameti" and its European context. *Festschrift für Nikola R. Pribić.* (Selecta Slavica 9.) pp. 221–228.

Litteraturvetenskaplig forskning vid institutionen för slaviska och baltiska språk. *Tidskrift för litteraturvetenskap.* h. 4. pp. 301–303.

Zaum' russa e poesia sonora Dada. *Il verri.* Revista di literatura. Mantua. No 29/30. pp. 95–105.

1984

L'acméisme et l'imaginisme russe. *Les avant-gardes littéraires au XXe siècle.* publié ... sous la direction de Jean Weisberger. Budapest. pp. 275–286.

How much reality can poetry sustain? *Text, Symbol, Weltmodell.* Johannes Holthu-sen zum 60. Geburtstag. München. pp. 421–438.

Hur den ryska litteraturen introducerades i Sverige. *Äldre svensk slavistik.* Bidrag till symposium hållet i Uppsala 3–4 februari 1983. Uppsala. pp. 72–77.

Mandel'štam and the Moscow Art Theater. *Theater and literature in Russia 1900–1930.* pp. 115–123.*

Osjet jezika. *Pojmovnik ruske avangarde.* Uredili Aleksandar Flaker & Dubravka Ugresić. Sv. 1. pp. 117–120.

A poem by Elisaveta Bagrjana and its translations. *Scando-Slavica* 30. pp. 95–101.

Prvobitnost-primitivizam. *Pojmovnik ruske avangarde.* Uredili Aleksandar Flaker & Dubravka Ugresić. Sv. 1. pp. 131–138.

Russkaja literatura v Švecii (iz istorii rasprostranenij). *MAIRSK* informacionnyj bjulleten' 9. pp. 11–14.

Translator's view of Edvard Kocbek. *Obdobje ekspresionizma v slovenskem jeziku, književnosti in kulturi.* Ljubljana. pp. 519–523.

Den unge Lagerkvist, filmen och avantgardismen. *Tidskrift för litteraturvetenskap* 1. pp. 4–14.

Us and them. Virginia Woolf and Russian literature. *We and they.* National identity as a theme in Slavic cultures. Copenhagen. pp. 211–221.

1985

"Frozen time" as a paradigm in modern Slavic poetry (Mandel'štam, Kocbek, Miłosz). *International journal of Slavic linguistics and poetics* 31–32. pp. 283–294.

How to translate avant-garde poetry. Some attempts with Chlebnikov's "Incantation by laughter". *Velimir Chlebnikov.* pp. 133–150.*

Koliko realnosti poezija moze podnijeti? (Milosz, Mandeljstam i "poetika dos-tance".) Zagreb. *Književna smotra* Godište 17. broj 57–58. pp. 131–137.

Nordijski mit i ruska avangarda. *Pojmovnik ruske avangarde.* Sv. 4. pp. 187–201.

Pervobytnost' – primitivizm. *Russian literature* 17. No. 1. pp. 39–44.

1986

Food images in Čechov. A Bachtinian approach. *Scando-Slavica* 32. pp. 28–40.

1987

(with Anna Ljunggren) Elena Guro's diary. *Russian Literature* 21. pp. 141–156.
Russia and the myth of the North: The modernist response. *Russian Literature* 21.
pp. 125–140.

2. Books edited by Nils Åke Nilsson

1950

Rysk lyrik. I urval och översättning. Stockholm. 108 p.

1954

(with Göran Lundström) *Berättelser ur båda fickorna.* Tjeckisk humor, satir och
berättarglädje i urval. Stockholm. 255 p.

1957

Den vita svalan och andra bulgariska berättelser. Stockholm. 259 p.

1958

Berömda ryska berättare. Från Tjechov till Sjolochov. I urval. Stockholm. 270 p.

1959

Modern rysk humor. Urval och inledning. Stockholm. 97 p.
Rysk lyrik. Ett urval från Pusjkin till Pasternak. 2. omarbetade upplagan. Stockholm.
99 p.

1960

Det nakna ansiktet. Ny polsk lyrik i urval och översättning.
Dostojevskij, Fjodor. En samlingsvolym. Urval och förord. pp. 7–14.

1961

Vesirens elefant. Berättelser från Jugoslavien. Stockholm. 241 p.
24 stora ryska berättare. Från Tjechov till Pasternak. Stockholm. 304 p.

1965

Modern rysk berättarkonst. I urval. Stockholm. 181 p.

1966

Berömda ryska berättare. Från Tjechov till Sjolochov. Ny utgåva. Stockholm. 159 p.
Rysk lyrik. Ett urval från Pusjkin till Pasternak. 2. omarbetade upplagan. Stockholm.
99 p.

1967

Rysk berättarkonst. Urval och inledning. Stockholm. 207

1975

(with Bengt Jangfeldt) *Vladimir Majakovskij. Memoirs and essays.* Stockholm. 196 p.
(Stockholm studies in Russian literature. 2.)

1976

Boris Pasternak. Essays. Stockholm. 215 p. (Stockholm studies in Russian literature. 7.)

1979

Art, society, revolution. Russia 1917–1921. Stockholm. 271 p. (Stockholm studies in Russian literature. 11.)
Russian romanticism. Studies in the poetic codes. Stockholm. 226 p. (Stockholm studies in Russian literature. 10.)
Swedish-Polish literary contacts. Stockholm. 156 p. (Kungliga Vitterhets historie och antikvitets akademin. Konferenser 3.)

1981

Du måste vittna. Poesi och reportage från Polen. Stockholm. 145 p.

1982

(with Inge Jonsson) *Romanen under nittonhundratalet.* Stockholm. 152 p.
Studies in 20th century Russian prose. Stockholm. 249 p. (Stockholm studies in Russian literature. 14.)

1984

(with Lars Kleberg) *Theater and literature in Russia 1900–1930.* Stockholm. 123 p. (Stockholm studies in Russian literature. 19.)

1985

Velimir Chlebnikov. A Stockholm symposium April 24 1983. Stockholm. 150 p. (Stockholm studies in Russian literature. 20.)

1987

The Slavic literatures and modernism. A Nobel symposium August 5–8, 1985. Stockholm. 318 p.

3. Articles on Slavic literature published in Swedish journals

1944–1945

Ryssland i bild. Vol. 1–2. Stockholm. Chapt. 9–10. pp. 257–322., 12–13. pp. 353–416., 16. pp. 483–512., 19. pp. 577–608., 24–27. pp. 737–864., 30. pp. 929–960.

1956

Strindberg på rysk scen. *Meddelanden från Strindbergsällskapet.* No. 20. pp. 5–16.

1957

Dudintsev "Ej av bröd allenast" *BLM* 26 pp. 444–445.
Ibsen på rysk scen. *Ord och bild* 66 pp. 218–223.
Litterär revolt i Östeuropa. *BLM* 26 pp. 39–42.
Polsk generation 55. *Lyrikvännen* 4 h. 2. pp. 12.

1958

Boris Pasternak och doktor Zjivago. *BLM* 27 pp. 139–144.

Brev från Warszawa. *BLM* 27 pp. 571–573.
Hos Pasternak. *BLM* 27 pp. 618–622.

1959
Livet som extas och offer. Kring Boris Pasternaks lyrik. *BLM* 28 pp. 372–382.

1960
Ivo Andrić. *BLM* 29 pp. 590–594.
Tjechov som dramatiker. *Kulturkontakt* 7 h. 1. pp. 4–10.
Diskussion: *Kulturkontakt* 7 h. 1. pp. 10–12. (Lars Levi Laestadius) pp. 12. (Sam Besekow)

1962
Ensam man vid lägereld. Osip Mandelstams poesi. *Ord och bild* 71 pp. 422–427.
Ung man med äpple i handen. Om Evgenij Evtusjenko och hans poesi. *Ord och bild* 71 pp. 90–96.

1963
Alexander Pusjkin – en rysk nationalskald. *Operans programblad* säsongen 1962/63:7 pp. 1–3.
Drömmen om det poetiska universalspråket. Velimir Chlebnikov och hans poesi. *BLM* 32 pp. 381–388.

1964
Parabelns bana. Andrej Voznesenskij. *Ord och bild* 73 h. 2. pp. 145–153.

1966
Blok och De tolv. *Ord och bild* 75 h. 2. pp. 141–146.

1968
Fångar i spegelvärlden. Kring Nabokovs författarskap. *Ord och bild* 77 h. 1. pp. 28–32.
Lyckan om 200 år. (Anton Tjechov). *Studiekamraten* 50 h. 4. pp. 77–79.

1972
Osip Mandelstam. *Lyrikvännen* 19 h. 5. pp. 20–24.

1974
Adam Mickiewicz och hans krimsonetter. *Lyrikvännen* 21 h. 3. pp. 30–33.
Människor och mat hos Tjechov. *Gastronomisk kalender*. Stockholm. pp. 7–14.

1975
Rysk litteratur och skandinavisk. *Rysk kulturrevy* 7:3. pp. 3–7

1976
En rysk exlibriskonstnär. *Rysk kulturrevy* 8:3. pp. 2–4.

1977
De ryska poeterna och Finland. *Rysk kulturrevy* 9:3. pp. 3–4.
Polsk surkålsgryta och litauisk issallat. *Gastronomisk kalender*. pp. 55–63.
Vasko Popa. *Lyrikvännen* 24 h. 1. pp. 31–33.

1978
Dostojevskij i Bad Ems. *Rysk kulturrevy* 10:4. pp. 5–7.

1979
Konsten och kommissarierna – Ryssland 1918. *Vetandets värld.* Stockholm. pp. 87–91.

1980
Bruno Schulz – författare och tecknare. *Slavisk kulturrevy.* 1:1. pp. 9–11.
Jugoslaviska bilddikter. *Slavisk kulturrevy* 1:1. pp. 15–17.
Polsk litteratur – en exportvara? *Slavisk kulturrevy* 1:1. pp. 3-6.

1981
Anton Tjechov. *Folket i bild/Kulturfront* h. 16. pp. 22.
Blaga Dimitrova. *Lyrikvännen* 28 h. 3/4. pp. 192
Czeslaw Milosz och poesins distans. *Du måste vittna.* pp. 111–121.*
Dagbok från Beograd. *Slavisk kulturrevy* 1:2. pp. 28–32.
"Du måste vittna." *Lyrikvännen* 29 h. 3/4. pp. 234–237.
"Jag är polack och jag skriver på polska." – Om nobelpristagaren Czesław Miłosz.
Slavisk kulturrevy 1:2. pp. 3–5.
Lodz – textil och kultur. *Du måste vittna.* pp. 53–64.*

1982
Dagbok från Zagreb. *Slavisk kulturrevy* 1:3. pp. 22–27.
Antiutopi och utopi i Tarkovskijs film "Stalker". *Rysk kulturrevy* 14:1. pp. 2–5.
En artikel i "Kultura". *Slavisk kulturrevy* 1:3. pp. 3–5.
Jugoslavien: En mångfald som också skiljer åt. *Allt om böcker* No. 5. pp. 36–37.
Polonäsen – ett tema i polsk litteratur. *Slavisk kulturrevy* 1:3. pp. 16–18.

1983
Ryskt avant-garde. Konsten som sprängde alla bojor – och blev bannlyst. *Månadsjournalen* 5. pp. 5–15.
Soldaten Svejk på svenska. *Slavisk kulturrevy* 1:4. pp. 20–26.

1984
Snoilsky. Prešeren och den slovenska poesin. *Lyrikvännen* 31:3. pp. 174–177.

1985
Sverigebilden i rysk litteratur 1890–1917. *Att vara svensk.* Föredrag vid Vitterhetsakademins symposium 12–13 april 1984. pp. 119–130.

Stockholm Studies in Russian Literature

Published by the University of Stockholm
Founded by Nils Åke Nilsson
Editor: Peter Alberg Jensen

Subscriptions to the series and orders for single volumes should be addressed to any international bookseller or directly to the publishers:
ALMQVIST & WIKSELL INTERNATIONAL, Box 638
S-101 28 Stockholm, Sweden

Universities, libraries, learned societies, and publishers of learned periodicals may obtain the volumes of the series and other publications of the University of Stockholm in exchange for their own publications. Inquiries should be addressed to Kungl. Biblioteket, Box 5039, S-102 41 Stockholm 5, Sweden, or to Stockholms Universitetsbibliotek, Universitetsvägen 10, Frescati, 106 91 Stockholm, Sweden.

1. NILS ÅKE NILSSON, Osip Mandel'štam: Five Poems. Stockholm 1974, 87 pp.
2. BENGT JANGFELDT/NILS ÅKE NILSSON (editors), Vladimir Majakovskij. Memoirs and Essays. Stockholm 1975, 196 pp.
3. CAROLA HANSSON, Fedor Sologub as a Short-Story Writer. Stylistic Analyses. Stockholm 1975. 136 (+ 62) pp.
4. SVEN LINNÉR, Starets Zosima in The Brothers Karamazov. A Study in the Mimesis of Virtue. Stockholm 1975. 237 pp.
5. BENGT JANGFELDT, Majakovskij and Futurism 1917–1921. Stockholm 1976. 133 pp.
6. PER ARNE BODIN, Nine Poems from Doktor Živago. A Study of Christian Motifs in Boris Pasternak's Poetry. Stockholm 1976. 179 pp.
7. NILS ÅKE NILSSON (editor), Boris Pasternak. Essays. Stockholm 1976. 214 pp.
8. CHARLES ROUGLE, Three Russians Consider America. America in the Works of Maksim Gor'kij, Aleksandr Blok, and Vladimir Majakovskij. Stockholm 1977. 175 pp.
9. BARBARA LÖNNQVIST, Xlebnikov and Carnival. An Analysis of the Poem *Poèt*. Stockholm 1979. 166 pp.
10. NILS ÅKE NILSSON (editor), Russian Romanticism. Studies in the Poetic Codes. Stockholm 1979. 226 pp.
11. NILS ÅKE NILSSON (editor), Art, Society, Revolution. Russia 1917–1921. Stockholm 1980. 271 pp.
12. LUDMILA HELLGREN, Dialogues in Turgenev's Novels. Speech Introductory Devices. Stockholm 1980. 148 pp.
13. BENGT JANGFELDT (editor), V.V.Majakovskij i L.Ju.Brik: Perepiska 1915–1930. Stockholm 1982. 299 pp. (+ 32 pp. ill.).
14. NILS ÅKE NILSSON (editor), Studies in Russian 20th Century Prose. Stockholm 1982. 246 pp.
15. MAGNUS LJUNGGREN, The Dream of Rebirth. A Study of Andrej Belyj's Novel *Peterburg*. Stockholm 1982. 179 pp. (+ 8 pp. ill.).
16. KURT JOHANSSON, Aleksej Gastev. Proletarian Bard of the Machine Age. Stockholm 1983. 170 pp.
17. KAZIMIERA INGDAHL, The Artist and the Creative Act. Study of Jurij Oleša's Novel Zavist'. Stockholm 1984. 172 pp.
18. ANNA LJUNGGREN, B. Pasternak's Juvenilia. Six Fragments about Reliquimini. Stockholm 1984. 172 pp.
19. LARS KLEBERG/NILS ÅKE NILSSON (editors), Theater and Literature in Russia 1900–1930. Stockholm 1984. 123 pp.
20. NILS ÅKE NILSSON (editor), Velimir Chlebnikov. A Stockholm Symposium. Stockholm 1985. 150 pp.
21. MÄRTA BERGSTRAND, Från Karamzin till Trifonov. En bibliografi över rysk skönlitteratur i svensk översättning. Stockholm 1985. 430 pp.
22. LARS KLEBERG/HÅKAN LÖVGREN (editors), Eisenstein Revisited. A Collection of Essays. Stockholm 1987. 145 pp.
23. PETER ALBERG JENSEN/FIONA BJÖRLING/BARBARA LÖNNQVIST/LARS KLEBERG/ANDERS SJÖBERG (editors), Text and Context. Essays to Honor Nils Åke Nilsson. Stockholm 1987.

ISSN 0346-8496
ISBN 91-22-00879-9